CHASING
THE RAINBOW

CHASING
THE RAINBOW

THE STORY OF ROAD CYCLING'S WORLD CHAMPIONSHIPS

GILES BELBIN

Aurum
Press

Brimming with creative inspiration, how-to projects and useful information to enrich your everyday life, Quarto Knows is a favourite destination for those pursuing their interests and passions. Visit our site and dig deeper with our books into your area of interest: Quarto Creates, Quarto Cooks, Quarto Homes, Quarto Lives, Quarto Drives, Quarto Explores, Quarto Gifts, or Quarto Kids.

First published in 2017 by Aurum Press
an imprint of The Quarto Group
The Old Brewery
6 Blundell Street
London N7 9BH
United Kingdom
www.QuartoKnows.com

ISBN 978 1 78131 631 3
Ebook ISBN 978 1 78131 632 0

10 9 8 7 6 5 4 3 2 1
2021 2020 2019 2018 2017

Typeset in Minion Pro, Avenir Next and Futura by Jade Wheaton
Printed by CPI Group (UK) Ltd, Croydon, CR0 4YY

CONTENTS

FOREWORD
A MESSAGE FROM THE UCI PRESIDENT

For as long as we can remember, the title of UCI World Champion has gone hand in hand with the rainbow stripes, and the quest for the distinctive rainbow jersey has produced some of the most gripping pages of cycling's history.

Since the 1920s, the world's greatest road cyclists have made it their goal to claim the jersey that only the UCI World Champion has the right to wear.

Every UCI Road World Championships has had its own drama, its own story, its own champions. Some of the winners have been favourites before the race, while others have surged from near anonymity to take the sought-after title. Some have coped with, even revelled in, the pressure on race day while others have suffered from the weight of a nation's expectations.

While each race sees its share of joy, disappointment, delight and frustration, in the end there is just one winner, one person who can spend a year in the much coveted rainbow jersey.

This book recounts the tale of each edition of the UCI Road World Championships and how they unfolded. Interviews, anecdotes and insights help provide in-depth and often moving accounts of the races and stories behind the athletes who were Chasing the Rainbow.

Brian Cookson
UCI President

AUTHOR'S NOTE

Union Cycliste Internationale (UCI) sanctioned world championships exist for many forms and disciplines of cycle sport: road, track, mountain bike, cyclo-cross, BMX, trials, artistic, cycle-ball and Para-cycling. Within those disciplines categories can range from junior, through the under-23 category to amateur and then elite (professional) riders.

This book concentrates on the UCI's road world championships and specifically the elite category of road races for men and women (elite men were previously categorised as 'professional' in the days there was an amateur classification), although junior, amateur and under-23 races are occasionally touched on and there is a separate chapter covering the introduction of time trials in the 1990s. To this end, in the context of this book, unless otherwise stated, all references to world titles, numbers of rainbow jerseys or 'the Worlds' refer to elite road race world championships only and do not include world titles won in other disciplines or categories.

For ease of reading I have shortened all references to the Giro d'Italia, Tour de France and Vuelta a España to the 'Giro', 'Tour' and 'Vuelta' respectively. All references to other bike races are given their full titles in English, for example the Tour of Flanders rather than Ronde van Vlaanderen. Finally, all translations from foreign language texts are my own.

Giles Belbin, February 2017

1

INTRODUCING THE WORLDS: DOHA 2016

Doha, 15 October 2016:

Darkness is falling in Qatar. It is the evening before the men's elite road race, the final event of the road world championships, and I am in the luxurious Marsa Malaz Kempinski Hotel in Doha. Sat opposite me is the president of the Qatar Cycling Federation (QCF), the man who has played a bigger part than most in bringing the Union Cycliste Internationale's (UCI) flagship event to the Arabian peninsula for the first time – Sheikh Khalid bin Ali Thani.

The UCI has long sought out new horizons beyond the traditional European heartland of the sport for these championships – whether it be Canada and Venezuela in the 1970s, the USA in the 1980s, Japan and Colombia in the 1990s or Australia in the 2000s. Sometimes the Worlds have followed an already booming scene in a nation on the back of impressive results by riders from that country – see the USA, Colombia and Australia

– while on other occasions the championships have been used to spread the reach of the sport into new territories and linked to a nation's desire to show itself to the world and to try to increase cycling participation within its borders – see Venezuela, Japan and now Qatar. It is at best questionable whether bringing the world championships to Qatar, a country where the average temperature for six months of the year is over 30 degrees, will significantly boost the nation's cycling participation rates, despite Sheikh Khalid telling me that every new road built in Qatar now includes a cycling section and that construction of dedicated cycle paths continues to grow.

Arguably it is domestic sporting success that most fuels public participation and there is no better example of that than in Britain. Since the 2008 Beijing Olympics, Britain's elite cyclists have been on the crest of a wave, claiming multiple Olympic golds and world championships on the road and track as well as winning, at the time of writing, four Tour de France titles. In 2015 it was reported that the rate of participation in *sportives* in the UK had grown by 240 per cent in five years, something that the cycle sport and membership director at British Cycling, Jonny Clay, said had been driven by the success of riders such as Bradley Wiggins and Laura Trott.[1] The lesson? If you want your population to get on a bike you need someone to inspire them. Just three Qatari cyclists competed across all twelve events of the 2016 Worlds and just one made it to a finish line – Afif Abdullah finishing sixtieth in the men's time trial. History will dictate whether the 2016 Worlds were a success. Perhaps a Qatari child with talents lying latent watched Abdullah's ride and was suitably inspired to have a go themselves. Unlikely perhaps, but you never know. 'A journey of a thousand miles starts with one breath,'[2] wrote Phil Jackson, the legendary basketball coach in his book *Sacred Hoops,* borrowing from the ancient Chinese philosopher Lao Tzu.

'It is not popular here but that is not the issue,' Sheikh Khalid says. 'The issue is how to make it popular … If the UCI and us [the QCF], in charge of cycling, want to promote cycling we must make every effort, use every support, every sponsor, and government to promote cycling. We don't sit back and say: "Well we don't have cycling here so then we should not have cycling competitions here." No. How can you say that? We don't have people here interested in cycling so forget them? No.

'We have participated in promoting cycling in the region and in the world and also we carry a message to the world, a message of peace. Sport is the only thing that unifies all the world together. Every time you host a competition, and you get athletes and spectators coming from different areas of the world and touching first-hand another country, then their perception of the country is different completely ... It brings the whole world together.'

Spreading a global message of unity through sport, in other words. It seems a noble pursuit that even the sceptics among us would surely embrace.

***

The long and often sinuous world championship road that wound its way to Doha for the 2016 Worlds began in the late 1880s. On Christmas Eve 1889, the French long-distance specialist Charles Terront won a 100-mile road race in Birmingham billed as the road world championships. He was the only one of eight starters who actually finished, with all the others 'defeated by the Siberian cold'.[3] Cycling as a competitive pursuit was still in its infancy and newly formed national federations were battling for control over the international governance of the sport. In 1900 the UCI was formed after several nations broke away from the International Cycling Association (ICA) that had been established in 1892 and was predominantly a British-run institution. With the continental racing scene blossoming, many member nations felt that Britain, which combined the voting power of England, Scotland, Wales and Ireland, enjoyed unmerited power in the administration of the sport. And so the representatives of the national cycling federations of France, Italy, Belgium, Switzerland and the United States founded the UCI, with the aim of 'justly representing the interests of cycling countries'.[4]

The ICA had been organising world championship events since 1893 when the first track championships were held in Chicago. In August 1900, just four months after its foundation, came the first UCI-sanctioned track world championships. Held at the Parc des Princes velodrome in Paris there were four events – a sprint and a stayers race for professionals and amateurs.

Despite the upswing in popularity in road racing in the late 1800s and early 1900s, a period of which all of road cycling's five most important one-day classics (Liège-Bastogne-Liège, Paris-Roubaix, the Tour of Lombardy, Milan-Sanremo and the Tour of Flanders) as well as its two most important stage races (the Tour de France and the Giro d'Italia) were introduced, it was not until 1921 that the UCI introduced an official road cycling world championship. It took the form of an individual time trial and was restricted to amateurs. Sweden's Gunnar Sköld won that first 190-kilometre race in Copenhagen. The following year Britain's Dave Marsh prevailed on home roads, becoming Britain's first official amateur road world champion before the format was changed to a massed-start road race for the first time in 1923.

For the professionals there was no such championship. Instead the one-day GP Wolber, introduced in October 1922, took on the mantle of road racing's unofficial world championships, with only those who had recorded top-three placings at the major one-day races in France, Belgium, Italy or Switzerland during the season, securing an invite. It was a prestigious event, but it was not the world championships.

It would not be until 1927, some six years after the inaugural road Worlds, that professionals took to the start line of a UCI-sanctioned world championship road race for the first time and it took another thirty-one years for women to get their race. By then the rainbow jersey, that simple white cycling jersey with its five coloured bands, mirroring the colours of the Olympic rings – blue, red, black, yellow and green – and running horizontally across the middle, had become one of the most sought-after prizes in the sport. Introduced in 1927, the jersey is unique, a visible and tangible symbol of achievement that stays on a rider's back all season. Win the Worlds and the rainbow jersey remains yours until someone takes it off you.

***

DOHA, 16 OCTOBER 2016:

Darkness is falling in Qatar. It is the day after I had sat down opposite Sheikh Khalid and now all the races are over. The curtain has come down on the latest instalment of the story of the world championships. Slovakia's Peter

Sagan has just won his second rainbow jersey in succession, winning a sprint finish after an epic race in the desert. It was a good day. A good way to end the championships.

In the post-race media conference Sagan is wearing his rainbow jersey. He is in a playful mood, laughing and grinning. He is relaxed and the epitome of cool. He sings the *Star Wars* theme tune. Badly. Charisma pours from him in waves, the perfect world champion. 'Ah, everybody is happy again,'[5] he says.

2

IT'S AN ITALIAN AFFAIR

Nestled in the Eifel mountain range of western Germany, sitting beneath an imposing twelfth-century castle, lies the small town of Nürburg. Surrounded by lakes and by the peaks of long-extinct volcanoes, it is a place for hiking on spectacular trails that strike through the forests and meadows that bless this area of Germany. It is also a place to press the pedal to metal and to listen to the thunderous roar of finely tuned engines. For the quiet village of Nürburg is home to the Nürburgring, one of the most famous motor-racing circuits in the world.

Work began on the Nürburgring in the summer of 1925. In just two years construction of the circuit, comprising northern and southern loops around the village that could be joined to make a 28.3-kilometre lap, was completed and it opened in June 1927. After a motor-cycle race on the opening day, 85,000 people poured into the circuit on 19 June to watch Rudolf Caracciola become the first man to cross the finish line at the Nürburgring in a car. 'When we came to the newly opened Nürburgring in 1927, we opened our eyes,' Caracciola later said. 'We had not experienced such a thing before.

There lay in the middle of the Eifel mountains a road, a closed loop with nearly 180 curves ... a trail with slopes that caught the engine sharply to the lungs, but also with unspoiled views far across the country, valleys and villages.'[6]

A little more than one month after Caracciola's win, the northern loop of the new circuit was the host of the 1927 edition of the UCI's road world championships. Since the introduction of the championships, the issue of opening the race to professional riders had been debated. As public interest in the event grew, so the voices of those arguing for a professional race grew louder, but there remained resistance. The world championships were the pinnacle of the amateur calendar and some thought including a race for professionals, who already had numerous and increasingly prestigious races, would negatively impact the standing of the event. They counselled against including competitors who, in their eyes, were solely motivated by money. But the debate continued until 1927 when the UCI decided to hold a single race that was open to both amateurs and professionals with the titles awarded to the best placed in each classification. The controversial decision meant that the Nürburgring would play a significant part in the history of cycling: it was going to be the circuit on which cycling's first professional road world champion would forge their win.

The northern loop of the Nürburgring was a brutal examination of the strength and endurance of riders. The road twisted and turned and there were numerous climbs for the riders to tackle over the course of the 22.8 kilometre lap which had to be ridden eight times. The toughest part of the circuit came halfway round with a five-kilometre stretch of near constant climbing up to the Hohe Acht section of the circuit, named after the highest peak in the Eifel mountains. In their book *Van de Nurburgring tot Zolder,* authors René Jacobs and Hector Mahau describe the circuit as 'Undeniably the roughest and most selective course in the history of the world championships,'[7] while the Italian daily *La Stampa* called it 'a continuous rollercoaster tormented by countless curves.'[8]

It was a contentious choice of venue with many unhappy at the severity of the route. Commentators questioned the suitability of using a motor-racing track for a bicycle race and continued to debate the merits of the participation of professional riders. This was a new race for professionals at a time when it remained far from certain whether professional cycling even needed an official world championships, let alone what true standing the winner might enjoy in the eyes of cycling fans and media. The UCI's decision to opt for a single-race format also complicated matters. What if a famous, handsomely paid professional was beaten by a plucky but unfancied amateur? What then for the credibility of the Worlds? 'Sportingly, this project is really wonderful,' wrote André Sans in the newspaper *Paris-Soir,* 'but practically it presents many pitfalls and already the application of the formula to the road world championship of 1927 has not resulted in what was expected. Constructors are uninterested because they do not want to run the risk of having their champions beaten by amateurs, either after a regular race or after a puncture.'[9] When thought of in those terms, taking to the start line was fraught with risk for the professional riders and their employers. To be deemed worthy, the world championships needed a big-name winner.

***

Even before the race started it was clear that any well-known winner would not be French, simply because no top French professionals made the journey. The country was among the loudest voices in asking the worth of this new entrant on the cycling calendar, questioning whether such a race merited being called the world championships. This was a time when France was enduring some lean years in its own biggest races. Since the end of the First World War, Henri Pélissier had been the only French rider to record success in either the Tour de France (1923) or Paris-Roubaix (1919 and 1921), with those races now being dominated by riders from Belgium, Italy and Luxembourg. The 1927 Tour finished just four days before the world championships, with André Leducq and Antonin Magne the best placed of the French riders, finishing fourth and sixth respectively. Both were just twenty-three years of age and neither made the journey to Germany. 'Better to sacrifice one world championship than two careers,' wrote the magazine *Le Miroir des Sports.*[10]

In stark contrast stood Italy. France's neighbour from across the Alps had boycotted the inaugural amateur championships in 1921, upset at the decision to run the event as a time trial, before Libero Ferrario claimed their first title two years later in the first Worlds run as a massed-start road race. From that moment Italy embraced the Worlds as much as any other nation and now, with countries permitted a maximum of six riders across both categories, they brought four professionals and two amateurs to Germany. Included in their ranks were two of the biggest names in cycling: Alfredo Binda and Costante Girardengo.

Girardengo was the original *Campionissimo*, the Champion of champions. By 1927 he was nearing the end of an illustrious period that had already included two Giro titles and nine national championships as well as the Tour of Lombardy three times and five Milan-Sanremo wins (he would take a sixth in 1928). Meanwhile, the twenty-four-year-old Binda was busy supplanting Girardengo at the summit of Italian cycling after coming to prominence in the 1924 Tour of Lombardy. He finished fourth but had climbed the famous 10-kilometre Passo del Ghisallo alone at the head of the race and mixed it with Italian cycling royalty in the closing kilometres. He was living in France at the time, but when it was discovered that Binda was Italian, Italy's cycling press suddenly sat up and took notice of this relative newcomer.

Soon they could not have missed him even if they tried. In 1925 Binda rode his first Giro and won it by nearly five minutes ahead of Girardengo. It was the start of the passing of the torch. By the time of the 1927 Worlds, Binda had secured a second Giro crown, a couple of national titles and two wins at the Tour of Lombardy. He was successful and he was stylish and he would dominate Italian cycling into the early 1930s. The French climber René Vietto once said Binda had such a smooth action that he could cycle with a cup of milk on his back without spilling a drop.

The timing of the Worlds helped the Italians. With the true worth of the Worlds to the professional peloton being questioned, the cream of riders who had just completed the Tour de France were otherwise engaged with lucrative post-Tour assignments. On the day of the Worlds for instance, Luxembourg's Nicolas Frantz and Belgium's Maurice De Waele, first and second in the Tour respectively, were racing against each other in a nocturne on the Parc des Princes track in Paris, coincidently joined by Leducq and Magne. In contrast, for obvious and commercial reasons, Italy's best riders had been focused not on the Tour but on the Giro, a race that had finished some six weeks earlier. Unsure of his condition, Girardengo had not ridden that Giro, but Binda rode and ruled the race, winning twelve of the fifteen stages and claiming the overall title by more than 27 minutes. Such was his dominance that Binda was the overwhelming favourite to win the Worlds, despite the presence of Girardengo and a strong team of Belgian professionals, every one of whom had won at least one Classic.

The day of the race was cold and wet. A stiff wind blew and it was not long before riders were falling off the back and retiring. By halfway, a leading group of twenty riders had formed with all six Italians present. Belgium and France each had just one rider in the break, the amateurs Jean Aerts and René Brossy respectively. Aerts would go on to be the sole Belgian finisher, taking fifth overall and the amateur title, while Brossy finished ninth, the only French rider to complete the race. 'The popular little rider was keen to save the honour of our colours,'[11] reported *Paris-Soir*.

The Italians went to work on the sixth lap. Girardengo made his bid on the steep 3-kilometre climb to the Karussell hairpin, prompting a reaction from Binda and Piemontesi who dragged Brossy and Germany's Bruno Wolke with them, followed by Aerts. Binda then launched his move with around 30 kilometres to go, also on the climb to Karussell. Once he had attacked no one could go with him and in the space of 6 kilometres Binda opened a gap of more than two minutes. The race was over. Binda's winning margin over Girardengo was more than seven minutes. It was a stunning display of power, his performance head and shoulders above everybody else. In its account of the race, the British magazine *Cycling* described Binda as a 'remarkably improved rider'[12] somewhat overlooking his previous performances and illustrating the blinkered view of the British specialist cycling press, who viewed both professionalism and massed-start road racing on the Continent with sceptical eyes.

Italy had dominated the race. After Binda came Girardengo, Domenico Piemontesi and Gaetano Belloni, with Aerts the first non-Italian, nearly 12 minutes behind. The experiment of starting amateurs and professionals together and running effectively two races in one had not worked. The incongruous sight of awarding amateur world champion status to a rider who had crossed the line fifth meant the race was dubbed a fiasco by *Cycling*. But the Italians did not care. A new era had begun and in Binda they had road cycling's first professional world champion. 'You can view it an exaggeration to cry for a cycling race,' wrote Giuseppe Tonelli in *La Stampa*, 'but all of us Italians present at that time felt a lump in our throats and a tear in our eyes.'[13]

3

THE AGE OF THE POWERHOUSE NATIONS

In August 1928 the Italian publication *Sports Giallo* published a cartoon. It pictured a large and fierce-looking official, dressed in a suit and holding two fearful cyclists under his left arm with their backsides raised into the air, their fingers adorned with jewels. The man's right hand is raised above his head, his palm open, poised, ready to come down with force and punish the two riders tucked under his arm, like a schoolmaster dealing with a pair of naughty schoolboys. The riders have a look of shock and bewilderment on their faces. The man in the suit is a representation of the *Unione Velocipedistica Italiana* (UVI) – then Italian cycling's governing body – and the two cyclists are Italy's greatest and wealthiest riders: Alfredo Binda and Costante Girardengo.

If Binda had brought glory to his country in 1927 following his win at the Nürburgring, twelve months later the reaction to his performance in defence of that inaugural Worlds title could not have been more different. And not without good reason. In the late 1920s Binda and Girardengo were engaged in an intense battle for Italy's affections and, for each of them, preventing the other from winning prestigious races was nearly as important as trying to win themselves. In 1928 that was plain for all to see on the roads of Hungary.

The 1928 race started in Budapest and headed north to the town of Balassagyarmat before turning south and heading back into Budapest for the finish. En route were a number of tough climbs, poorly surfaced dirt roads and cobblestones. The UCI had decided the running of a single race for amateurs and professionals the previous year had not worked and so they split the field and ran two races. Just sixteen riders lined up at the start of the professional race, with teams limited to a maximum of three riders each. The amateurs were set off 50 minutes later.

While France sent only one professional rider, the national champion Ferdinand Le Drogo, for Italy Binda and Girardengo were joined by the 1920 Giro champion and multiple classics winner Gaetano Belloni, who had finished fourth the previous year. Belgium had its national champion Joseph Dervaes alongside Jules Van Hevel and Georges Ronsse. Van Hevel was thirty-three years old and had won the Tour of Flanders and Paris-Roubaix in 1920 and 1924 respectively, while Ronsse was just twenty-two but had already won Paris-Roubaix and Bordeaux-Paris. It was a strong team and one which the Italians would have to watch.

Which was exactly what they did. They watched. When Van Hevel escaped the pack after around 50 kilometres, Binda and Girardengo just looked at each other. When Ronsse made his move to bridge across to his compatriot soon after, Binda and Girardengo looked at each other again. Binda finally began to try to chase but when he looked to his rival to help none came. Twelve months earlier Girardengo had launched the first attack that had ultimately led to Binda's win and he was not going to the front of the chase now to help his biggest rival to a second Worlds win.

In contrast to the Italians, the Belgians worked together and by the 90-kilometre mark Ronsse and Van Hevel had built a lead of 12 minutes. Not even halfway and the Italian race was done with all three riders abandoning the race. After dominating the previous year, Italy would not record any finishers in Hungary. They were a team ripped to the seams by the intense rivalry of their two stars. The nation was embarrassed.

With 100 kilometres to go the 1928 Worlds was already two-rider affair. But Van Hevel was dogged by bad luck – first he suffered a flat tyre and then he collided with a cow on the road, injuring his leg. He remounted before falling away, leaving Ronsse to ride alone to the finish, crossing the line more than 19 minutes ahead of second-placed Herbert Nebe of Germany. Only eight riders finished and Ronsse's winning margin remains the largest in the history of the Worlds. No other time gap comes close.

In the days that followed the race, the UVI released an official communication confirming that, after conducting an investigation, its two greatest stars were to be suspended from all competition for six months. The UVI's communique, signed by its president Ernesto Torrusio, stated the suspension was for 'not having defended with faith and determination the prestige of Italian cycling whilst engaged in this most important world competition.'[14]

The decision of the UVI was welcomed by most observers. *La Stampa* wrote of Binda and Girardengo being 'blinded by deplorable rivalries, personal and completely inappropriate in a race abroad where they are riding in the good name of Italy.'[15] Before the announcement of the ban the two riders had been due to take part in a track meeting between Italy and the Netherlands. Fans had planned a protest against the pair. 'A great number of the public, who had not heard of the suspension went armed with "stink pots", bombettes and squeakers in order to show their wrath,' reported *Cycling*. 'However, they were doomed to disappointment. The two had gone shooting.'[16]

Unsurprisingly the riders considered themselves hard done by. Binda said that he had tried to chase Ronsse's move for 7 or 8 kilometres while Girardengo and Belloni refused to help. 'Then I stopped, it is true,' Binda said. 'But if you give me six months, the others should get six years, because they did absolutely nothing.'[17] For his part Girardengo pointed to the previous year's events, saying: 'Why ride and sacrifice myself for him?'[18]

'I understand the severity of the measure that strikes me,' Girardengo later said. 'I do not think I deserve it … I knew the importance of the race. [I] aspired to win it. I understood that in no better way could I honestly end my career … Torrusio will judge.'[19]

In the end the suspensions imposed by the UVI lasted only two months. On 26 October the Italian National Olympic Committee announced that the suspensions had served their purpose in giving an effective warning to Binda and Girardengo as well as other riders who competed abroad and that 'in consideration of the sportsman-like spirit in which they have welcomed the serious measures,'[20] the suspensions were lifted and the riders free to race again. Eight days later Binda lined up against his Worlds teammate Belloni, who for reasons that remained unclear had escaped any sanction, at the Tour of Lombardy. In a race marred by rain and floods, Belloni won while Binda suffered a number of punctures but was still there at the end to contest the sprint for the win, crossing the line just behind Belloni. But Binda's season's travails were not yet over and he was later disqualified for an illegal bike change.

***

In 1929 Georges Ronsse successfully defended his title in Zurich. Again countries were restricted to just three riders. This time Binda had different teammates – Leonida Frascarelli and Domenico Piemontesi – who were charged only with working for the man from Cittiglio. As the race approached its closing moments, and following strong attacks from Binda, Luxembourg's Nicolas Frantz and France's Marcel Bidot, a group of five had established a decisive lead. In that leading group were two Belgians: Ronsse and Joseph Dervaes, two Italians: Binda and Frascarelli, and Frantz.

Twenty thousand expectant fans crowded into the final, barricaded section of the race, lining the cobblestoned final straight, craning their necks to get a glimpse of the action. They had all paid one franc for the privilege of being close to the finish and were treated to the sight of five riders battling it out for the win. Frantz went early in the dash to the line, hitting the head of the race with one kilometre or so to go. He was still there, with Binda on his wheel, with just 200 metres left. Binda was perfectly placed – surely it was a formality for the great man. But then Ronsse made his move. From fourth in line the defending champion powered round Binda and Frantz to throw his bike across the line and claim a narrow win ahead of Frantz. A single second separated the first five riders and as the crowds poured around Ronsse, Binda was left stunned. He looked at Italy's newsmen aghast, speechless, unable to explain what had happened in the final moments of a race that was seemingly his for the taking.[21] It was the first time a sprint had settled the professional Worlds.

In just its third year, the world championships already had its first back-to-back champion. Ronsse had demonstrated his versatility, first by riding alone to a record-making victory in Hungary and then by timing his final sprint to perfection in Switzerland. In Britain there was still no officially sanctioned massed-start road racing, a legacy from the National Cycling Union's decision to ban racing on open roads in the 1890s. As a result the spectacle of a bunch race rather than a time trial was seen by many in Britain as a curious oddity perhaps best illustrated by reference to *Cycling's* race report which described Ronsse's win as a 'placid story of grouped riding, strenuous up the hills, easy going downhill and along the level.'[22] It was a view supported by the fact that every starter made it to the finish – the only time that has happened in the event's history.[23]

While Binda faced some criticism back home for his passive sprint, he had at least restored some pride for his country following the debacle in Budapest. The following year his world championship redemption was complete when he led the Italian team to a one-two finish ahead of Ronsse in the Belgian city of Liège. But again his success was not without complications.

Since 1925 the *Campionissimo* had ruled the Giro. Just once in that time had he failed to win Italy's national tour and by 1930 such was his dominance in Italy's showpiece event that the Giro organisers were fearful of yet another Binda win. The public were growing tired of reading about the Binda show and it was demonstrated in diminishing newspaper sales. The race organisers wanted a more competitive race and they hit upon the novel way of achieving it by paying Binda 22,500 lire to stay away – the amount he had worked out he would win at the Giro.[24]

Instead Binda went to the Tour. Alongside him in France was Learco Guerra, a talented rider from Lombardy who had turned professional in 1928 following encouragement from none other than Girardengo, who viewed the rider as someone who could challenge Binda now that his own legs were growing weary. Guerra won the second stage, inheriting the yellow jersey and holding it for a week. Binda meanwhile lost over an hour on stage seven to Hendaye, then won stages eight and nine in the Pyrenees before abandoning the race following a mechanical problem on stage ten. After retiring from the race Binda said: 'If I've abandoned it is because I have excellent reasons.'[25] But no one knew what those reasons were. It wasn't until 1980, six years before his death, that Binda revealed that he had been reluctant to ride the Tour at all and had instead wanted to focus on the world championships. In order to convince him to ride, Tour organiser Henri Desgrange had agreed to pay Binda a fee for each stage. Desgrange had known Binda was focused on the Worlds and would not continue all the way to Paris.[26]

And so it was left to Guerra, nicknamed 'the human locomotive', to fly the Italian flag at the Tour and he did so in style, winning another brace of stages and securing second place behind France's André Leducq. Guerra's performance catapulted him into the hearts of the Italian *tifosi* (fans). *La Stampa* called him 'the revelation of the race'.[27]

So when Binda, the man who abandoned the Italian team in the Pyrenees, beat Guerra, who battled to second virtually single handed in that race, to claim his second world championship title in a tight sprint, the response from the Italian public was perhaps more muted than might have been expected.

The 1930 world championships were meant to have been the glorious homecoming of Ronsse. For the first time the event was being held in Belgium and the country was expecting their defending champion to make it three wins in a row on the roads of the Ardennes. It was the centenary of Belgium's independence from the Netherlands, a fact celebrated on the front of the event's official programme and something that only added to the sense of expectation.

On the run in to the finish, Binda and Ronsse were together along with Guerra and Germany's Kurt Stoepel. With 150 metres to go Guerra sprinted to the front, laying everything on the line. Ronsse was not able to react quickly enough, but Binda mined the depths of his reserves to stay on

Guerra's wheel and pass his popular teammate in the final 20 metres to take his second rainbow jersey. Binda had prevailed over Ronsse, who finished third, reversing the result of twelve months earlier. But while Binda had the title Guerra had the love of the people. 'I can say that I do not know if Binda would have won without Guerra,' wrote Carlo Trabucco. 'The locomotive has been invaluable to the Italian champion. In the last 200 metres he was truly like a suction pump. Binda, on his wheel, has found victory. We therefore cannot separate the name of Binda from that of Guerra.'[28]

***

Fast forward twelve months and Guerra had the jersey as well as the plaudits. Instead of a massed-start road race, the 1931 world championships took the form of an un-paced time trial over a 172-kilometre course, starting and finishing in Copenhagen. The change in format came after representations to the UCI from national federations concerned at the dominance of the Italians and Belgians. The world championships were meant to be an individual event and teamwork of any kind was officially against the regulations. Some federations felt that the Italians in particular were guilty of ignoring this rule and were in effect riding as a team, even if the antics of Binda and Girardengo in previous years suggested just the opposite. The format change was put to a vote and carried, much to the annoyance of the Italians.

While long at 172 kilometres, the time trial was at least flat. The seventeen professional riders were set off at two-minute intervals, heading south-west towards the village of Baarse before turning 180 degrees and heading north, straight into a strong headwind.

Guerra stopped the clock in Copenhagen at 4:53:43, some 04:37 ahead of France's Ferdinand Le Drogo. In the amateur race Denmark's own Henry Hansen won, posting a time some 02:50 faster than Guerra on exactly the same route, creating the situation where the amateur world champion had outperformed his professional counterpart. Hansen's time was nearly six minutes quicker than that of the second fastest amateur, Italy's Giuseppe Olmo. With the roads remaining open to cars, *Cycling* alleged that Hansen had benefitted by sheltering from the wind amongst cars, reporting: 'There is no doubt that the winner, a popular local hero, was very unfairly helped in this way by the shielding movements of the motors, and such help made an enormous difference.'[29]

A similar accusation was levied at Guerra as well as allegations that he had received information as to his position relative to his rivals while out on course – another practice that was banned at the time. The Italian press took this as sour grapes from nations that, in their eyes, had tried and failed to break Italy's stranglehold on the event by changing the way it was run. 'It is not only the locomotive Guerra that rubbished your pride,' wrote Emilio Colombo in *La Gazzetta dello Sport*, 'it is all Italian cycling that beat you in a sport that you do not and cannot understand.'[30]

Guerra was a hero. *Corriere della Sera* described his ride as an 'irresistible march,'[31] while in his book on Italian cycling, *Pedalare! Pedalare!*, John Foot describes Guerra returning home in a train daubed in graffiti proclaiming: 'Long live Guerra world champion.'[32] Receptions were held in his honour and Colombo described him as 'an irresistible fighter, a complete rider.'[33]

***

Binda had finished sixth in Copenhagen, well over eight minutes behind Guerra, but in 1932 the *Campionissimo* roared back to claim his third title, setting a record for the men's title that, while since equalled by three others, remains to this day.

By his standards Binda had endured a disappointing 1932. His last major win had come in the autumn of 1931 at the Tour of Lombardy, achieved in some style with a long solo escape in the rain. Binda put his win down to the twenty or more eggs his Legano *soigneur* had passed to him to eat during the race.[34] The best he could do at the Giro was seventh overall and a couple of second places on stages while working for teammate Antonio Pesenti. Binda needed a big win to close his season.

Twenty-five riders started the race in Rome. At the end of the second lap Guerra led a group of twelve. Binda and his compatriot Remo Bertoni broke away on the final climb to Frascati. No one could go with them. The pair worked to build a lead of over five minutes before Binda beat his fellow escapee across the line by 15 seconds. During the race news came that Binda was not feeling well, that he had not slept the night before and had not done half the training he had planned.[35] Yet still he won. The following year he would win his fifth and final Giro title, taking six stages, the newly created mountains prize and the overall by more than 12 minutes.

In Rome William J Mills had been Britain's first representative in a professional world championships road race. He complained of sickness the night before the race but still started, then crashed after one lap, broke a wheel and retired. He was already 15 minutes down. His sickness was wearingly dismissed as being caused by nervousness.[36]

***

In six editions of the race three men had claimed the title of world champion. All three had been worthy winners who, importantly, had proved their credentials in other prestigious races as well as in the Worlds. Binda had reigned supreme over Italian cycling, winning multiple Giri as well as the Tour of Lombardy and Milan-Sanremo, Ronsse had won Paris-Roubaix and taken three Bordeaux-Paris titles, and Guerra was a multiple Italian champion who had won numerous stages at the Giro and Tour and finished on the podium at Milan-Sanremo. These were big-name riders whose championship-winning rides had only served to enhance the growing prestige of the Worlds.

In that time France, the country that boasted the most important race in the world, had featured on the podium only once, courtesy of Ferdinand Le Drogo's second place in 1931. In 1927 there had been just four days between the end of the Tour and the Worlds, but as the 1920s gave way to the 1930s there was now often more than two weeks between the events and sometimes as much as a month. Consequently, with the Worlds' standing growing and the movement in timing helping logistically, France's participation grew more serious. In 1930 André Leducq had ridden the Worlds for the first time a month after winning the Tour. It was the first time that the Tour champion had started the Worlds and Leducq was joined in the French team by Charles Pélissier who had won eight stages during Leducq's victorious Tour ride and finished second in another seven. While Pélissier and Leducq could only finish ninth and eleventh respectively in 1930, their involvement was indicative of growing French interest in the race.

In 1933 France hosted the Worlds for the first time with the race held on a racing circuit in Montlhery. The decision was motivated in part by the need of cycling federations to cover the costs of hosting the event. By using a closed, secure circuit instead of open roads, it was easier to charge an entrance fee to the thousands who now wanted to watch what was becoming an increasingly popular event. The circuit itself was 12.5 kilometres, with plenty of twists and turns and a single climb – the one-kilometre long, 12 per cent Côte Lapize.

France selected a strong team. Roger Lapébie was their national champion and he was joined by Antonin Magne, the 1931 Tour winner and runner-up to Lapébie in the nationals. They were scheduled to be joined by Paul Chocque, a rider some had earmarked as the favourite, but when Chocque had to withdraw at the last minute because of illness he was replaced by Georges Speicher.

Speicher was some replacement. Three weeks earlier he had taken the biggest win of his career, winning the Tour by four minutes over Guerra. He was already a darling of the French people, standing in the yellow jersey in front of a huge crowd in the Parc des Princes, and had been busy enjoying himself and celebrating his win. After being hastily thrust back into action, Speicher would make history as he delivered France's first rainbow jersey.

A storm brought thunder and downpours of rain halfway through a race that Speicher ruled right from the start. At the end of the opening lap he was at the head of the race and there he pretty much stayed. He broke away alone with 125 kilometres still to go and pulled out a huge lead. French cycling writer Pierre Chany described Speicher as riding with a sort of aura, without weakness, handling his bike with 'extraordinary dexterity'.[37] After a huge solo effort, Speicher crossed the line in 7:08:58, more than five minutes ahead of compatriot Magne. France had its first world champion and the title could not have been delivered with more panache or from a more popular rider. And it had come on home roads. It was the first time a rider had achieved the Tour/Worlds double, a feat that would not be matched for more than twenty years.

'A champion can win everything,' ran one headline in *Paris-Soir* in the days that followed the race. 'And Speicher is one.'[38] Through Speicher, France had finally arrived at the Worlds.

The race returned to Germany in 1934, scene of the first professional world championships seven years earlier. Rather than the notorious Nürburgring, this time a 9.4-kilometre circuit in Leipzig was used. It could not have been more different. Where the Nürburgring was hugely challenging, the Leipzig course was flat and frankly dull.

In the days before the race the German President Paul von Hindenburg had died. Adolf Hitler, who had become Chancellor of Germany in early 1933, then declared himself joint President and Chancellor, before later abolishing the office of President and announcing himself as the Führer of the German Reich and People. So the 1934 world championships were run in a country under Nazi rule. It meant that the winner would be presented not only with the rainbow jersey but also be photographed draped in a sash carrying the swastika, all presented to a soundtrack of Hitler-endorsed military marches.

Karel Kaers was the recipient of the jersey. Kaers was just twenty years old and he became the youngest male road-race world champion, a distinction he still holds. His victory came from nowhere. He had only been riding at the highest level for just over a year and only had one road win to his name – the Grand Prix d'Ostende. The Belgian, large for a cyclist at just under two metres tall, was more of a track rider with two national junior track titles his stand-out results.

Yet Kaers shocked the world, beating more fancied riders like Guerra and Magne. The course did not lend itself to serious breakaway attempts. Instead the bunch rolled round the circuit, shedding some of the twenty-six starters as they went. The finale came down to a fourteen-rider sprint and the young Belgian won the dash to the line ahead of Guerra, who claimed his third podium spot in five years. The reaction was muted, with at least one writer highlighting the irony of having a road-race champion who was more regularly seen on the track than on the road.[39]

'Both "champions" [professional and amateur], were they sent next week against the same field and over a real road course as to distance and gradients, would not be anywhere near the leaders at the end,' opined *Cycling* in its race report. 'The French commentators say he [Kaers] is a worthy champion, but he is not the road champion, for it was not a road race!' [40] But Kaers would later prove his worth, winning the Belgian national title and the Tour of Flanders during a career shortened by the outbreak of war.

***

If the Leipzig course was deemed too easy for a professional world championships, the 1935 race made up for it in spades. Held in Floreffe in the Belgian province of Namur, the race included sixteen ascents of the 3.8-kilometre long Bois de la Haute Marlagne. Among the twenty-nine riders that started were former champions Guerra and Speicher, but it was Belgium's Jean Aerts who triumphed and rode the final 50 miles 'through a roar of cheering that must have been unique in the history of the world's title race.' [41] Aerts had won the amateur title in 1927 and his 1935 win meant he was the first man to have both the amateur and professional road-race titles amongst his *palmares*.

***

'So it's true. I'm a world champion. The rainbow jersey is in the suitcase. There is no doubt.' So wrote Antonin Magne in *Paris-Soir* on 8 September 1936. 'Of course, I went to Bern with the hope of defending myself, but I knew that to win, one would have to be very strong and have a little luck. I had that luck...' [42]

The luck Magne referred to was to not suffer a puncture. On the flinty roads of Switzerland, the pouring rain that fell during the race loosened grit and stones, the result of which was a myriad of punctured tyres that ruled many riders out of contention.

The rain and wind that arrived during the race made conditions tough. Magne got away with Denmark's Werner Grundahl and Belgium's Gustaaf

Deloor. Deloor punctured, leaving Magne and Grundahl at the head of the race with a two-minute gap on the chasers. Over the course of the next five laps they worked together to increase the lead to three minutes.

'At each passage my comrades – [Emile] Ignat in particular – shouted at me,' Magne wrote. '"Attention! Sprinter!" They meant that Grundahl would be formidable in a sprint finish.' [43]

With three laps to go, Grundahl lost the wheel of Magne and then suffered a puncture himself. He would finish fifth. Magne, meanwhile, powered on alone to claim a terrific solo win, with a gap of more than nine minutes on Italy's Aldo Bini. In the first professional road race to be held during September, just nine riders were classified. 'What a beautiful thing, what a Champion,'[44] commented none other than the original *Campionissimo* and now Italian national team coach, Costante Girardengo. Others meanwhile pointed to the number of riders who had fallen or had punctures. Magne responded: 'You forget, sirs, that a cautious rider in good condition punctures less often than others!'[45]

***

A little under a month before the 1937 championships in Denmark, the Belgian team had departed from the Tour en masse, with their leader Sylvère Maes still in yellow just three days before Paris. Their departure came following rows with the French team and the race organisers over the application of penalties and bonuses between Maes and France's Roger Lapébie. Lapébie had received illegal help on a number of climbs in the mountains but was only docked 90 seconds while Maes was penalised 25 seconds for co-operating with Gustaaf Deloor, while chasing back to the head of the race after suffering a puncture. Deloor was Belgian but was riding as an individual and so co-operation between Maes and Deloor was against the rules. The Belgians felt the penalty levied against Lapébie was insufficient while the one imposed on Maes was excessive. That, coupled with a 'convenient' level-crossing closure that further impeded Maes' chase of Lapébie after his puncture, led to the Belgian walkout.

Eloi Meulenberg, a twenty-four-year-old, three-year professional, had been part of Maes' team in France. He had won four stages before heading home to Belgium. In Denmark, Meulenberg would restore a little joy to Belgian cycling. Part of the decisive five-man break that finished the race more than six minutes ahead of the rest of the race, Meulenberg first chased down any attacks his fellow escapees tried to make in the final kilometres and then waited patiently for the sprint, winning by a couple of lengths. At 297.5 kilometres the race, held on a flat 8.5-kilometre circuit north of Copenhagen, remains the longest in world championship history.

Belgium's supremacy at the world championships was confirmed a year later. Described by *Cycling* as the hardest road championships held to that point, the 1938 race was the first hosted by Valkenburg in the Netherlands and the first to go over the infamous Cauberg, the short but steep grind that would later become synonymous with the one-day Amstel Gold spring classic. In 1938 the peloton would have to scale it twenty-seven times.

There also featured a tricky and narrow one-kilometre descent of the Geulemerberg and sand-strewn surfaces that was described as more like the turf of a trick cyclist. The race was hit by thunder, lightning and rain. In short it was an extraordinary and brutal day, the kind that stands out in the annals of a race's history and helps to forge its identity. Of the thirty-six starters only eight finished with the entire teams of Italy, Germany and Denmark abandoning the race. Even the great Italian Gino Bartali, who was coming off the back of his first Tour win and was the pre-race favourite, could not handle things and climbed off with around 15 kilometres to go. Such days are the stuff of legend.

With 30 kilometres left to ride, a leading group of four had established itself at the head of the race: Switzerland's Paul Egli and Leo Amberg, Belgium's Marcel Kint and Piet Van Nek of the Netherlands. When home favourite Van Nek finally fell away, it left a three-up sprint to sort the podium places.

Despite being outnumbered by the Swiss, Kint, nicknamed the 'black eagle' because he wore a dark cycling jersey and had beaked nose, was too fast. The sprint was, in the words of Pierre Chany, a 'simple formality.'[46] *La Stampa* meanwhile described Kint as the perfect athlete for a road race: 'intelligent, brisk, durable and fast.'[47]

Kint did not know it yet but he would become the longest serving world champion in history. The 1939 championships were scheduled for early September in Varese, Italy, but on 30 August, with the world in turmoil and Britain's declaration of war on Hitler's Germany just days away, the French sports-paper L'Auto, carried a front-page headline that simply read: 'See you later, world championships!'[48] Given the situation in Europe the UCI had made the decision to postpone the event even though it had already started. L'Auto wrote that it was envisaged that the championships would resume, 'probably next month.'[49] As it turned out, Kint would not be called on to defend his jersey until September 1946.

4

MARCEL KINT
(1938)

It is mid-November. In the dark and the rain I am driving around the side-streets of Kortrijk, Belgium looking for No.21, Proosdijstraat. My satnav is telling me I've arrived, but I can't see the bike shop I'm looking for; all I can see are houses. I park the car and retrace my route on foot. Then I see light drifting onto the pavement from an open garage door and a sign that says: '*P.V.B.A; Marcel Kint; Velos in T'Groot.*' My satnav was right, I am indeed where I need to be.

Inside stands a slim man, I'm guessing in his thirties, with a shaved head, wearing a scarf and headphones. He is working at a computer mounted on a counter. Behind him runs a long and narrow storeroom and workshop filled to the brim with bicycle parts. Later he will show me around a little and tell me that the premises runs for nearly 100 metres behind the street, but for now he just gently smiles, removes his headphones and offers his hand. This is Marniek Kint and I'm here to talk with him about his grandfather, Marcel.

***

'I was not exuberant, have never been a rider of many words.
What did I have to say anyway?
I laboured on the bike to have a better life and that's all.'[50]

Marcel Kint

In 1938 Marcel Kint won the rainbow jersey in Valkenburg, prevailing in a three-man sprint after one of the toughest races in the event's (then) short history. As described in the previous chapter the outbreak of war the following year meant that Kint held the jersey for eight years, becoming the longest-serving world champion in history.

Today Marniek, runs the bicycle business that his grandfather established after his retirement in 1951 and which still carries his name. Marniek takes me through to the businesses *salon*, an oasis of style and calm in which he displays the company's work and cycling accessories in a gallery-like setting. While Marniek makes coffee I am left to wander happily around the room, enjoying a few moments to look covetously at the stylish and closely detailed machines on show, wonderful examples of Marniek's handiwork, all lovingly crafted in the name of his grandfather. Then we sit down with our coffees and Marniek begins to tell me all about his grandfather.

***

Marniek Kint:

I knew my grandfather very well. He taught me to drive a car. He had a hobby keeping pigeons and when I was around twelve years old, something like that, my father thought it was better to help my grandfather with his pigeons than to go to the football. So every Friday, Saturday and Sunday we went together on the road, flying his pigeons. I grew up on the other side of the street here, where my parents still live, and my grandfather lived here, this was his house. On Wednesday afternoons we worked together with our grandparents ... we lived, not together, but very closely.

He was a very quiet person concerning his sport and his cycling victories. The only times I heard something about his past as a cyclist were when journalists came to the house for any reason. Maurice Desimpelaere, the Belgian rider who won Paris-Roubaix in 1944, lived 10 kilometres from here and he and my grandfather were friends. So he came often to see my grandfather and chat and I would be there drinking cocoa and listening. My grandfather was not like other people who would scream, 'Yes I was world champion, yes I won the Belgian championships, blah blah blah.' No. He worked a lot. It was normal for him, well, perhaps not normal ... it is difficult to explain...

The life of my grandfather: He was born in 1914. Because of the world war he didn't see his own father for several years. They were not rich people and he had to work at a young age and so cycling for him was an opportunity to earn more money. He was grateful that he could do it. Being a world champion for him was just ... if you work hard you can finish first and that was it. For him it wasn't something special that you then had to talk about.

He started cycling in 1931. He was seventeen years old and working in a factory for Bekaert, a big company from Zwevegem where he was born. One of his colleagues was the other type of man, he was shouting, 'I'm a cyclist, I can win!' My grandfather said to him: 'Maybe you should work instead of talk because you don't know, maybe I am better than you.' But he didn't have a bike because they didn't have the money. So his colleague was teasing my grandfather and after a while he said, 'OK, I will ride in a race.' He didn't win that race but his colleague was way, way behind him. That was the first time he rode a race, I think he finished third or fourth and he felt good. It opened his eyes ... he thought maybe I can ride a bike better than other people, why not?

I don't want to read you his *palmares,* but I think it is seventeen pages of top-ten positions. In his first year, 1931, he won two races already. The next year, 1932, 1, 2, 3 … 12 races in his second year cycling. And if you win all the time … well it's not easy money, and they maybe won only the equivalent of five euros today, but back then it was a nice amount of money.

Kint finally turned profession in 1935 and three years later won his rainbow jersey.

Due to the win in Valkenburg he became public property of a sort. He didn't like it, it was not for him. He had some more money because of his win so decided to start a bar … a café. If you have a bar your fans will come to drink and so it will make extra money. But really he didn't like to be at the centre of everything. He was world champion and he loved cycle racing and to do that as a job, but he didn't like all the fuss about it.

But it changed his life because it meant he could invest in the bar. It was the reason that he built bikes afterwards and it was the reason he was famous and successful with his bikes. I mean in those days if you were world champion in cycling … it was *the* sport … if he hadn't won in Valkenburg maybe I wouldn't be here now making bicycles. It changed a lot.

In 1939 Kint had gone to Italy to defend his title but, with war imminent, just four days before the race the world championships were postponed. The event wouldn't be held again until 1946.

Due to the world war the national federation decided that if you want to keep on riding as a professional you had to choose between two licences – A or B. If you had licence A, you were in the higher category but you had to go to Milan, you had to go to Paris and so on to race because the Germans would let you travel. But if you had the B licence you weren't allowed to go abroad and had to stay in Belgium. My grandfather, as world champion, was supposed to be category A, but he refused. He said he wanted to be category B because if he had to go to Italy, to Spain, to France it would cost him a lot of money and the profits would not be enough. But the national federation said no, you are world champion, you are not allowed to be category B, you have to take licence A. So my grandfather said in that case he would stop riding. He didn't ride for two years.

When the Worlds returned in 1946 Kint went to Switzerland to defend the jersey he had won eight years earlier. He was alone at the front of the race until his compatriot Rik Van Steenbergen rode across bringing the Swiss rider Hans Knecht with him. Van Steenbergen then fell away leaving Knecht to beat Kint in the final 500 metres. It was later reported that Kint was held back by Swiss fans on the run in to the line.

He never said a word about it to us. No, nothing. I mean, to the journalists yes, but to the family nothing. I know that if I had been my grandfather in 1946 I would have … ah, let's just say I would have been very unhappy.

My grandfather was away alone in front of the race. It was Rik Van Steenbergen's first world championships, of course – because of the war. He was nineteen years old I think, very young. I suppose he thought he could be better than my grandfather. He did everything to catch up with my grandfather with Hans Knecht, the Swiss, on his wheel and then in the last five or ten kilometres he was dead, you know what I mean, he had nothing left. So only Hans Knecht and my grandfather were at the front. My grandfather was faster than him but Knecht was from Switzerland so he had a lot of supporters there to cheer for him.

Some supporters went on the road and caught my grandfather, they stopped him, they held him and they pushed Knecht, for maybe 10 or 15 seconds. If you're standing still and the other rider is riding 30km/h or something it is impossible to catch up. So he lost. My grandfather said afterwards that he was thinking of not finishing, he was very mad. But he did finish, for the money I suppose because second place also had some bonuses I think.

In Belgium the two groups of supporters argued, so they had to make it up. The manager of Rik Van Steenbergen suggested to my grandfather that they ride on the track during the winter and so they were paid to race together. That was the deal afterwards and they won several six-day races together. It was a good mix for my grandfather and they earned a lot of money so that was good for him – at the end of his career it was a good option. Of course, for me, I'd rather be world champion, but at that time, after the war, money was also important so I can understand his decision but I am not a very big fan of Van Steenbergen.

Kint's war-interrupted career lasted for sixteen years. As well as the Worlds he won Paris-Roubaix (1943), La Flèche Wallonne three times (1943–45) and Gent-Wevelgem (1949), before retiring in 1951.

I think for him it was just his job, it was a way to earn more money than by working normally in the factory. But he was proud that he achieved everything he did – that he was the world champion, that he won the Belgian national jersey, that he won Paris-Roubaix … that he proved to himself that he was a good cyclist. If you don't win you cannot say to yourself you are doing well, you can only do that when you win, but it was only to himself, not to the public or to other people … it was not in his personality to talk – blah blah blah, no.

After retiring, Kint immediately started his bike-building business.

He had another goal in his life – to use his experiences of riding a bike to build one. Mercier, my grandfather's sponsor, was a bike-building company in France and he had seen a lot of things with them. So he gave himself a new goal, to make his own bikes in Belgium. He started that in 1951. He finished riding and immediately he had a bike shop above his bar. It grew very fast and then they moved here in 1956. He made the bikes himself. In that time if you had a broken wheel or if your frame was broken you had to fix it yourself; every winter he had been to Mercier in Saint-Étienne in France to build his own bike.

I have seen paperwork from those days and they employed fourteen people here, building a lot of bikes. In those days cars were very expensive and so the bike was the main way of getting around. People wanted bikes and what was better than buying a bike from the world champion next door? He was well known in Belgium and so it was easy for people to say, 'Ah, you are Marcel Kint, I'll buy a bike from you.'

My father continued the business … as I continue now as a third generation. I always say I was just born here in Kortrijk and all this was my grandfather's and my father's doing. I didn't do anything but what I can do for him now is to make sure people don't forget him. Of course I am very proud. Who has a grandfather with such a career in cycling? I'm also proud to make my own bikes for our family's bicycle business. I have two children and a wife and my own life but I am working, honouring his memory. When I was young, in school, and I said my grandfather was Marcel Kint people said, 'Who is Marcel Kint? We know Johan Museeuw and we know Eddy Merckx, but that's it!' Now, after seven or eight years working here, many people know Marcel Kint because we try to promote our bicycles and we are still connected to the person who started everything. There is always a connection to my grandfather in the bikes we build. It is due to him I am working here and I'm happy that we can do it.

5

THE WORLDS RETURN

The world championships had been dominated by Italy, Belgium and France during the pre-war years. Other nations had come close to the top step but none had reached it. Over the years the championships had begun to assume greater importance in cycling's annual calendar. In 1927 sixteen riders from six countries had started the first professional road race; by 1938 that number had grown to thirty-six riders from twelve nations, and with some memorable races and incidents, the event was slowly forging its own history and identity. Now, after an eight-year hiatus, the UCI's flagship event returned after the defeat of Nazi Germany with the task of regaining the momentum that had been building during the pre-war years.

In February 1946 and with Europe in the early stages of reconstruction after six years of hostilities, the UCI held its first post-war congress. During the meeting, held in Brussels under the presidency of Belgium's M. Alban Collignon, the issue of the next world championships was discussed. With few nations able or prepared to organise the event, the Swiss city of Zurich accepted the invitation to host the championships. 'It is our country's great honour and privilege to organise the first post-war world championships,'[51] reported the *Gazette de Lausanne*. Winston Churchill was invited as a guest of honour but he declined saying he was not undertaking public engagements.

Six months after that meeting in Brussels, thirty-two riders lined up in Zurich at the start of the 270-kilometre race. The cast of characters in the professional peloton had changed markedly since the previous championships, with just six riders from the 1938 race returning, including the winner Marcel Kint. Among the new faces were some noteworthy names riding their first professional Worlds, including future champions Albéric Schotte and Rik Van Steenbergen, and Emile Masson, the Belgian winner of the 1939 Paris-Roubaix.

During the UCI's February congress, Germany's readmission into the organisation had been rejected at the request of the committee while Italy was only provisionally readmitted after lengthy discussion and an intervention in their favour by France.[52] German riders were not issued the licences which would have enabled them to compete in races in Europe but Italians were free to race and they brought a strong team to Zurich, including Fausto Coppi. At the time Coppi had one national championship and one Giro title to his name, along with a single win in Milan-Sanremo, but this was his first start in the professional world championship race. Alongside him was his great rival Gino Bartali and the 1942 Milan-Sanremo winner Adolfo Leoni.

The day before Kint had claimed the professional title in 1938, the amateur race had been won the Swiss rider Hans Knecht. With Nazi Germany encouraging where possible the continuation of popular events such as cycle racing as a way of trying to appease occupied populations, both riders had ridden during the war and Kint in particular collected some notable wins including Paris-Roubaix in 1943 and three La Flèche Wallonne titles in a row (1943–1945). Now they would go head to head on a day of freezing rain when only seventeen riders made it to the finish.

With less than two laps to go Kint attacked and went away alone. The champion was riding strongly and seemingly towards a famous second title, but then two riders emerged from the pack behind and set off in fierce pursuit. There was nothing strange in that, but peculiarly the rider doing all the work was Van Steenbergen – Kint's compatriot and, on paper at least, teammate.

The other rider was Knecht. The Swiss merely sat on the young Belgian's wheel, presumably dumbstruck by his good fortune, as Van Steenbergen towed him up to Kint. It was a huge effort by the Belgian and by the time the two had made it across to Kint, Van Steenbergen was exhausted and had nothing left. He fell away on the final lap and finished third.

That left a stunned Kint and the home favourite Knecht to fight out the sprint. But the drama was not over, with Knecht allegedly then benefitting from some further unexpected assistance. While there is no photographic evidence to prove what happened, it was reported that in the final 500 metres fans spilled on to the course and held Kint back while pushing Knecht up the hill. The result was a first Swiss victory while Kint had to be content with second, ten seconds back.

The Swiss crowds were in raptures, celebrating wildly in the pouring rain, but the fallout in Belgium was huge. Kint was furious. He had been riding to what appeared to be a guaranteed victory until his young teammate had set off in pursuit. The supporters of both riders argued passionately over just what had happened on the roads of Zurich, although the two would later make up and appear together that winter on the track in six-day races, continuing that arrangement throughout the late 1940s and collecting several wins. In his book, *Campionissimes*,[53] the Belgian author and journalist Pierre Thonon questions the events of the race, writing that while it is difficult to say exactly what happened (and even harder to prove) it was well known that there was an agreement between the Belgian riders that, while riding as individuals (regulations still prohibited teams working together), if one of the team was leading the other riders would not actively hunt them down. Thonon writes that, in return, if a Belgian won the race they agreed to pay each of his three teammates 15,000 francs. This was a time when a world champion could command only a 1,500 franc premium for criterium appearances, effectively meaning that a Belgian winner would have to pay out 45,000 francs to his team, a sum that he could only earn back through more than thirty criterium contracts.

The inference is that for a Belgian rider the rainbow jersey would have come at a significant financial cost. Could that explain what happened in Zurich? Surely not. If a rider did want to 'not-win' a race because of the financial implications, then they would probably opt for a different strategy than one involving attacking with 35 kilometres to go, building a large lead before relying on a teammate to chase the break down while dragging a home-favourite with him, and then claiming partisan fans disrupted your final sprint while making sure no cameras were present. Surely it would be simpler to just say later that you were not feeling well. Van Steenbergen never really answered why he had chased his teammate so doggedly while Kint rigorously maintained that he was held back in that final sprint and that without that incident he perhaps would have won.

***

Held on a day of intense heat and on a 7.8-kilometre course described as being more fitting to a criterium or kermesse than a world championships, the 1947 Worlds became less of a bike race and more a trial of who would be the last to fall in the extreme conditions. 'The relentless sun, the overwhelming heat on this simple course, made the competition extremely hard and caused a total failure of all predictions,'[54] reported *Le Monde*.

Of the thirty-one riders that started in Reims, France, only seven made it to the finish. It was the lowest number of classified finishers in the history of the event and remains a record. The Dutchman Theo Middelkamp won, claiming the Netherlands' maiden win in the race. Twice a Tour stage winner and three times a national champion, it would prove to be the biggest win of Middelkamp's seventeen-season career, which also brought him Worlds podium placings in 1936 and 1950. Middelkamp had suffered a puncture on the final lap while part of the small leading group. He grabbed a replacement bike from the pits and continued on his way. The only problem was that the bike was not from his own cabin. The Dutchman had merely taken the first one he could find, sending all the support teams into a spin. He lost only 200 metres in the process and quickly made it back to the front group, taking a 10-second win over Belgium's Albert Sercu, father of the legendary track racer Patrick.

Among those who did not make it through to the finale were the previous year's winner Hans Knecht, Rik Van Steenbergen, Fausto Coppi, who had led the bunch for the opening few laps two days after taking the world pursuit title, and Ferdi Kübler, winner of two Tour stages the previous month. With more than a quarter of the race still to go, the field was down to ten riders – this on a pan-flat, smooth, 'easy', course with no climbing or technical descents. The heat and the merciless sun had burned off all but the hardiest. Never has the age-old adage that it is the riders that make the race not the course, been truer.

If Swiss and Dutch wins in the two years since the return of the championships after the war suggested a changing of the guard after the pre-war dominance of the Belgians, Italians and French, normal service soon resumed and 1948 brought the first of three straight titles for Belgium. It came courtesy of the man who would be dubbed the 'last of the Flandriens' by Belgian journalist Albert Bakert.

Synonymous with the Tour of Flanders, Albéric 'Briek' Schotte was born in Kanegem, West Flanders in 1919. Part of a large farming family, the young Albéric was charged with taking his brothers to school every day, six miles there and back, on his bike.

That 'training' in the end brought rewards. He rode his first Tour of Flanders in 1940, the youngest rider in the peloton, and came third. By the time he lined up in Valkenburg, the Netherlands for the 1948 Worlds he was a two-times winner of the Tour of Flanders and Paris-Tours. He later estimated that punctures and mechanical problems cost him up to four more Flanders wins.

The return to Valkenburg also meant the return of the Cauberg, depicted on one race map as a fierce dog waiting to bite the riders. In 1938 only eight men had made it to the finish here. A decade on the peloton fared little better. 'After twenty-seven "Caubergs" only 10 pros make the finish line,'[55] ran the headline in the Dutch daily *Leidsch Dagblad*.

Described as a 'Race of Giants,'[56] more than 200,000 people flocked to the circuit. Among them were thousands of Belgians who had crossed the border to watch one of their own try to take the title in a race they had last won a decade before. The war accounted for much of that period and immediate post-war races had not brought courses suited to the Belgians' strengths. Belgium still boasted many of the world's best riders in tough one-day races such as Paris-Roubaix, the Tour of Flanders, Liège-Bastogne-Liège and La Flèche Wallonne where, from 1930 through to 1948, remarkably just five non-Belgian riders had triumphed across all four of those races. When the roads turned cobbled, or when the wind blew and the rain fell on races that brought a seemingly never-ending succession of steep and narrow climbs, the Belgians were still the masters.

Schotte laid his cards on the table early, first breaking away as part of a five-man group and then moving clear alongside Apo Lazaridès of France, and Kübler. The Swiss could not hold the pace, leaving Schotte to beat Lazaridès in the sprint by five bike lengths, much to the joy of the thousands of watching Belgians.

'As I write this report it is five hours after the finish of the race and the road traffic trying to get back into Belgium is still jammed outside my hotel,' wrote *Cycling*'s reporter. 'But the passengers are happily shouting 'Schotte! Schotte!! Schotte!!!''[57]

But what of Italy, the other nation that had ruled the pre-war years? The Italians, with the great Alfredo Binda now at the head of affairs, had selected a team that included both Fausto Coppi and Gino Bartali, who had claimed a famous second Tour win just weeks earlier. The two men were at the very height of a rivalry that would split Italy and the world of cycling. You were either a supporter of Coppi or a supporter of Bartali. It was impossible to be a supporter of both. The two riders were obsessed with each other and their rivalry hit arguably its lowest point in Valkenburg. In an echo of the Girardengo and Binda debacle of twenty years earlier, the two riders were suspended from racing for two months because of 'a lack of willingness to compete.'[58]

'We notice that the two Italian champions have not been mentioned,' *Le Monde* wrote at the end of its race report. 'Only concerned to watch each other ... Coppi and Bartali were victims of the manoeuvre of Schotte...'[59]

As Schotte had sped up the road, the two Italians had sat and watched – each fearful of making the move that would tow the other to a possible victory. The Italian fans whistled and jeered, but still neither did anything.

La Stampa described the two as 'playing an ugly game', and described Bartali as 'a lead ball and chain',[60] on the team as Schotte and the others powered away. Both abandoned the race some 70 kilometres before the finish. Coppi later relayed the discussion he and Bartali had shared before they stopped:

'When we learned that our gap was more than ten minutes,
 Bartali was remorseful,' Coppi said.

'We must save our honour. Are we going to Fausto?'

'I'm going to bed!' I replied.

'Well,' said Gino. 'Me too under these conditions.'

And we turned around together, without exchanging a word,
not very proud of ourselves... [61]

Individual riders were not given the right of appeal by the Italian cycling's governing body (the UVI) and so the professional cyclists' association appealed against the punishment dished out to both riders and their trade teams threatened action. On 2 October the UVI relented and voted to grant the two riders an amnesty. They were free to ride again. Three weeks later Coppi claimed his third straight Tour of Lombardy title in a show of force that saw him complete an 80-kilometre solo breakaway with a five-minute win.

But Coppi and Bartali would never again start a world championships together.

***

When Bartali had turned to Coppi in Valkenburg and asked if they were going to restore their honour, he could not have known that twelve months on Coppi would at least restore his, even if he did not return from Copenhagen with the rainbow jersey in his bag.

Coppi had enjoyed a terrific 1949 season, winning Milan-Sanremo before claiming the Giro and the Tour, becoming the first rider to record that particular double. He set about dominating the Worlds on a flat course that offered little in the way of a platform for him to launch a solo bid. 'The steepest pitch on the road course is 250 metres of 1 in 40! [2.5 per cent]'[62] reported *Cycling*.

This was Coppi's first concerted bid for the title and the Italian got straight down to business, bridging across to an early break just 30 kilometres or so into the 290-kilometre race and then, after that was caught, making sure he was part of the decisive move that went with around 80 kilometres remaining.

Coppi, Van Steenbergen and the Netherlands' Gerrit Schulte attacked and broke away before Kübler and his Swiss teammate Ernst Stettler worked together to get across. Coppi knew that Van Steenbergen was the faster sprinter. Even though he would go on to win Paris-Roubaix, Coppi's skill and grace truly came to the fore when the mountain roads of Europe tipped skywards. By contrast, the Belgian was at home on the flat gruelling roads of northern Europe. It was here, in northern France, Belgium, Denmark and Germany, that Van Steenbergen would enjoy his best days; Coppi knew he had to get away from the tenacious Belgian.

And so Coppi threw everything at Van Steenbergen, attacking relentlessly in the closing laps. Nothing worked, he simply could not get him off his wheel. And worse, Kübler hung on, too. 'The grimness of the effort was telling on the Italian's face. He used every road manoeuvre in those three laps to shake off the Belgian and get away alone,' reported *Cycling*. 'He needed only 50 yards and his great un-paced skill [time-trialling] would have done the rest. But the young road-cum-trackman would not be dropped.'[63]

Into the closing straight, in front of a large crowd sat beneath Danish flags, Van Steenbergen roared past the dejected Coppi. To rub salt into Coppi's wounds, Van Steenbergen's sprint offered a wheel for Kübler to pass the Italian maestro as well. After ruling the race with an iron fist, Coppi's reward was third and the acknowledgement of the cycling world that he had given it everything. Three years later Coppi would suffer a similar fate in Paris-Roubaix, again at the hands of the Belgian.

After the events of 1946, Van Steenbergen had come of age in the Worlds. His was a terrific display of tactical acumen – all he had to do was to stick with the Italian until the end and the title was his. He knew his strengths and what it would take to win and he followed his plan through perfectly. And there was far more to come in Van Steenbergen's world championship story.

The following year Briek Schotte completed Belgium's run of three straight world championship wins, claiming his second rainbow jersey in a race that passed many places synonymous with the battles of the First World War, including Ypres, Messines Ridge and the Menin Gate. The race was defined by a 130-kilometre escape by France's Antonin Rolland before Schotte broke away with the 1947 champion Theo Middelkamp. Schotte was so strong that he then rode away from Middelkamp to win by just over one minute in front of his home fans. It was only the second time that the same country had claimed three world championships in succession, matching Italy's three wins between 1930 and 1932. In seventeen races Belgium had claimed nine wins, with Italy's four titles the next best. The world championships were being ruled by one nation.

6

MAMAN: JE SUIS CHAMPION DU MONDE

With Belgium reigning supreme at the world championships, France and Italy, traditional powerhouses of cycling, had enjoyed slim pickings. At the Tour it was becoming a similar story. Since the end of the war the French had managed just one win in its own national race – Jean Robic in 1947. French cycling needed a new hero, someone to take on the might of the Belgians. That hero would come in the form of Louison Bobet who during the 1950s would become the first rider to win three consecutive Tours, as well as claiming four Monuments (including a win at the Tour of Flanders in 1955, out-sprinting Rik Van Steenbergen in a result so extraordinary that cycling writer Pierre Chany described spectators dropping cartons of frites in surprise) and France's first rainbow jersey in eighteen years.

By August 1954, when the Worlds returned to Germany for the first time since the war, the twenty-nine-year-old Bobet was in the middle of that terrific run of form. He was the darling of France. The 15-kilometre circuit in Solingen, a city in the west of Germany famous for the manufacture of blades, was described by Harry England in the pages of *Cycling* as a 'journalist's dream and the rider's nightmare ... undoubtedly the fiercest circuit I have ever seen in twenty-five years of race reporting.'[64]

The route constantly challenged the riders: narrow and twisting roads, S-bends, narrow bridges, tough climbs, sharp descents and even tramlines all came thick and fast. In total there were thirty-two climbs to tackle over the course of sixteen laps. There was not a moment's respite to be had; physically nor mentally. And on top of that it rained. A cold, dispiriting rain that stung the eyes, drenched the skin and sapped the spirit.

So perhaps it is not surprising that of the seventy-one starters only twenty-two made it home. First among them was Bobet. The decisive moment came after France's Robert Varnajo attacked on the tenth lap, taking Italy's Michele Gismondi with him and setting in motion a chain of events that would ultimately see a group of seven emerge at the head of the race with around 45 kilometres to go. In that group were four riders who were either already, or would become, legends of the sport: Coppi, Gaul, Bobet, Anquetil. No need for first names. Along with Varnajo and Gismondi they were joined by Switzerland's Fritz Schär. They may not have been household names, but on this day they matched the best the peloton had to offer.

This circuit provided the toughest test for even the greatest of riders. Anquetil lost touch, not yet the master he would one day become. Coppi fell and lost valuable time. He remounted but his race was effectively done. At the moment Coppi had fallen Bobet and Schär had launched an attack and cycling's greatest artist could finish only sixth. Switzerland's Ferdi Kübler, another fancied rider, had long since abandoned the race.

Entering the final lap Bobet and Schär were alone at the front of a rapidly tiring race. Following their attack they had built a lead of 30 seconds over Gaul. Bobet looked to have this race under control.

Then disaster struck for Bobet. On the final lap he had a puncture. After hours navigating this most brutal of courses in terrible conditions, Bobet's race was threatened to be derailed by something completely out of his control. But fortune favoured the brave. Luckily for the Frenchman he was close to the feed zone and he quickly collected a replacement bike. Even so, he lost a minute to Schär with less than 12 kilometres to go. 'After Kübler, Coppi. After Coppi, Bobet. This turned into a massacre,'[65] reported Claude Tillet in *Le Miroir des Sports*.

But Bobet was not going to quit. He launched a fearsome pursuit and hauled Schär back with 7 kilometres to go before passing the Swiss on the 2.3-kilometre final haul up the Balkhausen climb to the finish to take a solo win by 12 seconds. Then, Bobet, darling of France, resplendent in the rainbow jersey, grabbed the microphone and shouted six words: 'Maman, je suis champion du monde!'[66]

Later, after he had bathed and had a massage at his hotel, Bobet talked to reporters. 'You can never imagine how much I suffered after my puncture,' he said. 'I thought I had lost and I cursed the fate which had robbed me of the title of world champion that I had desired with all my strength and that, I think, I deserved ... No, for nothing in the world, would I like to relive those moments ... That was hard. Good God. You have to have suffered on a bike to understand.'[67]

***

Three years earlier, in 1951, the championships had returned to Varese, after twelve years the cancellation of the 1939 event that was due to be hosted by the Italian city. The circuit would be lined by over one million people, many of whom had poured over the Swiss border in the hope of seeing one of their star riders win a second rainbow jersey for Switzerland.

In Ferdi Kübler and Hugo Koblet, Switzerland boasted two of the finest riders in the peloton. Kübler had won La Flèche Wallonne, Liège-Bastogne-Liège and the Tour of Switzerland earlier in the year, as well as finishing third at the Giro. Koblet, meanwhile, had won the biggest race of them all – the Tour. Kübler had sat that race out. He was focused on the Worlds and headed to the Swiss mountains to prepare before arriving in Varese a week before the race, giving himself plenty of opportunity to ride on the circuit itself.

That circuit was 24.6 kilometres long and featured a 5-kilometre climb averaging 4 per cent, the short but steep Bodero with stretches at 9 per cent and a stiff climb up to the finish in Varese. It favoured climbers and looked tailor-made for Coppi. Italy had not won the rainbow jersey for nearly twenty years and the country dearly wanted to break Belgium's grip on the race. 'It seemed that each organizing country was striving to design a course which could favour its own nationals,'[68] wrote Pierre Chany. But as it turned out Coppi did not race.

Earlier that year his beloved brother Serse had died after a crash during the Giro di Piemonte. Fausto buried his brother and went straight to the Tour where he rode in a daze. His natural talent meant he was still in contention through the Pyrenees but he then lost 16 minutes on a stage to Montpellier when he was struck by a short-term illness. Coppi finished tenth in Paris but the illness returned as the world championships approached and he did not start. In *Fallen Angel,* his biography of Coppi, William Fotheringham writes that the Italian press speculated the illness was an excuse not to face up to the might of the Swiss, a claim Coppi denied, saying, 'I would have been stupid not to have seized the chance of competing in a world championship on a course which suited me, in front of my fans, at a time when the fatigue of the Tour was only a memory.'[69] Instead the Italian challenge was led by Fiorenzo Magni, who had won his second Giro earlier in the year.

By the end of the third lap nine leaders enjoyed a lead of over two minutes. The Italian favourites – Magni and Gino Bartali were booed and jeered by the home crowd as they sat in the peloton over six minutes back.

Magni then put in a huge effort. In two laps he went from being five minutes down to joining the leading group. Bartali then attacked from the peloton along with Koblet. Koblet fell away after a puncture while Bartali continued a furious pursuit on the final lap, trying to claw back a four-minute deficit much to the delight of a home crowd which was roaring him on, kept abreast of developments thanks to the commentary on the loudspeakers that dotted the course. Ultimately it was a doomed effort. Bartali had left himself far too much to do and could only finish ninth, just over one minute down.

At the front Kübler had a problem. He was outnumbered by three Italians with the kilometres counting down. But his preparation had been perfect and he knew the course better than anyone. Kübler controlled the closing moments, chased down any attacks and then launched his own sprint from 300 metres out to win by three lengths from Magni and Antonio Bevilacqua.

'Undeniably our champion yesterday was stronger, his performance proves it irrefutably,' gushed the *Journal de Genève*. 'It was a good escape; He controlled it without exhausting his strength, he mastered his impulses and he had sufficient resources to contest the final "rush" without error, that is, taking the lead and not letting it go! The best has won and all the athletes will congratulate Ferdinand Kübler for this exploit which crowns his career and brings our riders to the pinnacle. After the Tour de France, the world championship, with two different men! That is to all our honour.'[70]

***

The following year Heinz Müller won Germany's first title in a bunch sprint in Luxembourg. It was a surprise victory; previously Müller had only won on home roads and this was by far the biggest win of his career. The jersey could have been Magni's but his saddle slipped as he started his sprint and he finished fourth. There was controversy in the amateur race when Piet van den Brekel was ultimately disqualified after first being hailed the winner and being presented with a bouquet of flowers. Then he was disqualified for allegedly changing his bike in the feed zone and the judges awarded the win to the Italian Luciano Ciancola who had finished second in a photo finish. The jersey was awarded to the Italian and the Italian national anthem rang out from the gramophone. Then Van den Brekel's disqualification was overturned but he was given second in the photo finish. Then the photo-finish images were deemed inconclusive and the result declared a dead heat. 'This was declared by the judge as his final decision,' reported *Cycling*. But there was one more final twist to come. 'Then the officials formally disqualified Van den Brekel for changing machines within the lines of the feeding area.'[71] All clear then.

It was during these 1952 world championships that the UCI declared at its annual Congress, held two days before the men's road race, that world championship races would no longer be an individual contest. Until now riding as a team had been against the rules, riders would start wearing the jerseys of their national teams but officially be forbidden from riding as a team. Aside from national championships, teamwork played a huge factor in every other race and the reasons for claiming the Worlds as an individual event were getting more and more spurious. As far back as the early 1930s some nations had faced accusations of effectively riding as a team during the Worlds and some riders had even been thrown out of races after the commissaries judged them to be helping a fellow countryman rather than riding for their own interests. From this point forward riding as a team was no longer against the rules. The controversies would instead now come when countries openly refused to ride as a team.

***

By the late summer of 1953 Fausto Coppi was regarded as one of the greatest cyclists that had ever turned a pedal. He was a five-times Giro champion and a winner of two Tours. He had multiple wins in both of Italy's most prestigious one-day races, Milan-Sanremo and the Tour of Lombardy. He had even won Paris-Roubaix in 1950, not bad for a man more at home in the mountains. And if war had not come in 1939 and interrupted his fledgling career who knows how many other big races he could have claimed? He was also twice a world champion on the track. But there was something missing. Alfredo Binda, that other great Italian master, had a jersey in his wardrobe that Coppi had not yet claimed. Binda's three wins in the Worlds had assumed even greater importance and for Coppi to truly inherit the title of *Campionissimo* from Binda, he surely had to fill that one void in his *palmares*. Coppi needed that rainbow jersey of road world champion.

On the front page of *La Stampa* on the morning of Monday 31 August 1953 ran a headline that Italy and the cycling world had long been waiting to read. It might have been simply expressed but the message was loud and clear: 'In Lugano Coppi wins the title champion of the world'.[72] After a startling display of grace and artistry, Coppi could now claim the undisputed title as the greatest cyclist the world had seen. The *Campionissimo* had ridden majestically and broken an Italian barren spell at the Worlds that improbably stretched back to 1932 when Binda took the third of his titles. *La Corriere della Sera* celebrated with a full-page spread with its correspondent Nicolò Samarelli describing Coppi's win as: 'The masterpiece of the champion. The most dazzling victory among many, also because it was the most coveted and not achieved until now.'[73] *Cycling*, meanwhile, said it was: 'A victory that all the cycling nations can acclaim … His newest crown will establish a legend, and the tale of his victory will become a classic.'[74]

Coppi had refused to ride in the Tour which had ended a little over a month earlier, telling journalists he wanted to try his luck once more at the Worlds. Coppi said that if he failed he feared he would never wear the rainbow jersey given his age. He prepared well, riding in only one race leading up to the event and ensuring he had at least one rider in the Italian team he could trust in Bianchi teammate Michele Gismondi. He based himself in Lugano three weeks beforehand, working with Gismondi and his mentor Biagio Cavanna. It was 'a day expected by Coppi for ten years,'[75] Pierre Chany later wrote.

Hours after the race the name of Coppi was still being chanted in the streets of Lugano. Thousands of his fans had come from Italy to witness his latest attempt on the rainbow jersey. Such was the magnitude of Coppi's dominance in the race that he had completed much of the after-race protocol before the second-placed rider, Germain Derycke of Belgium, had crossed the line. 'He was hugged, kissed, carried, cheered, taken to the UCI's president, invested with his championship vest, presented with flowers, stood to attention whilst his country's national anthem was sung, and the Italian flag went to the masthead … and then it was that the second man in the world's professional road championship, 1953, crossed the finishing line!'[76] reported *Cycling*.

The race was run over eighteen laps of a 15-kilometre circuit with a start/finish straight on a newly built road in the middle of an airfield around which the route circled. The route took in climbs and scenic Swiss villages, with stretches of *pavé* punctuating the smooth, and in places fresh, concrete. The works had been expensive and so spectators were charged for entrance to help to fund some of the infrastructure improvements the Swiss had made. The organisers were confident that the draw of the race would mean many would still come and their faith was rewarded when one hundred and thirty thousand turned up. The crucial climb was the Crespera, a 1.6-kilometre cobbled ascent averaging 6 per cent. It was no Alpine giant but it at least offered something of a springboard for an attack.

Coppi was patient. For the early part of the race he sat quietly in the peloton, at times more than three minutes behind the various leaders. Then, on the twelfth ascent of the Crespera, he stirred. It was time. In the space of little more than one lap, the graceful Italian turned a deficit of more than one minute into a lead of 01.20. The stands shook with excitement as Coppi showed his class. A cartoon drawn after the race depicts the great man in full flight but without a bike, pedalling only air, such was the freedom of his movement. Only one man could grimly hold on – Derycke. The gritty Belgian was made of stern stuff. He had won Paris-Roubaix earlier that year and would later go on to claim Milan-Sanremo (1955), Liège-Bastogne-Liège (1957) and the Tour of Flanders (1958). Derycke was no one-day novice and he clung on but ultimately Coppi proved too good.

Some books have claimed that Coppi waited until the final climb of the Crespera to drop Derycke, incredulously commenting that Coppi pulled out more than six minutes in the space of the final 10 kilometres. But contemporary newspaper accounts report it was actually on the penultimate lap that Coppi danced away after zigzagging his way up the climb, waiting for the steepest section – the hairpin just after the village of Stallone – to make his move. *La Stampa* reports that at the end of the seventeenth and penultimate lap Coppi already had a lead of just under three minutes.[77] Lugano was in a state of pandemonium. It was all over.

Far from cruising to his win Coppi carried on his time trial to victory. He crossed the line in 7:30:59, his winning margin more than six minutes with only five men managing to get within ten minutes of him. Coppi had obliterated the field in one of the greatest world championship rides of all time. But his life was complicated. Rumours of an extra-marital affair with Giulia Locatelli, the wife of a doctor, who would later be dubbed 'the White Lady', were gathering pace. Locatelli had first met Coppi five years earlier when she approached him for an autograph on behalf of her husband who idolised the rider. She quickly became obsessed herself and the two had grown close, too close not to be noticed by gossipmongers who were now talking in ever-louder voices. Locatelli had been in Lugano and was actually photographed with Coppi as he celebrated on the podium. Also there was Coppi's wife, Bruna. In a bid to avoid further controversy, that night Coppi went home with Bruna, Gismondi and Cavanna rather than attend the celebratory dinner. In *Fallen Angel,* William Fotheringham writes that instead of going to the dinner the foursome 'had a sandwich in Varese, where Cavanna joked that Coppi had better get him some sparkling wine because they had done nothing to celebrate the fact that his protégés had won both the amateur and professional titles [Italy's Riccardo Filippi had won the amateur race the day before].'[78]

Five days later Coppi was on the track to race at the legendary Vigorelli Velodrome in Milan. The authorities were overwhelmed by the sheer number of supporters that wanted to see their world champion on the boards and the event was stopped for an hour because of the numbers of people that packed the stands to capacity and spilled over into the centre of the track. Thousands more stood outside, chanting for their hero, hoping for a glimpse of the great man. And he did not disappoint. In front of his adoring public, the newly crowned road world champion rode the fastest 5-kilometre pursuit that had ever been recorded.

***

Belgium's Stan Ockers had rolled home third in the Lugano world championships that had been dominated Coppi. Two years later, after Bobet had taken his famous win in 1954, it was the turn of the Belgian to shine and for Coppi to fall away and abandon to a soundtrack of jeers from the fickle Italian crowd.

The championships were held in Frascati, 20 kilometres south-east of Rome, and the expectation in Italy was huge. On the day of the race, traffic built up on the roads since before dawn. It was meant to be a celebration of Italian cycling, but turned instead into a demonstration of what one person can achieve by sheer force of will.

After ten laps of the 21-kilometre circuit, the peloton trailed a leading group of twelve riders by more than eight minutes. The bunch seemed unwilling or unable to launch any kind of meaningful pursuit. In the peloton were plenty of former world champions: Bobet, Kübler, Schotte and, astonishingly, Coppi. The home favourite was eight minutes behind on home roads and apparently doing nothing about it. Nothing visible to the thousands watching anyway. The boos that rang out might have been heard across Italy.

But one man in that peloton was unwilling to give up. With 80 kilometres left Constant "Stan" Ockers decided that he was not going to sit in the bunch and watch the race pass him by. Instead Ockers, along with Italy's Bruno Monti and France's Pierre Molinéris, attacked.

On paper it seemed like a ludicrous move. Three riders more than eight minutes down chasing a large leading group was an attempt surely destined for failure. Ockers had other ideas. Incredibly, after just two laps of chasing, Ockers and Monti were within one minute of the leaders (Molinéris had fallen behind suffering with cramp) and by the time the bell signalled the final lap the determined Belgian was in the leading group. Meanwhile, Bobet, Kübler, Schotte and Coppi had all abandoned the race – 'when they could but finish like novices they retired,'[79] sniffed Cycling.

With 5 kilometres to go, just as the road rose up to 10 per cent, Ockers made his final and decisive move to ride to a win built on a simple refusal to give up. His final margin was over one minute ahead of Luxembourg's Jean-Pierre Schmitz.

Ockers' win had crowned an outstanding season for a man in the twilight of his career at thirty-five. He had claimed wins in La Flèche Wallonne and Liège-Bastogne-Liège earlier in the year.

It was the start of another period of Belgian ascendancy. Rik Van Steenbergen's team crushed the opposition in 1956 on the Danish roads of Ballerup, north west of Copenhagen. Perhaps it was riding on the hard and exposed roads of northern Belgium that perfectly prepared the Belgians for this Worlds, with five of the top six riders wearing the Belgian jersey. Only the Dutchman Gerrit Schulte was able to infiltrate their stranglehold on the top placings by finishing third. Van Steenbergen, with rain falling and flags buffeting at right angles to the road, won the final sprint ahead of his compatriot Rik Van Looy. Twelve months later, Van Steenbergen again won the final sprint, this time ahead of Bobet and André Darrigade of France. With the event hosted in Waregem, West Flanders, Van Steenbergen was on home roads as he equalled Binda's record of three wins and became the first rider to take back-to-back wins since his countryman Georges Ronsse in the late 1920s. With six riders in the top ten, Belgium's dominance was only slightly less clear cut than the year before.

***

No Italian had made the top ten in either the 1956 or the 1957 race, a disaster for a nation that, until then, since the end of the Second World War had only once failed to have a rider in the top five (1950). In the build-up to the 1958 race Italy held out little hope of anything other than another Belgian win. For *La Stampa,* the overwhelming favourite on a lumpy rather than hilly northern France route in Reims was Van Looy. 'Who is able to head off on a course like that of Reims but the unleashed Van Looy?' pondered Gigi Boccacini in the newspaper's preview. 'Nobody.'[80] The main hope, Boccacini concluded, was that an Italian escaped alone, 'and only [Ercole] Baldini is apparently capable of such a feat.'[81] As it turned out Baldini was the only rider they needed as he washed away memories of the fading champion Coppi with a performance every bit as stirring as Coppi's win five years earlier.

Baldini had won the Giro in June and he was not going to waste time in his bid to become just the third rider to win the Giro and the Worlds in the same year, matching Binda (1927) and Coppi (1953). As early as the first hill on the second lap, he followed a move by Bobet, teammate Gastone Nencini and the Netherlands' Gerrit Voorting, to open up a lead of 01.40 by the end of the lap. By the time that lead had been stretched to six minutes after 120 kilometres, heads in the peloton were being scratched.

With a little under 60 kilometres of racing to go, Baldini upped his pace and struck out alone. He rode a blistering lap to put distance between himself and those in pursuit and while his pace slowed over the final two laps, he completed a famous victory ahead of Bobet. Baldini had only been a professional for two seasons and now he was on top of the world. During the race Gino Bartali had followed the breakaway in a car and had returned to the press tribunes to speak worriedly to journalists: 'Voorting is broke, Nencini and Bobet are tired,' he said. 'Baldini is just riding elegantly. But I'm afraid for him. They went too early, the counter-move of the Belgians will rage with unheard of ferocity.'[82] But Bartali need not have worried. Baldini was too strong. His performance was described by *La Stampa* as 'a great escape crowned by a triumph that only a truly top-class athlete could achieve.'[83] At the age of thirty-nine, this was Coppi's final world championship race. He finished eighteenth, some seven minutes back.

While Bobet had been the best of the rest in Reims, the French sprinter André Darrigade had won the five-man dash to the line to take third. One year later he went two steps higher up the podium, winning an eight-rider sprint on the flat 10.2-kilometre motor-racing circuit in Zandvoort in the Netherlands. Darrigade had to change his bike three times but still easily prevailed in the sprint ahead of Italy's Michele Gismondi. In the peloton was Tom Simpson, making his professional Worlds' debut. He was Britain's sole rider and he finished fourth, at the time Britain's best result. 'He came to the world championships for experience so he said,' reported *Cycling and Mopeds*. 'He learned in the first 50 miles and then proceeded to put the learning to good use.'[84] Soon the world would learn just how good Simpson was.

7

A NEW ERA BEGINS

For decades many in the male-dominated world of cycling had seen a woman on a bicycle as unnatural, unseemly and certainly not something to be encouraged. But as the 1940s gave way to the 1950s slowly things began to change and women's cycling started to develop. Various unofficial national and road world championships for women had been held since before the Second World War, but it was not until the 1950s that officially sanctioned races started to appear. In 1951 France organised its first official national championships for women and in 1956 Britain held its own inaugural championships. It would take a little longer for the likes of Belgium (1959), Italy (1963) and the Netherlands (1965) to follow, but slowly progress was at last being made.

Millie Robinson had won that inaugural British national title. Robinson was a trailblazer. In 1955 she took part in a three-day women's race in France called the Circuit Lyonnais-Auvergne, winning all three stages and the overall title. The race was such a success that Jean Leulliot, a French journalist who created the magazine *Route et Piste,* as well as directing bike races, decided to organise a women's race in Normandy. It would run for five stages and he would call it the Tour de France Féminine.

Britain sent a team of six riders and dominated the race. With a total distance of 373 kilometres the race was split into six stages. Britain won three. June Thackeray took one and Robinson picked up two, including a decisive stage four during which she escaped, grabbed 13 seconds on the bunch and took the race lead. Robinson and Thackeray finished first and second respectively, with two other British riders also making the top ten. Robinson would go on to break the women's hour record in 1958.

Women's cycling was slowly on the up, at least in Britain and France, with a number of small races appearing on the calendar. But still the UCI remained unconvinced. In late November 1957 Britain tabled a motion at the UCI's congress in Zurich for an official women's world championship to be held. The motion was supported by a number of federations, notably France and the USSR. The resulting press release stated that 'in principle the international cycling officials are not opposed to the establishment of world championships for women; how the women's events will be organised will be elaborated on at a future session of this Committee. It is still to be considered as probable that the program of a women's world championships will include only a few sprints. In any case, they will exclude a road test.'[85]

After more work and lobbying by the federations, in the early spring of 1958, and following its Congress in Paris, the UCI confirmed the election of Adriano Rodoni as its new president and published a number of other decisions. Included among them was 'the creating, on a trial basis, of a female world championship in three disciplines (60-kilometre road, 3-kilometre pursuit, 500-metre sprint). France is responsible for its organisation.'[86] At last the cycling women of the world had their official world championships – they would be held in August and they would include a road race. Happily, despite initially being deemed only a trial, the women's world championships were here to stay.

***

Twenty-eight riders from eight countries started that inaugural women's road race in Reims, France. Among them was the twenty-four-year-old from Luxembourg Elsy Jacobs. Jacobs' elder brothers Roger, Edmond and Raymond were all cyclists and Elsy, inspired by them, borrowed their bikes to train. Soon she was racing herself and winning. By the late summer of 1958 Jacobs had been riding for five years and had become one of the most popular women in the peloton, commanding high appearance fees after moving to France and becoming a full-time cyclist the year before.

Jacobs was Luxembourg's sole entrant. Britain was well represented with a full complement of six riders, matching the teams of France and Belgium, while the Soviet Union took five. The federations had promised the UCI they would fully support the event should it be organised and they were true to their words.

Jacobs was no sprinter and her race tactics by now were well known. She would attack hard and early and look to break out alone from distance. If she arrived at the finish with anyone else she knew she was not going to win. She may not have possessed a quick turn of speed, but strength, stamina and courage she had in abundance. And so Jacobs focused on constructing her race around the hills that punctuated the 20-kilometre circuit.

On the second lap, just as the toughest part of the circuit approached, Belgium's Yvonne Reynders attacked, prompting a flurry of activity. Reynders could not stay at the front but her move created a leading group of seven over the top of the circuit's first major climb.

There was more than half the race to go but Jacobs wanted to put on a show. On the second climb, the Côte de Calvaire to the village of Méry-Prémecy, she struck out alone. The rest of the chasing group of sixteen riders would not see her again until the finish. The full British team was there, three Soviets were there. It would not matter – they couldn't catch Jacobs. She was too strong. She had nearly one minute at the end of the second lap and she would only pull out more time on her ride to the finish as she powered to a famous win. Jacobs was a study in concentration and discipline, never wavering, never once looking like she might be caught despite all cycling logic dictating she surely must be.

In the end Jacobs won by nearly three minutes from the next best rider, the Soviet Union's Tamara Novikova. Jacobs had just become cycling's first official female world champion on the road. A new era of women's cycling had begun. Later that year Jacobs set a new benchmark for the hour record on the track at the Vigorelli Velodrome in Italy. Her mark of 41.347 kilometres would stand for fourteen years.

Twelve months on, Reynders, the daughter of a coal merchant who trained by making deliveries to her father's customers on her bike in Antwerp, won a final bunch sprint in Belgium. Reynders had been the rider who had first ignited the race the year before but had ended up in twentieth position. This time any serious attacks on the flat 4-kilometre circuit in Rotheux-Rimière, south of Liège, were snuffed out. In the sprint Reynders waited for her time and then attacked on the right-hand side of the road while the other leading riders went left. 'I drove alone on the right side of the road,' she said after the race. 'I was afraid of the moment when I would be leading, not looking behind me. A few times I turned my head toward the finish line ... I kicked and kicked but did not seem to move forward ... I did another last effort and suddenly heard the announcement that a Belgian is world champion.'[87] It was to be the first of four road titles for Reynders.

8

YVONNE REYNDERS
(1959, 1961, 1963, 1966)

This story starts with an email to a Belgian contact who once helped me with an interview for a magazine article on the rider Herman Van Springel. 'I don't suppose by any chance you know Yvonne Reynders?' I asked my contact. 'Sorry, I don't know Yvonne,' came the quick reply. 'But maybe you can contact the restaurant *Casa Grinta* in the Belgium village of Terhagen. It is not only a restaurant but also a museum of bicycle racing. Yvonne has her own table in that restaurant.' That put me on to Paul Van Bommel.

Van Bommel is a chef and a collector of cycling memorabilia. The restaurant to which my contact directed me no longer exists – Van Bommel retired and closed it a few years ago – but when it was open he used the floor space above the restaurant to display his extensive cycling collection. He had tables named after famous Belgian cyclists and had their pictures and their stories printed on them. One day, four-times road world champion (seven-times if you include her titles on the track) Yvonne Reynders visited the restaurant and looked around. 'Typical, no women,' she said to Van

Bommel. That made him think. He decided to make an Yvonne Reynders table and when it was finished he invited her back to his restaurant to see it. They have been firm friends ever since and he now knows as much about her life as a cyclist as anyone. Today, with Reynders approaching her eighties, he sometimes helps her with interviews, assisting writers like me who want to learn more about her career.

I learn all this over lunch at Van Bommel's home. After a couple of introductory emails and a few phone calls, I'd been invited to Belgium to meet Paul and talk about Reynders' career with the blessing of the woman herself. Van Bommel spent all day with me. He fed me, took me to see his huge cycling collection, which includes the rainbow jerseys of Reynders and which will soon be displayed in a new museum to be built in his village, and introduced me to his friend and fellow collector Patrick Den Hert, who in turn showed me the world championship jerseys of Rik Van Steenbergen and Stan Ockers – a rare treat.

But before all that, before the lunch he had so kindly laid on and before the hour enjoyably spent not even scratching the surface of his cycling collection, we spent two hours talking about Yvonne Reynders and her career, during which we called her at her home, put her on speakerphone and asked her directly about her world championship story.

***

Paul Van Bommel:

At first Yvonne was into athletics. She had a very difficult youth. She was constantly in conflict with her father – with her mother her relationship was very good, very close – but her father was a tyrant and she always was in conflict with him.

She did the shot-put and the discus and she became Belgium champion. A neighbour of hers had tried cycling but he wasn't very good, so he said to Yvonne, 'You're an athlete, here's my bike, try one race.'

YVONNE REYNDERS (1959, 1961, 1963, 1966)

She finished two or three minutes before the second-placed rider even though she had never before ridden in a race. That was the start of her cycling career – this was at the beginning of the 1950s.

One year she rode sixty-four races and won sixty-one times, she was really outstanding. The parents of Yvonne had a coal shop and she delivered the coal to their customers. She had a *triporteur*, you know what that is? It's like a cargo bike, with a large area at the front to carry loads. She delivered 10kg sacks of coal using it and she carried 24 sacks – 240kg of coal on the bike! She went along the *Nationalestraat* in Antwerp and it was like Paris-Roubaix, all cobblestones. Some people wanted coal delivered to the fifth, sixth, seventh floors of buildings and to earn extra money she carried the coal up all the stairs – there were no elevators so it was good training.

Then she used to go training after work. One day Rik Van Steenbergen was training with another cyclist and looked up the road and saw another rider. 'C'mon,' he said, 'we're going to get up to him.' So they start racing, pacing each other, trying to get over. It took them about 20 minutes of chasing together before they finally got to the cyclist. It was Yvonne. And she was alone.

So she became very strong. She was also very strong in the mind because she always had to fight the supremacy of her father. One time after a race she took her bike and she threw it in the cellar and said, 'That's it.' He was always drunk, he fought with the fathers of other girl cyclists so she was really ashamed of him. She said: 'This is it, I'm finished with you. It's not possible anymore.' But he bought her a new bike and said, 'OK, I'm sorry, I went too far.' He bought her a new bike and she started racing again.

Reynders' cycling career started at a time when competitive women's cycling was still very much in its infancy.

Women's cycling at that time was more popular here than in the Netherlands just over the border, but still it was frowned on a bit. I had a customer and her grandmother was a Belgian champion but her grandmother's husband and children didn't even know she was a cyclist! One day her husband was reading the newspaper and saw his wife was Belgian champion – he didn't know anything about it. It brought shame at that time for a woman to cycle … this was a little earlier than Yvonne's era but it really brought shame to some. But Yvonne's parents really were supportive of her cycling. It was actually her father that started the women's cycling federation here in Belgium.

In Antwerp there was a *sportpaleis* where riders could go training on the track but women weren't allowed. Even though by then she was three times world champion she wasn't allowed. So she put on some men's clothes and a false moustache and then she went training. Some cyclists went to the boss of the *sportpaleis* and told him Yvonne Reynders is here training. He went down to the track and said, 'Come on, off the track, you – it's not allowed.' She carried on. It took more than an hour before they could catch her … she was playing with them and everybody was laughing. One week later she went to the wife of the director of the *sportpaleis* and said, 'I am three times world champion on the track and I can't train? This is crazy.' The wife talked to the director … and then she could go training. It was thanks to her that women started to be able to go to the track.

Reynders was selected for the first women's world championships in 1958 where she finished twentieth. One year later, in Rotheux, Belgium, she took the first of an eventual four road titles.

Yvonne Reynders:
The course was not that hilly. It was pretty flat with only small hills. There was a long straight and then a U-turn. It rained that day so everybody had to take care and in places the road became very narrow. A lot of riders fell

there. At one point I had to go off the road and ride around the back of the spectators. I remember there was a girl in a miniskirt who stepped back and we collided and I fell on her. I was angry about that.

There was a breakaway and I rode hard up to it. The breakaway was with Beryl Burton and some other British riders. For the sprint I was told, 'Yvonne, you have to go to the right because the British always ride on the left side of the road. You have to go on the right, it is your only chance because they will go with each other in the sprint.' So after the U-turn I went to the right and everyone else followed the British on the left side. There was a policeman on a motorbike. He was like, 'Oh, a Belgian in front!' and so he helped me a little bit, helped to keep me out of the wind. I went alone on the right side and I heard everybody cracking behind … and I became world champion.

My father was jumping like a crazy man – his feet were higher than my handlebars! He was so happy that his daughter was world champion.

Two years later Reynders had her second win on the Isle of Man after having to switch bikes because of a mechanical fault.

I had to provide for myself. I had to pay for my travelling and everything. At the Isle of Man … I'd never had any problems with my bike before but during that world championship race the brake cable broke so I had to take my second bike, which was very heavy. I was really angry that it had broken and that I had to ride back up to the peloton. There was a breakaway that had gone, so I asked, 'Are there Belgians in the breakaway?' No, no Belgians. But Burton was in the breakaway, [Elsy] Jacobs was in the breakaway, and so I said to myself, 'I have to go across.' So, on my second bike I made the catch. Then Jacobs said to me, 'Come on, Yvonne, you are the strongest, you take the front.' 'But I've just come from the peloton up to you,' I said. I played a game, pretended I was very tired but really I wasn't.

Then we went up a small climb and I ended up at the front just because I was so strong, but I thought there are still two or three laps to go so it is too early to be alone. I let them come back to me and I carried on pretending I was tired. Halfway round the last lap I went away alone to the finish. I had a lot of adrenaline that day because of what had happened to my bike.

Most girls went to a world championship one week before and they would ride the course a few times to learn every corner, every U-turn, every climb. But I used to take the train just two days before and went up the climbs on my bike with all my clothes and belongings in my luggage. I only rode the course once. I didn't do any more laps because I thought if I ride it a lot I'm just going to hate the course when I want to be focused on it. Just once and I know where the turns are, where the climbs are … where the downhills are … only once, no more training on there.

In 1967, during the world championships in the Netherlands it was reported that Reynders had failed a doping control. She was disqualified and given a ban of three months there and then. An angry Reynders quit the sport for ten years.

At Limburg I was accused of doping … but I didn't take anything so I quit. I still talk about it because it was unfair how I was treated. It was an ideal course for me that year, with the Cauberg. I couldn't lose there.

Paul Van Bommel:

She is very angry about that. I don't know what happened but she said to me: 'I never, ever, doped and I swear it to my mother.' I believe her. She was very angry and so she retired. Then, after ten years, she started again and became Belgian champion then went to the world championships and came third. She said after all those years that she was the old lady, you know? Everybody was like fifteen years younger than her. It was crazy –

everybody was looking at her like she was an old woman. And she became Belgian champion for the third time. Everybody was very, very surprised.

Yvonne Reynders:

Winning is winning, and winning a world championships is great and so I have no preference between them. But at another race once, in France, the women were riding on the same route as the men but we started halfway round. The men had already started when we set off. I went off the front because I wanted to catch the train to go home early – ride hard, win and go home. I said to a teammate, 'Come on, we're going to leave them behind,' but she couldn't follow me and so I was alone. After a while I heard a car with music behind me and I thought, 'Oh, they're coming back to me.' But then I saw all the brands of the men's teams and realised it was actually the men. It was the start of a long climb and suddenly there was Raymond Poulidor with all of the others. I went uphill alongside Poulidor and he couldn't leave me, he couldn't drop me. Then on the downhill, because I was lighter – Poulidor was 20kg or something heavier than me – I had to let him go. But on the climb I was with the men. That was good. I didn't know I could follow the guys.

9

A VERY BELGIAN CONTROVERSY

In the closing metres of the 1963 world championships the man everyone expected to win finally hit the front of the race. Belgium's Rik Van Looy, dubbed the Emperor of Herentals, had been at the top of the sport for seven years. He had turned professional in 1953 with the Gitane-Hutchinson team and took his first classics title in 1956, winning Gent-Wevelgem. He won Milan-Sanremo in 1958, the first of eight Monument wins. He was a force in the Grand Tours and during his eighteen-year career claimed thirty-seven stage wins across the Tour, Giro and Vuelta, winning the points jersey at the Tour and Vuelta and, improbably for a one-day specialist, the climbers' competition at the 1960 Giro. No less a judge than Jacques Anquetil once described Van Looy as his real rival in the Grand Tours, a man he had to watch in the mountains and on the flat.

By the time of the 1963 championships in Ronse, in the Flemish province of East Flanders, Van Looy was also a double world champion. In 1960 he had taken his first rainbow jersey after holding his nerve and timing his sprint perfectly on an uphill finish at the the Sachsenring motor circuit in East Germany, the first and only time the event was hosted by the German Democratic Republic, beating defending champion André Darrigade by four lengths. Van Looy made it back-to-back wins the following year on a 13-kilometre 'bike riders' course'[88] of stiff climbs, heady descents and hairpin bends just outside Bern, Switzerland. After a 1961 spring campaign during which the Belgian had won Paris-Roubaix and Liège-Bastogne-Liège, the latter being a victory that *La Stampa* described as being 'imposed with absolute superiority',[89] and in the process becoming the first man to claim all five Monuments, Van Looy had been the overwhelming favourite among the press pack in Switzerland. He did not let the scribes down. Van Looy sat and waited and moved to the fore only when Raymond Poulidor made his bid with around 7 kilometres go, quickly reeling the Frenchman back and holding off a strong effort from Italy's Nino Defilippis, who came past six riders in the final 50 metres to take second. Poulidor finished third, the first of four podium positions for the Frenchman over the course of his career. Alas the man known as 'the eternal second' never would make the top step.

Now, two years on from his second Worlds win and with the line fast approaching in Ronse, Van Looy was on home roads and seemingly heading for a third title. Earlier in the race Britain's Tom Simpson had been part of a two-man break along with Ireland's Shay Elliott. Simpson had won the 570-kilometre Bordeaux-Paris earlier in the year and though he wore the jersey of Great Britain he lived in nearby Gent and was fiercely popular with the Belgian fans – when Simpson walked out of his front door to drive to the race that morning there was a simple message for him, painted on the road: 'Simpson, Champion.'[90]

For 13 kilometres Simpson and Elliott led the race in front of hundreds of thousands of fevered Belgian supporters. A roar had gone up around the course when news of his attack was announced over the loudspeakers, but Simpson was a marked man and Elliott had already been at the front for more than 70 kilometres. The break was doomed to failure. Early during the penultimate lap they came back into the fold once more, their adventure over. Simpson, the Brit who Belgians had taken to their hearts, would have to wait for another day.

Now it was the turn of the real Belgians. In the closing moments Van Looy launched wave after wave of attacks in a bid to get free from the marauding pack. He was wary of working with Simpson, preferring instead to tempt Poulidor into his wheel, a man he was confident of beating in a final sprint. But Van Looy's efforts did not work and with the finish line approaching the leading group still numbered twenty-nine riders. Then Van Looy hit the front at a ferocious pace. One of the greatest one-day racers in the history of the sport had clear air between him and the line with less than 100 metres to go. Surely the race was over and Van Looy was about to join Binda and Van Steenbergen with three world titles. But then appeared a man who until now had been sitting anonymously in the bunch. His name was Benoni Beheyt and he also wore the jersey of the Belgian national team. What was about to happen would cause uproar throughout the Belgian cycling world.

Beheyt was just twenty-three years old, and in only his second year as a professional, but he was no novice. He had already won Gent-Wevelgem, taken top-fifteen places at both the Tour of Flanders and Paris-Roubaix and finished second on the final stage of the Tour in Paris, when he was second to Van Looy.

To watch the footage now is to relive the drama of that hugely controversial few seconds. In the final sprint Van Looy is on the right-hand barrier. He is ahead by at least a couple of bike lengths when he begins to veer sharply across the road. Fast approaching is Beheyt, looking intent on competing the sprint despite reportedly complaining of cramp earlier in the race and, on that basis, refusing to offer a lead-out to his leader.[91] Across comes Van Looy, from the barrier to the centre of the road. Beheyt is now half a wheel behind and the rest of the bunch are three lengths or more back. Still Van Looy comes across; he is now a metre or more the other side of the centre line, pushing Beheyt further and further to the left.

Then comes the brief but fateful moment. Beheyt appears to pull on Van Looy's jersey. The youngster seems to actually tug back the old master. The leader of the team is apparently pulled back by a young teammate whose single best result is first in a semi-classic one-day race. Regardless of the whys and wherefores, and never mind the evidence of the footage showing

Van Looy veering wildly off his line, from this moment Beheyt was doomed to become persona non grata.

As the pair pass the finish line, Beheyt raises one arm in celebration. Then, almost immediately he looks over at Van Looy, who quickly loosens his toe-straps and looks back in indignation, putting an arm out as if to say, 'What the hell are you playing at?'

As he was hoisted on to the shoulders of the crowds at the line, Beheyt barely raised a smile. This was not the demeanour of a man who had just claimed the biggest win of his young career. He appeared to carry instead the air of someone who was fearful of what was about to happen to him. There is a picture,[92] taken after the awards ceremony, that shows Beheyt in the rainbow jersey with the winner's medal around his neck. His head is bowed. Van Looy stands at right angles next to him staring angrily into space. It seems to speak more than words ever could.

Afterwards Van Looy was apoplectic. In his book on Jacques Anquetil, *Sex, Lies and Handlebar Tape,* Paul Howard tells how in an interview with the French magazine *Lui* Anquetil described Van Looy having to be held back from physically confronting Beheyt in the changing room after the race, shouting 'I'd paid him to help me.'[93] It was said that Beheyt would never win another race. It did not quite turn out that way. He managed to win a handful of races after 1963, including a stage at the Tour the following year, but five years after his Worlds win he was out of the sport.

***

In between Van Looy's second win and Beheyt's alleged act of treason, Jean Stablinski had listened to *La Marseillaise* ring out in Salo, Italy after claiming France's third title in nine years. Stablinski's 1962 win was superbly forged, a tactical masterclass of riding during a 296-kilometre race over twenty-three laps of a testing circuit above Lake Garda that included a short but challenging 12 per cent climb just one kilometre from the finish.

Stablinski attacked from a small leading group at the end of the penultimate lap and in 3 kilometres opened a gap of 30 seconds. By the time he crossed the line he had 01.22 over second-placed Shay Elliott, despite having to call the service car forward after puncturing 6 kilometres from the finish. Thousands poured onto the road to mob the Frenchman. Stablinski and Elliott were firm friends and rode for the same Helyett team. 'The strongest man won,'[94] said Elliott afterwards.

Stablinski had worked in the mines of northern France from an early age to provide for his family after his father died and when asked afterwards about suffering during the race he simply said, 'Of course, it's hard … But it's much less so than at the bottom of the mine, believe me.' He lamented the fact that he would now have to forego wearing the tricolour jersey of French national champion, which he had won for the second time two months before, for the rainbow bands. 'I like the tricolour jersey,' he said. 'I will have to put it in the wardrobe now and replace it with the rainbow jersey. It will be very heavy to wear and much less pleasant for me.'[95]

**

Over thirty years of world championship racing some of the greatest names in cycling history had enhanced their *palmares* by claiming the rainbow jersey: Alfredo Binda, Antonin Magne, Ferdi Kübler, Fausto Coppi, Rik Van Steenbergen, Louison Bobet and Rik Van Looy among them. But one name was missing from that particular roll of honour: Jacques Anquetil.

By the time the Worlds returned to France in 1964, Anquetil had claimed five Tours, two Giri and the Vuelta, the first rider to win all three Grand Tours. A stage racer *par excellence,* he was tremendous against the clock, winning multiple Grand Prix des Nations titles and breaking the hour record on the track. He was the king of the peloton, but at the world championships it had been a different story. In nine starts Anquetil's best performance had been fifth in 1954, his race debut. Anquetil's relationship with the French public was complicated. He was portrayed as a cold and calculating rider, a winner without charm who was just too dominant to be likeable. 'Each time he wins the ill-feeling grows,' reported *Le Miroir des Sports* after his 1962 Tour win. 'He says it can't be helped but it is obvious he's disturbed. He can't be blamed for the incompetence of the rest.'[96]

Instead the public fell for Raymond Poulidor, the man that Anquetil so often beat into second place in a rivalry that came to define both men's careers. For nine years their paths crossed on the roads of Europe and although by far the most successful of the two, Anquetil was fixated on his rival, unable to understand why Poulidor was able to win the one thing denied to him – the unconditional love of the French fans. 'Their rivalry lasts 24 hours a day,' Anquetil's director sportive Raphaël Géminiani once said. 'Some nights even I can't sleep for thinking about it.'[97]

The 1964 Worlds were held under the gaze of Mont Blanc, on one of the most difficult courses in the history of the championships. The tough course meant that Anquetil was installed as one of the favourites. In fact *L'Equipe* were so confident of an Anquetil win that they were promoting the idea of a road/pursuit double for the man who had just claimed his fifth Tour win.[98]

Less than two months earlier Anquetil and Poulidor had ridden shoulder to shoulder up the Puy de Dôme during the Tour in one of the race's most iconic moments, each refusing to cede to the other. Poulidor took some time out of Anquetil that day. He had won the battle but Anquetil would once more win the war, again taking yellow in Paris. Now they were on the same national team and, like Binda and Girardengo and Coppi and Bartali decades before, the intense rivalry would dominate their performances. Quite simply, neither could stomach the thought of helping the other to victory and the team was divided with its two star riders riding not only against the rest of the peloton but against each other. In the words of Pierre Chany, for three successive years (1964–1966) by having eyes only for each other, they 'offered gifts'[99] to the other riders. Gifts that came in the form of rainbow jerseys.

Sixty-five thousand people lined the Sallanches circuit to watch the Netherlands' Jan Janssen profit from inability of France to work as a team, crossing the line with both hands raised, looking dapper in dark sunglasses despite the rain that had fallen on the race. Earlier in the year Janssen had won the points jersey at the Tour and he would go on to win Paris-Roubaix and the Vuelta in 1967 and then the Tour in 1968. At the time, though, this was by far the biggest win of the twenty-four-year-old's career. Poulidor finished third, Anquetil seventh. Paralysed by a rivalry that would see them finish second and third in 1966, unable to work together to overhaul Rudi

Altig in the final sprint, neither would ever win the rainbow jersey despite it certainly being well within their capabilities.

In the 1964 amateur race a nineteen-year-old rider from Belgium took his first rainbow jersey. His name was Eddy Merckx. After Merckx's win *Cycling* spoke to a Belgian *soigneur* about the rising star. 'The one thing the crowd did not realise on Saturday was that Eddy Merckx is a greater trackman than he will ever be on the road,'[100] he told the magazine. Soon the world would find out that would not be the case.

10

MR TOM AND THE YORKSHIRE HAUSFRAU

In four decades of road world championships, Britain had produced just one winner – Dave Marsh, who took the amateur title in 1922. That would all change during the 1960s, a decade in which the country would record four road world-title wins, with Beryl Burton winning the women's title in 1960 and 1967, Tom Simpson taking the professional men's race in 1965 and Graham Webb winning the amateur title in 1967. After decades of nil-returns, from 1960 to 1967 Britain was suddenly flushed with success.

Leeds-born Burton was not part of the six-woman strong squad that Great Britain had sent to the first women's world championship in 1958. Instead she made her debut the following year. Burton was at the beginning of a startling thirty-year career that would see her amass seven world titles (two on the road, five on the track), amongst a haul of national records and titles simply too exhaustive to list here in full. Suffice to say she claimed thirteen pursuit and twelve road-race national titles and for twenty-five years in a row she won the Best British All-Rounder title, awarded to the nation's most complete time trial rider. Burton remained an amateur throughout her career, combining her cycling with her work on a rhubarb farm, but her success was far-reaching. The Germans dubbed her the 'Yorkshire hausfrau' and it was in East Germany, in 1960, that Burton claimed the first of her two road world championships.

Burton was in commanding form. Earlier in the week she had won her second world pursuit title and now she led the thirty-strong field at the end of every one of the race's seven laps. She spent the final 35 kilometres alone at the head of the race, holding off a chasing pack of thirteen. It was Elsy Jacobs who had provided the initiative for Burton's solo move, making a signature bid to escape the pack at the halfway stage. Burton matched Jacobs' attack and wanted them to work together to force a lead, but ultimately Jacobs could not match the Briton's pace and fell back, leaving Burton to ride to victory while dragging her lead out to over three minutes. 'Now she had the circuit and the race organisation to herself,' reported *Cycling and Mopeds.* 'The car immediately behind her contained six spare bicycles and there was time for her to run through all if fate decreed and still win handsomely … Beryl the peril of East Germany. They will not easily forget her!'[101]

It was the first time that any rider had won world titles in the pursuit and the road race in the same year. In the *Daily Express,* Ronald White reported: 'The army of foreign journalists here are widely acclaiming Beryl's unique double. One told me "Even the maestro Fausto Coppi could not do it!"'[102] Unlike the feted Coppi, after her unique double Burton, described as the 'ultimate amateur',[103] simply went back to work, shunning all offers to go professional before claiming a second title seven years later when the race was held in Heerlen, the Netherlands.

Before that 1967 race Burton had been distraught. She had worked hard over the off-season, putting in the miles, but she had lost her world pursuit title. The jersey in an event in which she had ruled, taking five world titles in the space of eight years, had been wrestled away by Russia's Tamara Garkushina, at the start of an unbelievable eight-year Soviet dominance of the event. Burton had managed only third, a great result for many but a disaster for her. 'I've failed, there's only one medal which matters,'[104] she said.

But Burton's performance one week later in the road race again prompted seasoned journalists to compare her performance on the roads of the Netherlands to Italy's legendary rider: 'This was like one of Fausto Coppi's great wins, two Belgian and Italian journalists said to me after Beryl Burton had crossed the line,'[105] reported *Cycling's* Alan Gayfer.

On the first lap of the 55-kilometre race, Burton went to the front and drove a fierce pace, pulling out a gap and taking just one rider with her, the Soviet Lyubov Zadorozhnaya. For one lap Zadorozhnaya stuck with Burton but then, on the second climb of the 2.4-kilometre hill outside Ubachsberg, Burton went away and Zadorozhnaya was left to ride herself to second place. Zadorozhnaya later said she would have done herself some harm if she had tried to stay in Burton's wheel.

Forty-three seconds lead at the end of the second lap became 01.47 at the finish. The Soviet Union had four riders in the top-six, including second and third, but Burton had been the star of the show, untouchable and in a class of her own. She later observed drily that she had ridden harder races.

From its inception to Burton's second win, the race had been ruled by the trident of Jacobs, Reynders and Burton, as well as Soviet athletes benefitting from state-sponsored support that was later revealed to include doping. [106] But it was Reynders who was really the woman to beat, with the Belgian claiming four titles in the space of eight years. In 1961 she took her second title, winning on the Isle of Man despite the strong efforts of Jacobs to break away alone. Reynders had to switch machines during the race, forcing her to launch a furious chase to get back up to the leaders. With 200 metres to go Reynders still had enough in the tank to hit the front with a devastating turn of speed, power past Burton and Jacobs and become road cycling's first official double women's world champion.

After Marie-Rose Gaillard had retained Belgium's grip on the women's title the following year, leading a one, two, three for Belgium in Italy ahead of Reynders and Marie-Thérèse Naessens, Reynders took her third title in 1963. A stiff wind blew down the finish banner in Ronse making a tough course harder still and Burton crashed out and had to go to hospital. There was now no disputing Reynders as the dominant rider in world championship races, in six years she had won three titles. 'Oh, I was nervous,' Reynders said after her third win. 'Three, four days before the race … Oscar Daemars scolded me because I went to see the course only the day before the championship

... In group training others were right over their bikes on the uphill while I was singing and very easily climbed to the top.'[107]

After wins for the Soviet Union's Emilia Sonka in 1964 and East Germany's Elisabeth Kleinhans-Eichholz in 1965, Reynders added a fourth title in 1966, in a race during which a leading group of five formed that included Burton, Jacobs and Reynders. Burton did all the work, the rest unwilling to help. 'Every time I turned round to speak to Reynders or Jacobs about leading they made it quite clear they wanted nothing to do with me,' Burton said afterwards. 'It was like beating your head against a brick wall.'[108] In the sprint Reynders calmly took the win ahead of an eighteen-year-old Keetie Hage. Burton finished fifth.

As it turned out the four-times champion would not ride in another Worlds for ten years. It meant that there was an Yvonne Reynders-sized hole in the peloton when Burton claimed her second jersey in Heerlen. Reynders had travelled to the Netherlands to defend her title but then, on 28 August 1967, the Dutch newspaper *Leidsch Dagblad* ran the following story:

The first result of the doping tests during the world championships exploded like a piece of trotyl [TNT] in the Olympic Stadium when Saturday afternoon UCI secretary René Chesal stepped out of the door of the boardroom at the stadium with a ballpoint written communiqué, the result of an emergency meeting of the UCI board convened after receiving the results of the doping tests.

Chesal read: 'Yvonne Reynders and Alex Boeye, both Belgium, Kevin Crowe (Australia), Freddy Ruegg (Switzerland) and Dieter Kemper (West Germany) have been detected as doping. The consequences are: 1. They are disqualified. 2. They may not start in Amsterdam. 3. The amateurs are suspended for three months and the professionals (Kemper and Ruegg) receive fines of 2,000 francs. There is no protest allowed against the investigation or the verdict.'[109]

Reynders was incensed. She furiously denied, and continues to deny to this day, any wrongdoing. In fury she quit the sport. The suspension may only have been for three months but she would not return to cycling until the mid-1970s.

After the race Burton was asked about Reynders' absence: 'Were you happy that Yvonne Reynders was not riding?' 'Frankly it didn't matter,' she replied. 'She would have been at the back shattered with the others anyway.'[110]

***

When *Cycling* ran their preview of the 1965 world championships the magazine installed France's Jacques Anquetil and Italy's Gianni Motta as favourites and listed Michael Wright, a British-born rider raised in Belgium who spoke little English, as Britain's best hope, while forecasting that Tom Simpson should make the top ten.

Two weeks later the front cover of the same magazine carried a picture of Simpson crossing the finish line in Lasarte, northern Spain. His mouth was gaping, his eyes were narrowed. He was pictured alone, with only pressmen on motorbikes behind. In fact, out of shot but just three lengths back, was the German rider Rudi Altig. Above the picture ran a simple headline: 'Simpson is Champ!'[111]

Before the championships, held on a lumpy 19-kilometre course starting and finishing just outside Lasarte, 10 kilometres to the south-west of San Sebastián, Simpson's 1965 season had been mixed, to say the least. He had had plenty of decent placings, including third in a legendary edition of the mammoth Bordeaux-Paris that saw Jacques Anquetil record a famous win just twenty-four hours after claiming the ten-stage Dauphiné Libéré, but he had recorded no victories and had been forced to abandon the Tour after injuring his hand, leaving him with 'severe blood poisoning, bronchitis, a kidney infection and one abscess after another.'[112] Simpson had just seven weeks to get ready for the Worlds.

More than 50 years later Barry Hoban, winner of eight Tour stages and Simpson's teammate in Spain, told me that Simpson had spoken with the rest of the six-strong British team in the weeks building up to the race in order to garner their support, offering a financial reward should he be successful. Sure enough his team worked tirelessly and cleverly for him.

Hoban got in the early break and on the second lap Simpson and Altig rode across, along with Sebastian Elorza of Spain. Hoban helped to drive the pace for 200 kilometres, ensuring no one could make it up to the break. 'Barry Hoban was magnificent,'[113] Simpson later said. As Hoban kept the pace high, the rest of the team behind handled any attempt from anyone to get across. Alan Ramsbottom was particularly strong, closely marking French champion Henri Anglade. The pair were former trade teammates, but had history. Ramsbottom had been accused of not being available to support Anglade at a race in 1964 after a mix-up in schedules that came after Ramsbottom felt his own chances during a stage of the 1963 Tour had been hampered by having to wait for the Frenchman.

Poulidor, Anquetil and Van Looy were among the favoured riders that had not made the break, with the rivalry between Anquetil and Poulidor again referenced in the post-race reports in relation to France's poor showing. 'The duel that should have been at the front between Anquetil and Poulidor took place at the lowest levels of the competition,' reported *Le Monde*. 'The two French champions will together return back to back, one to his native Normandy, the other to the Limousin: they both gave up, as did the champion of France, Anglade.'[114]

Two laps from the end, when the break's impetus was wavering, Simpson and Altig struck out for victory. The two worked together, knowing that this was their opportunity to make history. They increased their gap until it was clear one of them would be claiming the rainbow jersey for the first time. Altig was a strong solo rider; three years before he had humiliated his teammate Anquetil in the prestigious two-up Italian time trial Trofeo Baracchi, carrying the French time trial specialist to the win. Anquetil was so exhausted that when he entered the finale at the Vigorelli Velodrome he promptly crashed into a post. Two years later Altig had ridden the Baracchi with Simpson and had set an equally ferocious pace, nearly riding the Briton off his wheel. Now, Simpson called out to Altig: 'remember the Baracchi!' and the two formed a pact – work together until the final kilometre when it became each man for himself.

After more than six and a half hours of racing, with minutes in hand over the rest of the race, the final, uphill sprint beckoned. Just as Altig went to change gear Simpson stomped on his pedals and rode away. There was nothing the German could do to pull him back. 'Nine times out of ten I beat Simpson in a sprint,' the German later lamented. 'This had to be the tenth time.'[115]

Crowds surged around Simpson. He may have been British but he was well-loved on the Continent and had a huge following in Belgium where he lived. His manager, Gaston Plaud, was crying. The president of his supporters' club in Gent, Albert Beurick, was crying. The promoter of the Gent six-days, Oscar Daemers, about to open a new track, was rubbing his hands in glee. The crowd was chanting Simpson's name and journalists were throwing microphones at him, shouting questions. The British contingent chanted '*El Campeonato, El Campeonato.*' Tommy Simpson, Mr Tom, had won the rainbow jersey. 'This lean, sallow-faced Briton pedalled to the peak of his years of challenging Europe's kings – the rainbow jersey of a world champion and the professional road race title,'[116] wrote Ron White in the *Daily Express*. 'I'm hoarse from shouting and cheering, you've never seen scenes like this in all your life – world champion Tom Simpson,'[117] reported *Cycling*'s editor Alan Gayfer.

Simpson later told *Cycling* the story of that final sprint. 'What happened was quite simple,' he said. 'I heard Rudi change gear and I thought his chain was slipping. You only get opportunities like that once in a lifetime and I jumped at it.'[118] Less than two weeks later Simpson won his first race as world champion – the Tour of Lombardy – by three minutes ahead of Italian favourite Motta. 'He wears the rainbow jersey,' reported *La Stampa* of Simpson's arrival alone in the stadium in Como. 'His face is covered with mud. He dangles on the bicycle demanding from himself extreme reserves of energy. The public, for a moment, are quiet, in absolute silence. Then someone claps their hands. Others copy him. Simpson goes around and crosses the finish line amid the din of a huge ovation … his face lit by a perpetual smile that seems to have fun with everything and everyone.'[119] Simpson was the toast of the cycling world.

***

Twelve months on from Simpson's win, the man who had left Spain disappointed after trailing in the Briton's wake cut a very different figure. Rudi Altig had fractured his hip at the Vuelta in 1965 but had still managed to match Simpson until the very last moments in Lasarte. Now, at the Nürburgring, Altig secured Germany's second men's title following Heinz Müller's 1952 win.

This time round Simpson retired, fatigued by the energy-sapping 22.8-kilometre course and with too much racing in his legs. As the final lap approached a four-man break went that included Motta, Poulidor, Italo Zilioli and Jean Stablinski: two Frenchmen, two Italians. Behind them sat some big names, including Jacques Anquetil and two young riders that were already beginning to make their indelible mark on the cycling world –Felice Gimondi, a twenty-three-year-old Italian, and Eddy Merckx, of Belgium, just twenty-one.

Anquetil, ignoring the fact he had two supposed teammates up front, rode hard to join the front group. Then Gimondi launched his bid, taking a 25-second lead at the bell. Altig, meanwhile, was gathering himself, having struggled as the race progressed and after earlier going to the back of the peloton to be sick. Anquetil led the pursuit of Gimondi who then saw his chances scuppered by a puncture. Anquetil pressed on at the head of his small group, which still included Poulidor, but seemed to be unsure of exactly what to do. With around 10 kilometres to go, and much to the puzzlement of the French, Altig was able to catch a lift up to the front group on the wheel of Anquetil's teammate Lucien Aimar.

Altig had learned from the previous year. Today there was to be no waiting around in the sprint. Rounding the final corner into the 500-metre long finishing straight he launched his move, opening a sizeable gap. Anquetil set off in hot pursuit. With 200 metres to go the Frenchman was gaining. Altig dug again, pouring every effort he had into the pedals. The German crossed the line with his right arm raised to be lofted onto the shoulders of his waiting fans. Anquetil was left to take second with Poulidor third.

Once again Anquetil and Poulidor's rivalry meant that neither man had won. Anquetil did not take his place on the podium and accusations flew in the French press. Anquetil and Altig had resolved those differences that had been so visible at the Trofeo Baracchi in 1962 and were now close friends, their families had stayed together and the two riders had ridden the course together in the lead-up to the race. Why had Aimar, like Anquetil a member of the Ford-Hutchinson trade team, helped Altig across to the break? In *Sex, Lies and Handlebar Tape*, Poulidor maintains that there was nothing sinister in Aimar's actions. 'No, Aimar's not compromised,' Poulidor told author Paul Howard. 'He [Anquetil] was scared I would win, and I perhaps didn't want him to win either. It was our bad blood that allowed Altig to come back.'[120] In the same book, published in 2008, six years before his death, Altig tells Howard that he thinks the truth will now never come out, saying only that, 'the truth is that he was second and Poulidor was third.'[121] Anquetil's second place was the best he would manage at the Worlds. Howard concludes that it seemed that throwing away the best opportunity Anquetil had to fulfil a lifetime's ambition was preferable to putting everything on the line and running the risk of losing out to Poulidor.

***

In contrast to Anquetil's travails at the Worlds, Eddy Merckx was in only his second full year as a professional in 1967 when he took his first professional world title. Some described his season-long targeting of the event as a gamble that had paid off. If the notion today of anything that Merckx tried or targeted being deemed a gamble seems slightly absurd given his complete domination of the sport from the late 1960s to the mid-1970s, it should be remembered that of all his major victories at the time, 'the Cannibal', had 'just' two Milan-Sanremo wins to his name.

Merckx had taken the amateur title three years earlier when he won a race in which he would not have competed without his mother's intervention, When subjected to medical tests before selection he had been told that he had a problem with his heart and would not be considered for the team. His mother Jenny did not believe it. She questioned the chief selector and then talked to the family doctor. He told her there was no problem with her son's heart. Merckx rode and Merckx won. A pattern that would soon become familiar.

Three years on, the day after Graham Webb followed in Merckx's trail to claim Britain's second amateur title, Merckx became just the third amateur champion to go on to take the professional title, matching the achievement of his compatriot Jean Aerts (1927/1935) and Switzerland's Hans Knecht (1938/1946). Merckx's win was crafted in the style to which the cycling world would soon become accustomed – in short he was at the head of the race from the first moment until the last.

When Gianni Motta attacked just 5 kilometres into the 265-kilometre race in Heerlen, the Netherlands, a small group of riders went with him. The circuit had one significant climb and Motta's had been a long-planned attack, with the Italian under instruction to strike out early whether or not anyone went with him. Merckx went with Motta, as did Jos van der Vleuten of the Netherlands, Ramón Sáez of Spain and Bob Addy of Great Britain. The race had only just started and yet it was in many ways already over. Only one man would later infiltrate this leading group, Van der Vleuten's teammate Jan Janssen, the 1964 champion, who put in a huge effort in to claw back two and a half minutes to join the leaders.

Merckx took the sprint ahead of Janssen and Sáez. Motta, whose aggressive race plan had prompted the whole thing, finished fourth. The reign of the Cannibal was about to start.

***

The following year brought a win for Vittorio Adorni, an Italian trade teammate of Merckx, who got himself into the early break and then struck out alone for a win of nearly 10 minutes after the pre-race favourites, Anquetil, Gimondi, Merckx, Van Looy and Poulidor, all sat behind in the same group unwilling or unable to make any move. In the women's race the Netherlands' Keetie Hage took her country's first title. Adorni's win came with the second largest margin in history while Hage was just nineteen years old and riding only her second Worlds after taking second behind Reynders in 1966. It felt like the start of the changing of the guard in women's cycling.

The decade came to a close in Belgium with wins for the Netherlands' Harm Ottenbros and the USA's Audrey McElmury. Merckx had been the overwhelming favourite on home roads in Zolder but was so closely marked that the 300,000 spectators that packed the roadsides saw him ride round the circuit thirty times in the shelter and anonymity of the peloton. Boos rang out and on the final lap, 300 metres from the finish, Merckx cycled off the course towards his hotel. Ottenbros was the first of the sixty-two riders who crossed the finish line. His best victories until then had been a brace of stage wins at the Tour of Switzerland. McElmury, meanwhile, took a first elite road title for the USA in the pouring rain in Brno, Czechoslovakia. McElmury crashed on the penultimate lap but was still able to record a win of over one minute from Britain's Bernadette Swinnerton. It had been a remarkable period for Britain at the Worlds with four wins and a further two podium placings across the women's and men's amateur and professional races. But it would be another eleven years before a Briton would again make a Worlds podium.

11

BARRY HOBAN

In 1965 Barry Hoban, then a second-year professional with a couple of Vuelta stage wins already to his name, was instrumental in guiding Simpson to his famous win. For more than 200 kilometres Hoban was at the sharp end of the race, working for Simpson.

Hoban would go on to enjoy a highly successful career of his own, winning eight Tour stages and Gent-Wevelgem as well as taking podium spots at Paris-Roubaix and Liège-Bastogne-Liège. Today he lives in Wales, in a house remotely situated high on a steep and narrow road. Hoban had warned me it would take some finding and when he calls me to see where I am, it turns out that I am not where I thought I was. Eventually, after a few U-turns and driving up and down precipitous Welsh roads while praying I won't meet a car coming the other way, I turn into a driveway that I'm still not totally convinced belongs to Hoban. Then I see the cycling paraphernalia dotted around a garden that overlooks a spectacular valley and I know that I've found him.

We settle in Hoban's comfortable sitting room and for the next two and a half hours this most engaging of interviewees tells me about his career and that September day in 1965 when he helped Tom Simpson to bring the rainbow jersey to Britain.

***

Barry Hoban:

Tom and I were very similar types of riders in that Tom was a very good individual pursuit rider [Simpson won the national amateur title in 1958] and I was British amateur pursuit champion twice, in 1960 and 1961. The continental gurus used to say, 'Give me a pursuiter and I'll make a bike rider out of them,' because they knew they could go fast. Tom was like that, he could win time trials and he could win road races and so could I. He was good on the track, I was good on the track. And so when Tom started doing things … I thought if Tom Simpson can do it then I can do it.

There was a guy in Harrogate, Ron Kitching, who was Mr Cycling really. He had a cycle shop and he was one of the first guys to import stuff from the Continent. He used to go to France and he could speak French and he got very friendly with André Bertin who had this team and he gave me a letter of introduction to go there – that's how I went.

I rode the Tour de l'Avenir in my second year and there was a guy there, a journalist, who just sort of cottoned on to me. He followed professional races and said to Antonin Magne, 'That Barry Hoban … he's riding in northern France, he's got some ability.' Next thing the club president gets this letter from Magne saying he was interested in signing me as a pro for Mercier-BP. That's how it all started.

In September 1965 Hoban headed to northern Spain for the Worlds after a difficult second season that had been affected by the amount of racing he'd had during his first year as a professional.

There was no selection process really, any rider that was riding on the Continent was going to be selected. We were certainly far superior to the riders riding in Britain and so the team was basically the British riders who were racing on the Continent. It was a strongish team, not a large team, but it was all that Britain had. I mean if you were riding for a pro team then you weren't there because you were useless, you had to have certain capabilities. In those days British Cycling, the BCF, they had no money at all. They never ever paid one penny of my expenses at the Worlds. Nothing. You had to sort everything out yourself. You made your own accommodation arrangements and travel arrangements. We didn't stay as a team.

In 1961 I'd gone to the Worlds in Switzerland where I represented Britain in the pursuit championships. Tom rode it as well as riding the road race, and Tom was camping! He was there camping by Lake Zurich. You think now, 'What? Camping?' but that's how it was. I think at the Worlds in 1965 Tom and I stayed at the hotel where the British team management was staying but we paid all our own bills. Vin Denson was camping somewhere. I don't know where Michael Wright stayed or Alan Ramsbottom. We all made our own way there.

In Britain, in Yorkshire, we used to finish up on the moors with no one there, you didn't finish in towns – they wouldn't let you. So getting to the Continent it was, 'Wow, the roads are closed, the police have stopped the traffic. What?' It was a magical place. I would have probably paid to have ridden my first Tour de France I wanted to ride it so badly. That's how it was. So you went to the Worlds on the off-chance you could do something. When you look at it now, I mean there is only one place that counts in the world championships and that obviously is first. Second, third, fourth … they don't count. That jersey counts. That jersey is going to make whoever wins it a lot of money and that's what it's all about. It wasn't so commercial then, it was more a sort of folklore – it was, 'Well, I want to ride the Worlds,' and yes it was costing you money to do it, but hey.

In France the Tour finished and the riders were earning their money riding criteriums, driving here, there and everywhere. There weren't really any substantial races around that time after the Tour. So they introduced a race in the 1960s – Paris-Luxembourg – to give a bit of preparation to the guys who were riding the Worlds. You had stages of about 220–230 kilometres and it was nice having two or three days like that where you weren't driving everywhere.

I had no idea how I was going to get down to San Sebastián. When I got to the finish of the first stage of Paris-Luxembourg this guy came along and said, 'Hey, Barry!' It was a friend, a supporter of mine from Leeds who'd come over to get a glimpse of continental cycling. He'd not planned anything at all. I asked where he was going after the race and he said he didn't know. I said, 'Oh, I've got to get down to San Sebastián'. 'I'll take you down,' he said. He had this big Ford Zodiac. We drove down to San Sebastián in it, slept in the car, my bike was loaded in the back. We just pulled over, dropped the seats back and curled up there. We got to the hotel and I had no idea how I'd get back.

I went round the circuit with Tom beforehand. There was really only one climb, it was a good circuit for anyone who was in form. Tom had already spoken with the guys on the team who were living in Belgium and had said, 'Look, if you're prepared to help me as much as you can I'm prepared to pay x amount. Naturally, I'll decide who helped me the most and who gets what. If you all help me the same it gets split equally.' I forget how much it was but it was a reasonable amount of money.

I had the same conversation with him, it might have been in Spain or during Paris-Luxembourg. I was starting to go OK but I wasn't flying; I had knackered myself in my first year as a pro. I'd ridden the Vuelta again in 1965 but picked up some stomach infection and I was vomiting. I finished but I was knackered. Tom and I had ridden a few races together, gone to Britain and ridden London-Holyhead, so almost certainly we talked then … if … if … if.

On the morning of a big race you're a little friskier before the start. With road racing you can't plan, you have to plan en route. If you're riding Paris-Roubaix or the Tour of Flanders, you know you have to keep at the head of affairs and then say, at such a point I'm going to make things happen. But the Worlds, because it's a different circuit each year, people don't know. Nowadays teams would have gone down and recce'd the circuit but that wasn't done in our day at all.

Tom said, 'Look, be careful on the breaks, you know what is going to happen.' People say that I said afterwards we had to be careful of the Portuguese. Well, yes, there were a lot of Portuguese riders but there were also the Spanish riders. When you rode in Spain, the Spanish and the Portuguese guys were like bloody mosquitoes at the start. They just couldn't take it easy until someone was away up the road … bingbang, bingbang, bingbang, all the damn time!

Sure enough, early in the race an early break went and Hoban was there with them. After three laps Simpson rode across along with Germany's Rudi Altig and Spain's Sebastián Elorza. From that moment the race was truly on.

Off they went and I was with them straight away. I was quite happy to flow along, I knew what I was going to do. I wasn't going to ride eyeballs out, there was a long way to go. A couple of laps later Tom came up with Altig and said, 'Right. I think this is a good break, Barry. I don't want anyone else to come from behind.' It was split. There were no French riders there. So I started giving it full welly … I wasn't looking at the finish, I was looking at maintaining the breakaway so that Tom would have the chance to go for the win.

Franco Balmamion was probably the fancied rider in that break. He was a very astute rider and he'd won the Tour of Italy twice yet he never won a stage, he was a very clever rider. Once we got into that break I told Tom I'd ride for him. I was the type of rider that if I said I'd do something then I'd do it. I didn't need to sign a contract, my word was my bond.

So I got stuck in. A lot of the riders in there were riding, the Spaniards were riding, Peter Post was riding and Altig and Tom were riding as well. There were one or two, like Balmamion, who were being crafty and soft-pedalling. But then you never know. Some riders you could tell when they were suffering and there were other riders where you just couldn't. You'd think is he just being crafty or what? And he was a rider with a reputation. I remember Tom saying, 'Barry, how are you feeling?' I said, 'Well, the legs are beginning to hurt a bit now.' He said, 'Well, if you feel like falling off, fall off in front of Balmamion!'

Behind, there were attacks. Van Looy was there, Stablinski was trying to get up. There were a lot of good riders behind. One rider who never gets much publicity was the only rider who was messing with them behind – Alan Ramsbottom. If you want to disrupt a chase you ride second-wheel and you open a gap. Riders have to come round you all the time and you are breaking up their momentum and Rams was doing that extremely well. Riders told me afterwards, 'Bloody hell, Rams did a damn good job behind.'

The arrival of Simpson and Altig into the leading group was the real impetus for the break. Then, with two laps to go Simpson and Altig broke away.

Without Tom coming up I would have sat on that break. As for the group as a whole, certainly Tom and Altig and even Balmamion would have had hopes of doing something. If the bunch was together they wouldn't have had those same hopes, so it was in a few riders' interests in the group to keep the ball rolling.

You had Post and Den Hertog from Holland. You had little Kunde from Germany. There was a Swiss rider – Binggeli – and Elorza from Spain who had come over with Tom and Altig. For over 100 miles I'd been giving it full welly and if Tom hadn't been there I'd have been soft-pedalling and saving something for the final, but Tom was there … and he'd promised to make sure it was a good pay day.

I also knew that Altig, great rider though he was, was handicapped. He'd crashed in the Tour of Spain and broken his hip. What Altig did in that race was amazing considering the accident he'd had.

I was still in the group when they attacked. Then it split. I managed to stay with the group for another lap I think before finally the elastic broke. I don't know which of them went first because I wasn't right up the front at the time. But riders are conscious all the time of who is doing what and Tom and Altig were reasonably friendly, they'd been in the same team and had turned pro at roughly the same time. They'd have been looking around and thinking it was about time they were going, they didn't want to be carrying all those guys to the finish – you never know, there were guys like Peter Post who was a damn good road rider. They must have decided right, let's go. They were talking quite a bit together. They had come across to our break together and then they went away together.

I knew that Tom was an ace at preparing specially for a race, when he centred himself on a race not much was going to divert him from it. When he won Milan-Sanremo, Tom had ridden Paris-Nice beforehand. We had two days between Paris-Nice and Milan-Sanremo, but Tom didn't bother riding the last stage of Paris-Nice. He went for a nice gentle training ride, he had his hair cut and he went to Milan. He was preparing himself. When Tom set his stall out you knew – you could tell. His bike was immaculate, not that it wasn't always in good nick, but it was especially immaculate, he wasn't leaving anything to doubt. I saw that in San Sebastián.

Simpson and Altig reportedly made a pact; ride together to the final kilometre and then race it out for the jersey. Simpson won the sprint by around five lengths.

The thing is that Tom would've been able to tell. You can tell when you're going uphill if the person with you, or the people with you, haven't quite got it. And Tom would've sussed that. Tom knew what had happened to Altig and would have been thinking, and this is me saying this, but Tom would've been saying to himself, 'Rudi, it's not your day today, mate.'

In sport you get a moment when everything clicks and you get overdrive; you don't always have that but Tom had overdrive that day. And they spoke to each other … We ride, share the work, ride, and then the last 300 or 400 metres, you go there, I'll go here and the strongest man wins. Which is what happened. If Altig had been in that same position with Tom but hadn't had the accident then it wouldn't have been the same result because Altig was a great rider who could sprint hard.

By the time I crossed the line I knew Tom had won. I knew it had been a good pay day! When I realised Tom had won I just felt that I had done my job that day.

After the race Hoban went back to his hotel and began to think about how he was going to get home.

It was pandemonium. I didn't see Tom at the finish line and so the first time I saw him was at the hotel. Tom was going to disappear pretty quickly because the following day he was riding a criterium near Brest. The organiser had put on a plane and so Anquetil, Altig, Stablinski and, as world champion, Tom were on the plane. Tom had just taken delivery of a new car, a BMW TI – turbo injection 1800, a grey one and said, 'Barry, do want to drive my car back? I'll meet you at the Gare du Nord.' We had a quick glass of champagne and Tom gave me the keys to his car … 'See you at the Gare du Nord!' The next day I was in Paris, gave him his car back and I got the train with my bike and my bag back home to Béthune.

We didn't really discuss the race afterwards. You didn't in those days. There was a race, it had finished and Tom had the world champions' jersey. You were paid to ride your bike and win races. We were just doing our jobs.

Hoban's own best performance in the Worlds came in Gap, France in 1972 when he finished eighteenth.

The Worlds were always at the worst time of the season as far as I was concerned. If I rode a good Tour the banker was the criteriums. The top riders such as Anquetil and Merckx, the real top riders, they could afford to pay someone to drive a car for them, to rub their legs, to get their bike. I couldn't afford that so I did it myself. We used to average 4000 kilometres driving a week following the Tour. You were driving and racing every single day and some days racing twice. Consequently by the time you got to the end of the Crits you were knackered. In my car I used to have a sleeping bag and an alarm clock. Most of the track meetings were in the evening and after you got yourself sorted out and got paid it was knocking on 1am. At 2pm you might be riding 700 kilometres away. You'd drive until your eyes were almost closed then pull over, get into the sleeping bag, set the alarm for two hours later, get up and go again … it used to destroy you.

That year in Gap, Marino Basso won. Now Marino Basso had ridden the Tour that year and he had a whole load of Crits to ride in France but the Italian Federation said, 'Marino, how many criteriums are you going to ride? How much? If we pay you that money would you stay home and prepare for Gap?' They gave him that backing. If I had just had someone just to drive my car it would've been something.

The world title stays with riders for ever. They've been a world champion. It is one of the few things that stays because in cycling terms, on the Continent, the rainbow bands stay there. Any rider who has won the jersey but isn't the current champion still has the bands on the cuffs of their jersey. The Worlds are the pinnacle of a pro career.

12

THE DEATH OF A CHAMPION

On 14 December 2015 the *BMJ* (formerly the *British Medical Journal*) published a paper by Thomas Perneger, a clinical epidemiologist, titled *Debunking the curse of the rainbow jersey.*[122] For years cyclists and reporters had noted the frequency with which the results of a world champion failed to match up to their performances of the previous season when they had won the rainbow jersey. A good example, Perneger wrote, was Tom Simpson who in the months following his win in 1965 broke his leg skiing, went on to miss a large part of the following season and then, when he was riding, only managed to record a handful of second places. And Simpson was by no means the only rider to suffer. Was the jersey cursed? Cycling writers often asked.

Unsurprisingly, while giving evidence of the drop-off in results, Perneger's paper did not support the notion of a curse, instead concluding: 'The cycling world champion is significantly less successful during the year when he wears the rainbow jersey than in the previous year, but this is best explained by regression to the mean, not by a curse.'[123] That is to say a rider who wins the rainbow jersey more often than not has enjoyed a particularly successful season and then simply returns to a more average ('mean') year. However, if there was one rider who could have been forgiven for thinking the jersey was cursed, it would have been Jean-Pierre 'Jempi' Monseré.

Monseré was born in Roeselare, Belgium in 1948. He grew into a talented cyclist and at the age of twenty-one finished second in the amateur Worlds behind Denmark's Leif Mortensen. Monseré promptly turned professional with the Flandria team and just six weeks later he was awarded the win at the Tour of Lombardy after Dutchman Gerben Karstens failed a doping test. His professional career was not yet two months old and already the young Belgian was a Monument winner.

A little less than twelve months later Monseré was in Leicester, England, as part of a ten-man Belgian team that was keen to mount a concerted bid to reclaim the rainbow jersey. His selection had not been met with universal approval but his third place at the national championship behind Eddy Merckx and Herman Van Springel had sealed his spot. Belgium boasted a strong team. That year Merckx had won Paris-Roubaix, the Giro and the Tour, Roger De Vlaeminck had won Liège-Bastogne-Liège, and Van Springel was just three weeks away from the first of seven Bordeaux-Paris wins. But in Leicester it was Monseré who launched the Belgian bid to win the title. He was an ever-present in the moves that mattered, working to get across to the first meaningful break that went early in the race. When that was caught he was in a further group of seven that got upwards of 10 minutes ahead, and when that break was brought back he was in the chasing group of four that hunted down Italy's Felice Gimondi and France's Alain Vasseur, eventually catching them with 35 kilometres to go to make a leading group of six. Monseré was still there with a fast-approaching chasing group just seconds behind when the six wound up to contest the finish.

The day before Monseré had watched the amateur race and had seen Denmark's Jørgen Schmidt make his move inside the final kilometre to take the win. Monseré had seen where Schmidt had launched his attack and decided that was the crucial point.

And so, just as Schmidt had the day before, Monseré attacked before things came down to a sprint. Just as it had worked for Schmidt so it worked for Monseré. He held on to a two-second lead ahead of Mortensen, the same man who had beaten him to the amateur title the year before. Gimondi, who was considered by many the strongest and best performer on the day, took third. Only Karel Kaers had won the world championships when younger than Monseré. At the finish Monseré said that Gimondi had offered a financial reward to secure his support in the run-in. He said he had replied, 'I want to become world champion.' Gimondi fiercely denied the accusation and even threatened to sue, garnering support from Merckx among others. 'The Italian racer is honest,' Merckx said. 'His professionalism cannot be doubted. I am convinced certain allegations are absolutely baseless.'[124]

'I have never ridden with such ease,' Monseré said afterwards. 'Before I have always been the victim of my own lack of confidence but this time it was different.'[125] Even Merckx was impressed, saying his young teammate had ridden a great race and pointing out that it was not easy to make it to all the breaks. Gimondi, meanwhile, who finished third, called it a 'bitter end to a great race.'[126]

Ten days after Monseré's win his father, Achiel, the man who had encouraged his son to start cycling, died of a heart attack. Seven months later, on 15 March 1971, Monseré was riding a kermesse race in and around Retie, a small town in north-east Belgium. He was preparing an assault on the spring Classics and was riding in the bunch at the head of the race on the road between Gierle and the small town of Lille when he collided with a car. He was catapulted into the air and killed instantly. His team manager Noël Foré was one of the first on the scene. 'Most riders hoped for a moment that he would only be unconscious,' he said. 'But I saw he was already dead.'[127] A young life and a young career had been brought to a sickening end. Monseré had been wearing his rainbow jersey. A monument now stands where he fell.

Fate was not finished with Monseré's family. Five years after his death, Monseré's young son, Giovanni, was also killed after being hit by a car whilst riding his bike.

***

After Monseré's win *La Stampa* had dubbed the world championships a lottery, highlighting in a table that the past three men's races had all delivered surprising results and that none of the eventual champions had claimed a major race in the eight months building up to the championships that they then won.[128] The nature of the race, taking in multiple laps of the same circuit, meant that a strong rider needed a circuit of sufficient difficulty on which to launch their bid. If the route was not hard enough then the work of even the greatest rider would be easily matched and their efforts would end in vain. Favoured riders would simply be watched, marked and monitored by the rest of the bunch, just as Merckx had found out in Zolder in 1969. The result was that relatively unfancied riders had been able to spring a surprise on the rest of the bunch. Questions were being asked. For the rainbow jersey to retain its position as one of the most sought-after prizes in cycling it could not be thought of as being a lottery. An exciting race with a big-name winner was needed. Step forward Eddy Merckx.

In 1971 Merckx was at the peak of his powers. In the off-season he had signed for Molteni, taking his old Faema Director Sportif, Guillaume Driessens, with him. No one could challenge his might and in the nine months in the run-up to the Worlds in Mendrisio, Switzerland, among other races, Merckx won the Tour of Sardinia, Paris-Nice, Milan-Sanremo, Omloop Het Volk, the Tour of Belgium, Liège-Bastogne-Liège, the Dauphiné Libéré, the Midi Libre and then the yellow jersey and the points competition at the Tour. It had been another remarkable season but his win at the Tour had been bitter. Merckx was lying seven minutes behind race leader Luis Ocaña when the race reached the Pyrenees. In the midst of a severe hailstorm, Merckx went on the offensive. Ocaña matched him easily but then fell on the descent of the Col de Menté. Dutchman Joop Zoetemelk smashed into him and Ocaña's race was over. Merckx inherited yellow, although he refused to wear it the next day out of respect to the Spaniard and considered abandoning the race. After the stage Merckx said 'Whatever happens, I have lost the Tour. The doubt will always remain.'[129]

In Mendrisio Merckx was at last presented with a circuit just tough enough for him to use it to his advantage. The Novazzano climb was the principal obstacle and while only a touch over 2 kilometres long at around 7 per cent, it had to be tackled sixteen times during the 268-kilometre race and at least offered a launch pad for any race-winning move. Merckx made sure a teammate, Herman Van Springel, was in the break that went early but then went to work himself, putting the peloton under constant pressure.

On the thirteenth lap, with the first break caught, Leif Mortensen attacked. Five went with him: Cyrille Guimard of France, Georges Pintens of Belgium, Giancarlo Polidori and Felice Gimondi of Italy, and Merckx who then took up the reins. Within 10 kilometres the six had a lead of nearly 01.30. One lap later that had gone out to more than 14 minutes. There were 32 kilometres to go.

Merckx made his move on the penultimate lap on the second half of the Novazzano climb, cruelly distancing all those that had so far stuck with him apart from Gimondi. The Italian was not to be shaken and he stuck to the Belgian like glue.

They worked together, knowing that with a lap still to go it was in their joint interests to create an unassailable lead before worrying about the finish. Reflecting on the race some forty-five years later Gimondi told me he always knew he would not win but it did not stop him trying everything in the final lap to get away from Merckx. He tried on the final climb but Merckx came around and so they rode it side by side, each not willing to cede to the other. Then he tried twice more in the final 500 metres to shake the Belgian off his wheel, moving to the right, then to the left. He failed. With 250 metres to go Merckx came off the Italian's wheel with ease. It was over. All that was left was for Merckx to raise both hands in the air as he crossed the line and to then pay tribute to his great rival: 'Gimondi was riding better today than I have ever known him,'[130] he said. 'This victory is the one that gives me the most pleasure since my first Tour,' I experienced a very tough year, with constant questioning. So, I admit, for two months, in other words since the Ocaña offensive in the Alps [during the Tour], I doubted myself a little.'[131]

For the Worlds it was a welcome win. There was no bigger star in cycling than Merckx and his victory put a stop to questioning of the worth of the championships.

***

At the start of the 1970s, the Soviet Union's Anna Konkina took back-to-back titles in the women's race, first winning in Leicester in a dull race where the Soviets had three riders in the top four with only Italy's Morena Tartagni in second breaking their stranglehold. The following year brought the same result, Konkina first, Tartagni second, in a sprint in Mendrisio. Beryl Burton had been active throughout the whole race, attacking incessantly but with no other rider willing to help she came home in ninth. While she did not have the jersey, Burton was still seen by many as the strongest rider in the peloton. 'Whichever way you look at it she [Burton] is still the best woman rider in the world,'[132] said the USA's Audrey McElmury.

The women's world championships had belonged to a handful of riders from a few countries: Belgium, Luxembourg, Britain, the Soviet Union and the Netherlands. France's best result had come in 1959 when Renée Vissac finished fourth. That all changed in 1972 when Geneviève Gambillon won a six-strong sprint in Gap, to break her country's duck and, according to *Cycling*, secure the 'gold medal it needed to make the championships worthwhile.'[133]

Burton had again been the most aggressive rider in the race but had once more found herself overwhelmed at the end. It says much for her attacking instincts that this was the way she chose to ride. Burton rejected the tactical game of forcing the work on to others and biding her time. She knew one way to ride – hard, straight from the off, and if it worked it worked, if it did not, she knew she had left nothing out there on the road.

Burton's efforts set up an eight-rider breakaway early in the race that contained three former world champions – Burton, Anna Konkina and Audrey McElmury. Over the course of the race the Briton variously worked fruitlessly to get away or to chase down the few attempts by others to escape.

This time it was not the Soviets who rode Burton's coat-tails to victory, but a twenty-one-year-old nurse from Paris, Gambillon proving the old adage that the only time when leading a race matters is on the finish line. At last France had a female champion to stand alongside the likes of Speicher, Magne, Bobet, Darrigade and Stablinski.

In the men's race, Italy's Marino Basso won from an eight-rider sprint, beating compatriot Franco Bitossi, who had enjoyed a decent lead in the final 200 metres but tired badly. Two days earlier Merckx had said the Gap circuit was easy and therefore a circuit for Basso. 'Everyone laughed,' Basso said afterwards. 'But I thought he could be right and decided that wherever Merckx would go, then I would go with him and that is what happened.'[134]

***

By the time of the 1973 Worlds, Felice Gimondi had won two national titles, all three Grand Tours and two Monuments. The Italian was one of the best riders in the world. He was desperate to complete his set of jerseys by winning the one with the rainbow bands.

Gimondi had already stood on the Worlds podium twice but had twice heard the Belgian national anthem play as he watched Monseré and then Merckx collect the jersey he so coveted. This time around Gimondi felt things could be different. 'I can feel the win in my legs,' he reportedly told his manager Nino Defilippis two days before the race in Barcelona. 'All I need is your help to pull it off. Promise me this and I shan't bother you again, because it will be the last chance I will have to do it.'[135]

Defilippis listened and a plan was hatched around providing Gimondi with the best chance to win. The Italian team was together and focused with Gimondi keen to ensure he was never more than a wheel or two away from Merckx. Sure enough, Merckx was once again the agitator. With 90 kilometres to go he attacked on the famous Montjuic climb. Five followed: Freddy Maertens, Luis Ocaña, Domingo Perurena, Joop Zoetemelk and Gimondi. The crucial selection had been made.

On the same climb three laps later, Merckx went again. Zoetemelk and Perurena could not follow. Now there were four, but Gimondi was outnumbered. He was against two Belgians and a Spanish rider on home roads with the whole country cheering for him.

Maertens, the junior of the two Belgians, went to lead Merckx out. As the Cannibal came off Maertens' wheel so Gimondi came around Merckx. Maertens saw Merckx was beaten and tried to pull the Italian back but

Gimondi was not to be caught and he held the Belgian off. Just. Ocaña, the Spanish climber and the weakest sprinter of the four, took third ahead of an aghast Merckx. 'The single biggest day of my life,' Gimondi said. 'When one is thirty-one years old and wins the title in the last 10 metres it is something that you cannot explain. In those last 10 metres my entire career passed.'[136]

Pierre Chany wrote that Merckx had wanted to launch another attack before the finish but that Maertens, riding in his first Worlds, had dissuaded him, saying he was cramping and that he would prepare the sprint for him. 'I made the irreparable mistake of accepting Maertens' proposal,' Merckx said. 'I can only blame myself. In another race, I'd answer no, but here we both wore the Belgian jersey. Anywhere else I would have persisted in my attacks and Maertens could not have followed,' before adding: 'He launched the sprint very loyally; it was I who cracked behind him.'[137]

In the women's race Belgium's Nicole Van Den Broeck beat Keetie Hage in yet another bunch sprint. Initially it seemed the Belgian had gone too soon, but from somewhere she found a second kick and hit the front again in the final 100 metres. The Dutchwoman had nothing left to give and had to settle for second.

13

FELICE GIMONDI (1973)

Maurizio Evangelista is a former journalist and the founder of the Italian sports communications agency *Vitesse*. He is also the man who replied to a speculative email I sent to the organisers of the annual *Granfondo Internazionale Felice Gimondi*, asking if they could help me to make contact with the five-times Grand Tour winner who won the world championships in Barcelona in 1973.

It turned out I had struck pure gold. In a flurry of emails I learned variously from Maurizio that: Yes, he knew Gimondi well, in fact he had just written a book with him which was being published the following month. Yes, he had spoken to the man himself and he would be more than happy to talk to me. No, Gimondi doesn't speak English; did I have someone lined up to translate? Yes, Maurizio could help me with that if I needed someone. Gimondi's offices are in Bergamo, how was I getting there? Did I need a lift? What about to the airport afterwards? In short, in Maurizio Evangelista I had stumbled upon one of the most pleasant and helpful people you could wish to encounter. All I had to do was book my flight and hotel and then wait in the lobby at 10am on a Monday morning holding a laptop, a voice recorder and a list of topics to discuss. Everything else Maurizio sorted.

After he retired in 1978, Felice Gimondi entered the insurance business. We wait in a conference room at his offices. Across the corridor I can see Gimondi talking on the phone, above his head is a photograph of him and Merckx while in the hallway hangs a frame containing his 1965 yellow jersey. Telephone call over he comes to greet us and sits down. At first he is a little circumspect, as if he is trying to work out who he is dealing with and what my motivations are. Soon enough, though, he relaxes and before long he is laughing and banging the table in good humour while telling me his story.

***

Felice Gimondi:

I was passionate about cycling growing up and I looked at the world championships with a special feeling because I was excited by the jersey – the colours of the rainbow jersey. It was fantastic to imagine being a rider dressed in this jersey but I never really thought that one day or another I could get it.

The way I won the world championship was for me very special because it was a big surprise. In that situation, in a breakaway, I couldn't imagine I could be the winner. In comparison to all my other race victories, in all those other moments I was in some way the favourite or at least expected to compete for the victory, but that wasn't the case for the world championships. I was thinking maybe I'm too old, maybe it's too late.

The key to winning those world championships was to have the whole responsibility on my own shoulders and to be able to deliver. Nino Defilippis was the head of the Italian team when I won and he was a brave man and understood my situation. I did not have a great relationship with Gianni Motta. I'd had two years of riding with Motta in my team [Salvarani –

1970 and 1971] and I had been very disappointed when the team decided to sign Motta because I felt it was a lack of confidence in me. I asked why they signed him without asking me for my opinion, without checking what it meant for me.

I think for Nino Defilippis to have made the decision to choose me as the sole leader, I had at worst to come second to be at peace with my conscience and to reward Nino Defilippis for his choice. My need was to come second … please!

Franco Bitossi, Italo Zilioli, Marino Basso, Giovanni Battaglin … these were very good riders, all able to win. I mean Basso won the world championships the year before, so there were some very good riders in the team. The key was Defilippis' decision to say to me: 'You are the leader.' The alternative to me was Basso. If it came to a bunch sprint then Basso was the man or if there was an attack in the last kilometre then Bitossi was the man. That was exactly what we did in Gap in 1972 when Basso won. Then Bitossi was leading but Eddy Merckx – who was a good friend of Bitossi's – chased and brought the bunch up to him, then Basso won the sprint.

My plan was to stay close to Merckx. I stayed there all the time. At most there was only ever one other rider between me and Merckx. No more. I had Eddy constantly under control because I was expecting Eddy to go.

Sure enough Merckx attacked with 90 kilometres to go. Five riders went with him, including Gimondi. Merckx later attacked again leaving four out front – Merckx, Freddy Maertens, Luis Ocaña and Gimondi.

His first attack was not a strong attack; he just forced the pace and the others fell off the wheel. His strongest attack was on the penultimate lap but at that moment I realised that this Merckx was not the strongest Merckx. Once he tried this very strong attack it showed he was not so powerful because I lost no more than 20 metres and then made contact again. At that moment, at that key moment, I realised that today Merckx is very good, but he is not the perfect Merckx!

I was very sure of my condition because I approached the Worlds that year in a very good way having come through well in some difficult tests. I won the Coppa Bernocchi the week before and one week later I rode the Giro del Piemonte and won there. That is the proof that I was in really great condition and so I was in the perfect condition for the race.

There was a very good atmosphere in the team because Nino did everything in the proper way – I mean there was no playing on two tables. I had a good feeling with all my teammates. At dinner and in the evenings there was a good atmosphere and a really strong team spirit. It was something that made me even more powerful.

After Eddy attacked on the penultimate lap he was talking with Maertens. They were talking Flemish of course, so I didn't understand what they were saying. I was wondering if Eddy was asking Maertens to prepare a sprint because Maertens was a neo-pro and of course, even if that situation probably more favoured Maertens, he was so young that once Eddy asked for his help he couldn't say no.

In the last 5 kilometres, as the road was so narrow, I was staying all the time on Eddy's wheel, no way was I going to move from there. The key was that with one kilometre to go Eddy was launching Maertens to bring him outside to remove me from his wheel, but I stayed there. So at the end Eddy was going by himself. At that moment I was thinking Maertens' sprint was too long. Because of that, in effect Maertens was really preparing the sprint for me and not for Eddy. That was the key.

Honestly, the best Merckx could have won everywhere but he was not in his best condition that day. The point is that if Maertens had had the opportunity to do the sprint for himself he could have been the winner, no doubt. He was doing a very long sprint but despite that he was only a little bit away. That means that he was really the strongest, but at that moment because of the situation in the Belgian team he was not in the position to ride for himself.

This is one of the highest level world championships because of the four riders competing for the win. Merckx had won the Giro that year, Ocaña had won the Tour, myself and a young Maertens, who would go on to win two world championships and who was able to win seven, eight stages in a Tour … unbelievable.

We watch the video of the finish and Gimondi asks me to pause it with 250 metres to go.

This was the key moment because Eddy was coming out to go to the line but he was not so strong. That was why I was coming out at the same time because at that moment I realised that Eddy was not that strong. Eddy was trying to come out of Maertens' wheel but he couldn't come, so I then knew that was my moment to go.

Two years previously, in Mendrisio, Gimondi had been in another breakaway with Merckx. That day he came second as Merckx powered away to win. As we watch I wonder if Gimondi had used anything from that experience in Barcelona.

No, not really. Mendrisio was a two-man sprint, me and Eddy. We were only two with two laps to go and from that moment I was already completely aware I was going to be the loser, I had no dreams of winning. The sole goal was to remain with him up to the end. Eddy was doing unbelievable things to try to go solo. I was collaborating with him even though I knew I had no real chance. Eddy tried so hard at the end to have a solo win, but I was there. I suffered because it was so tough to stay with him.

I was looking at the legs. I did that my whole career, not only during the race but also at the start. I would look at Eddy's legs at the start and sometimes I would already know that today there is no way.

As we watch the sprint Maertens comes across and it looks like he and Gimondi touch in the final metres. Maurizio says you can see by the shadows that Gimondi held his line. Then chaos ensues as crowds of people descend on Gimondi.

I was very nervous after the race. My first thought was about my wife because she was pregnant and was due in two weeks' time. I was thinking that now that the race is over everything will be OK and I was hoping for some news from home. There were no mobile phones so you had to do the awards ceremony and the press conference with no contact with your family. I was feeling some pressure to find an opportunity to call home.

During the race there were some reporters who went to my home and my eldest daughter Norma was there. She was wearing an Eddy Merckx T-shirt with his face on it! Merckx was very upset afterwards but the most upset was Maertens. He was so young he had much more time to make amends.

Before a race I always thought that success was impossible, no way, there is no way I will ever be able to win. But once I won, for me everything was normal because I felt that if I won I had done my job. That was it. I didn't do anything special. This is my job. I have to win and I have won. There was no outward celebration, never any wish to celebrate myself. But obviously it is a special moment when you hear your national anthem and because there were so many Italian fans there.

But you can never be satisfied because the competition between riders, like with myself and Eddy, is a weekly story. It's like a television series. The next story comes the following week so it becomes a mental habit to stay focused on the next race. No one at that time was in the position to be satisfied.

In fact I didn't go back home but had to do three or four criteriums in Belgium and France. That tells you that it was just normal. And don't forget

Eddy Merckx. My road map constantly referred to Eddy Merckx. OK, today I won, I beat Eddy Merckx, but tomorrow…

Gimondi has described this 1973 race as his most memorable win over his great rival Merckx.

Yes, because of the manner of the win. Doing the same thing one thousand times I would never win. One of the main concepts during my whole career, and I say this now to all the young riders when I talk with them today, you must always be ready because the moment will come sooner or later and when it does you have to be ready. Then maybe you can take the win, otherwise, bye-bye. That's the lesson from this race. My whole career I had such a powerful opponent in Merckx, knowing that I would normally be defeated, not always but most of the time, but you never give up, stay concentrated, stay ready, don't lose motivation and one day or another the time will come.

The world championship is something that remains a milestone on your CV, even though for me I had other victories that mean the same or even more. In the second part of my career I realised that my power was decreasing. At that moment I realised how much I had spent in the first half of my career because of my fighting spirit and my giving everything. In the second half of my career I was thinking that if I could have managed my energy in a different way maybe I could have won even more. But then if I had not ridden that way maybe I would not have had the same reputation with the *tifosi*.

It wasn't that I was a protagonist at any cost, but if you are a top rider you know that people sooner or later will want something from you. That's the reason why when I was in some top races, like some classics in Belgium or in France, when I knew that the TV cameras were coming on I did everything possible to be at the front because I wanted to give people at home the feeling that I was in the thick of the action. Regardless of how the race would be, whether the course was suitable or not for me, my duty was to be there.

Gimondi is one of only three riders to win the Tour, the Giro, the Vuelta, the Worlds and Paris-Roubaix. Merckx and Bernard Hinault are the other two. I ask Gimondi how he sees his place in the history of the sport. He sighs and takes a while to answer.

I don't want to highlight myself too much, I never did. For me the main things were to be modest and to be honest. These were the ideals I have based my whole life on. Many sons and daughters go on the stage and say I am the son of ... I am the daughter of ... I never wanted such a thing. I wished only that Norma was proud and happy to say I am Norma Gimondi and that Federica was proud and happy to say I am Federica Gimondi. That's it. Not that I am the daughter of Felice Gimondi.

I have a special evaluation of my career. Of course these kind of victories show the most complete riders, but what I think is more important for me is how I was able to get a Grand Tour win when I was a new professional and then again when I was at the end of my career. For me to win the Tour in 1965 and then my third Giro in 1976 ... that is really meaningful. As well as Paris-Brussels, a race I won twice with a ten-year gap [1966 and 1976]. That means that your career has been long and consistent.

Every time the world championships bring a special story. I managed to win one but maybe it could have been two. I remember in 1966 I was away with two minutes lead, but behind Jacques Anquetil was doing everything he could to get back and I was caught. It's very strange how life turns out. At that time I was not such good friends with Anquetil but later we became friends because of our respective wives. During the criterium season we stayed and travelled together for weeks, so many of us brought our wives with us. That was the time to forge a better relationship with other riders and we became friends. It's a strange life because if I'd had that friendship with Anquetil those years before I could have become world champion at the Nürburgring as well. There were three French – Stablinski, Anquetil and Poulidor – and three Italians – myself, Zilioli and Motta. We were controlling each other and the bunch came back and Rudi Altig won. But

FELICE GIMONDI (1973)

I was quite happy afterwards because Rudi was a good friend of mine. He was a very special friend – we were teammates at Salvarani. I was always ready to work for Rudi.

And I am very grateful to Eddy. We are close friends. Eddy helped me to understand that in your career, as in your life, you can be the first, the second, the fifth, the tenth and no problem. The main thing is that you do your best everywhere, all the time, and that's it. That was a very important lesson for me. For my cycling career but even more in life.

14

KEETIE VAN OOSTEN-HAGE (1968, 1976)

In 1968, at the age of nineteen, Keetie Hage became the first Dutch woman to claim the world championships, winning from a sprint in Imola, Italy. Her elder sister Bella, who was also riding, waited eagerly after the finish to embrace her sibling, the pair of them products of the hard riding synonymous with their home province of Zeeland in the Netherlands. Eight years later, and having now married, Van Oosten-Hage would take a second world title. She would add four world titles on the track before hanging up her wheels in 1979. Such was her impact on the sport in the Netherlands, that today the annual award given to the Dutch woman cyclist of the year is named after her.

Fast forward nearly forty years and I'm in a car heading to Van Oosten-Hage's home in Zeeland. With me is Dutch sportswriter Leo Aquina, who has kindly set up the interview on my behalf and will be acting as my translator.

It is a grim day of cold wind and drizzle and Van Oosten-Hage welcomes us into her warm home. We settle in her dining room, complete with plates on the walls commemorating her achievements. Her two Dutch sportswoman-of-the-year trophies, dating from 1976 and 1978, are displayed discreetly on high shelves and the highchairs of grandchildren are placed around the table. She smiles at me and asks if I have really come all the way from England to see her. 'Yes,' I reply. She looks surprised. 'You are a two-time road champion Keetie,' I say. 'Of course, I would come from England to see you.'

**

Keetie van Oosten-Hage:

My father was athletic, he played football and other sports. When he stopped playing football he started cycling and he took us with him on rides with a touring club in Brabant, a nearby province. We were twelve or thirteen years old. Those were quite long rides, 200 or 300 kilometres. We went to Belgium and people told my father that his daughters were good at cycling and that we should start riding races.

My first race was in Belgium in 1966. I really remember it well because before I went to Belgium there were other Dutch girls who had ridden there but couldn't keep up with the speed – Belgium was much more developed in terms of women's cycling at the time. But I came second in my first race. I was there with Marie-Rose Gaillard, a Belgian who had won the world championships. The two of us escaped together and I got second.

There were races for women in the Netherlands from 1965 onwards but those were shorter, 30 or 40 kilometres. In Belgium they were longer – 60 or 70 kilometres. That's why we preferred the Belgian races.

In her first year of racing Hage finished second in the national championships, losing to her sister Bella, and the world championships where she finished behind Yvonne Reynders who won her fourth title.

KEETIE VAN OOSTEN-HAGE (1968, 1976)

There's an old Dutch saying: 'What is good comes fast!'

The 1966 Worlds were at the Nürburgring, the German race circuit. We rode a different route than the professional men but there was still a very steep climb on our circuit so that led to people dropping off. We ended up with four or five of us at the front. On the last climb I had to let the others go, but once they were over the top there was no tempo anymore and they all started looking at each other so I came back and then got second in the sprint.

I was surprised. I didn't really think it was special. I just rode and it went as it went. To come second it was just like, well, that's what happened. I did look up to Yvonne Reynders and the others who were up there at the top of the sport. I was like, OK, I really want to be there too. But once I got there all the things that I then did they were just the things I did, it was just normal.

I also realised that doing well in that race was partly luck. I rode the pursuit on the track and I realised that really I was not at the level of the others yet. There the difference in level was bigger.

Hage's silver medal was the first time a Dutch woman had been on the podium in the event's history.

We had a big party at the supporters' club back home in the village. Something new was that the journalists were interested and started asking me questions and doing interviews. I'll never really get used to that – even now. I had ridden an old bike during the world championships and the supporters' club managed to get me a new one. So some things changed, we didn't really have the money to buy proper, modern gear but now there were new facilities, new possibilities. In the year after there was a sponsor for tyres and clothing but not yet for the bike. But this was 1966 – it was already a big revolution.

I was still in school in 1966, a school for textiles. I was there until 1971. So I always trained in the evening. It was nothing compared to what the girls do today. I rode my bike to school and in the evenings, when I got back home, I did a lap around the island. That was in the beginning. Later I moved to a school in Goes and I had more time because the school was closer to my home and so I went training, like 60 or 70 kilometres in the evening, never much more than that. Mostly I trained alone … no trainer … not even measuring speed or distance or anything … just riding. There's a lot of wind here so that makes it hard … it made for good training.

We rode a lot of races in the Netherlands because the Dutch federation organised those races and they wanted to protect them, so they wanted to have the best women riding those races although we preferred racing in Belgium. In Belgium there were far more experienced riders, they were also ten or twelve years older than me. So it was more difficult. It was also difficult because really I didn't know anything about race tactics when I started going there, I had to learn everything on the job. My father always went with me but he was not a cycling expert so he didn't really know anything about tactics either. We really had to learn by racing, see what was happening. The Belgian girls, they were … they knew their racing, they knew their tactics so we really had to adapt to that.

In 1968 Hage won her first rainbow jersey, beating the Soviet Union's Bajba Tsaune in Imola.

In the build-up to the race I felt good. Three or four days before the race I won a bronze medal, my first bronze medal, in the pursuit in Rome. So that felt good, I felt in shape. But then two days before I had a training accident when I hit a van. I had a torn ligament in my little finger – my pinkie finger. The driver came straight across a crossroads and was too late to brake. The *soigneur* of [Gianni] Motta, the Italian professional, coincidentally happened to be driving by. He saw what happened and saw my bleeding finger and brought us back to the hotel.

It didn't really bother me. What was bothering me more was a woman from the federation who was sent with us to the championships. We didn't really get along and we had to sleep in the same room. She was smoking and I didn't like it … there was a bit of hassle. She was the federation's doctor's wife and they let her look after the women so we weren't by ourselves … but it would've been better to have been alone.

The course actually was a bit disappointing because it was quite flat and I would've preferred it hillier. I used to attack a lot but because it was such a flat course and because I was still looking up to the big women riders I didn't attack during the race as much as I normally did. That might have helped me save my energy for the sprint at the end.

I slept in all morning, which was a good sign because it meant I was relaxed. The other girls were actually annoyed at me sleeping all morning because the room was a bit messy and they were saying, 'You could have at least cleaned up your room!' But I was relaxed about it all. I was not normally relaxed like that; normally I would be very nervous before a race but this time I wasn't. One of the reasons might have been because there was no men's amateur race as it was an Olympic year so we raced in the afternoon rather than in the morning. That was why I could sleep all morning – maybe that was why I was feeling more relaxed.

We ended up with seven or eight of us going for the final sprint. There were no other Dutch riders in that leading group. There were no real attacks. Actually, the usual way the women's races were ridden back then was that riders would drop off the back and we would finish in a small group.

Going into the sprint I didn't really have anyone special to look out for. I didn't really know the other riders. There were Russians there and I didn't really know them, I'd never ridden against them. I didn't really look for a particular side of the road or anything, I was just sprinting. When I got into the lead there was still a long way to go. I don't know exactly how far but it felt like there was still a long way to go so it was really tough. My legs were hurting and I was thinking maybe someone will pass me but no one came.

Instantly there were many people, and police officers, crowding around me. The police were blocking the way to me, keeping people away. Italy is always a nice country to ride a bike because the people are always really enthusiastic, like in Belgium, and they also know their cycling. When I went racing in Italy with the rainbow jersey afterwards people would recognise it and I would hear people saying, 'Oh, there's the world champion,' but back in the Netherlands people wouldn't really notice or know what the rainbow jersey was. It was really the first time that so many people had gathered around me in the finishing straight so that was a bit overwhelming.

There was a lot of partying afterwards. We went to the hospital where the surgeon who had stitched my finger worked and he came to the party. We were staying in a spa hotel and he brought a band from the village and presents – a sign with Imola written on it.

Afterwards not much changed. I was still in school, life just went on the way it always did. There were eight children at home and the Dutch way is to just stay normal, you have to stay normal…

There's a Dutch saying: 'If you act normal, you act crazy enough.'

Yes. Life just went on. There were a few more journalists but you really can't compare it to the way it is now with the world championships. Also the province of Zeeland and this Dutch saying … here it is even more relevant … it is more sober here. People from Zeeland are really sober about everything.

Cycling for women in the Netherlands was still very much in its infancy and despite Hage's success she continued to face sexism.

Back home they never bothered me with sexist remarks, they just let me do my racing. But I trained a lot in Amsterdam, at the Olympic Stadium, where there was a cycling track and there I heard a lot of remarks like women should be doing gymnastics rather than riding a racing bike, things like that. There were a lot of professional riders that made sexist remarks, said that women shouldn't be on a racing bike ... that they should be in the kitchen and not ride a bike.

I just let them talk. It didn't bother me. When those remarks came, like I should be a ballet dancer or something, I just used to say: 'I'm no ballet dancer'. I used to answer back to them but I was never really bothered by it.

Eight years after her first world championships win Van Oosten-Hage, now taking her married name, went to Ostuni and won her second title.

Again it was in Italy, again in an Olympic year and again in the afternoon! It was way down south in the 'heel' part of Italy. There was one climb and there was a finishing straight, the last 5 kilometres was flat. In the previous years I had attacked a lot. A mechanic that had helped in 1968 was there helping us again and he told me before the race just one thing – you're allowed to attack once but no more than that. For the rest of the race stay in the pack, stay on the wheels and wait and wait and wait.

It was a sprint with a bigger group than in 1968 and I had a teammate, Truus van der Plaat, but she went sideways and blocked my way. I don't know if it was on purpose or not because Truss was also a good sprinter. At first I thought I was blocked but it was actually lucky for me because it was still quite far to the line and so I was forced to hold back. Then I went full out and won by a couple of lengths.

The main difference between my two wins was that the Dutch federation had developed and Dutch cycling had developed. In 1968 we went with three girls and in 1976 we had a full team of six. There was more interest from the federation and there were more competitive Dutch girls there – I mean I had a teammate in the front for the final sprint in 1976 and I didn't in 1968.

I'd had quite a lot of podiums in between my two wins, a lot of second or third places. The main reason was there was always one sprinter I couldn't quite beat. I think maybe I attacked too much, wasted too much energy during those races. The year before, in 1975, a different Dutch girl won [Tineke Fopma, Van Oosten-Hage was third]. She attacked on one side of the road while I was with the sprinters on the other side and she went on to the win.

It had been a long time since my first win, so I was getting more motivated … I also fell twice in the previous years. It was extra motivation to try to win it again.

In 1976 Van Oosten-Hage also won her second pursuit title. Afterwards she came under some pressure to help resolve some of the organisational issues within the federation and to try to move on people associated with the women's set-up who it was felt were not really helping the team. Her efforts were in vain and because of the fallout she was not selected for the 1977 championships. Van Oosten-Hage thinks this perhaps cost her two more world titles – in the road and pursuit. Even so, by the time she retired in 1979 Van Oosten-Hage had won six world titles, two on the road and four in the pursuit, and claimed a further twelve podium positions across both disciplines.

There is no particular race that I look back on and think I could've won that race if I'd done something differently, it's more a general afterthought that maybe, in hindsight, if I hadn't attacked so much maybe I could've beaten them. But most of the time when I was there with another rider I would be afraid of losing the sprint and would try to drop them beforehand; that's why I attacked so much, being afraid of losing the sprint.

KEETIE VAN OOSTEN-HAGE (1968, 1976)

My motivation came from being a top athlete and wanting to win everything I could win. At a certain point I felt I had won everything, only the Olympic Games was missing. In 1980 the UCI still didn't want women in the Olympics – the first time was in 1984. I would have continued cycling until 1980 for the Olympic Games but when the UCI decided they didn't want that I decided to quit. I had married in 1972 and after feeling that I had won everything I could win I also wanted to have children, so there was a reason to quit cycling.

Sometimes I forgot to enjoy my cycling because it is a lot of fun. If you choose to be a top athlete you have to choose to be a top athlete all the way, all the time. It's not just about riding a race, you have to train and you have to sacrifice a lot. You have to realise before you start that it means you can't party all the time – although back in the day we still had time to go out and have parties. Now they have less time to do that. I met my boyfriend who was not into sports at all … that boyfriend is my husband now and he had to get used to me being a top athlete. We had to sacrifice a lot for the sport. He had to adapt to that as well, which was quite special back then. He always came to the races. He always supported me.

15

MERCKX CROWNS A TRIPLE

Eddy Merckx's moniker of the Cannibal, first bestowed upon him by a young daughter of a teammate, did not come without reason. He was ruthless and all-conquering with an insatiable appetite for victory. By the summer of 1974 Merckx was the joint record holder for wins at the Tour and the Giro, equalling the exploits of Anquetil, Binda and Coppi respectively, and he was only one win away from Costante Girardengo's record of six wins in Milan-Sanremo, a mark he would later overhaul. He was firmly established as the most successful and dominant rider the world had ever seen. But now he had another record on his mind, another jersey to claim to raise him further still above all others in the pantheon of the greats. Alfredo Binda and Rik Van Steenbergen had three rainbow jerseys to their names. Merckx had two. It was time to win another one.

The Belgian's season had been hampered by illness and for the first time since 1965 he had not won a spring classic. As the year progressed he had set about making up for that disappointment, winning the Tour of Switzerland for the first time and claiming his third Giro/Tour double. Now it was late August and he was in Montreal. It was the first time the professional road race had been taken out of Europe and it came at a time when the Canadian city was working to establish itself as a truly global destination.[138] Two years after the Worlds Montreal hosted the Olympic Games, with the road race taking place on the same Mont-Royal circuit. Merckx was reportedly paid a fee of $2500 a day to ensure the world's greatest cyclist made the trip over the Atlantic for the Worlds.[139]

It was a tough route – 262 kilometres and twenty-one laps of a lumpy circuit, featuring a 2.5-kilometre climb to the finish. Once an early break had been caught, a long solo escapade from France's Francis Campaner, compatriot Bernard Thévenet went to work. On the twelfth climb of Mont-Royal, the Frenchman attacked and one lap later he was more than one minute ahead.

Thévenet may have been ahead but Merckx was in the bunch looking elsewhere, working out what would happen once they inevitably caught the Frenchman. He was concerned about the Italian team and in particular the threat of their up-and-coming star Francesco Moser. As the group pounded the pedals in pursuit of Thévenet, Merckx heard Moser instruct a teammate to take it easy. 'I realised that the man I was worried about was in trouble,'[140] Merckx later said.

By the final lap, Thévenet's lead was now down to 30 seconds and Merckx was leading the chase, followed by France's Raymond Poulidor and Mariano Martinez and Italy's Giacinto Santambrogio, the rider Moser had told to slow down. For 100 kilometres or so Thévenet had led the race in the hope of a famous and financially rewarding victory – L'Equipe's veteran correspondent Serge Lang told the Montreal Gazette that if Thévenet could hold on the win would more than double his earning power, a further indication of the commercial potential of winning the rainbow jersey. But Merckx was merciless and powered past the Frenchman on the final climb with Poulidor, Thévenet's teammate, following. 'It hurt me to pass him,' reflected Poulidor, 'but there was nothing I could do.'[141]

As if in homage to his beaten teammate, and wary of entering a sprint with Merckx, Poulidor immediately went on the offensive, taking six lengths out of Merckx as they reached the summit of the climb. But Merckx was not to be denied and made up the ground on the descent and pulled ahead. Poulidor managed to follow to ensure a two-man sprint for the win. Poulidor later said he had done all he could to shake the Belgian on the climb but to no avail. The result was obvious even before they crossed the line. Merckx looked behind, let Poulidor go to the front and then simply blasted by Poulidor when he felt like it. The Belgian won easily. 'Once he was with me I knew it was over. Merckx is Merckx. I had no chance against him in the sprint,'[142] Poulidor reflected.

Merckx had equalled the record of Binda and Van Steenbergen. But with his win came something extra. No rider had won the Giro, the Tour and the Worlds in the same year. Until now. Merckx had won the first triple crown of cycling, a feat that only one man has subsequently matched.

It had been a brutal test, a real example of what a Worlds race could be if the circuit presented was tough enough. As the laps went by and the speed picked up, so riders fell away and climbed off. The repetitive nature of riding a long race on a circuit, with the same climbs and descents and stretches of road coming in quick succession, hour after hour, with the pace winding up the whole time to a crescendo in the final few laps, does not suit all riders. From the 70 riders that started just 18 finished.

While Merckx had won, the French team received a great deal of praise for the way they rode. They had entered the race without great expectation. It had been twelve years since Jean Stablinski had last won the jersey for France. Poulidor was now thirty-eight and Thévenet was not yet quite at the peak of his career – although he would only have to wait another season to win his first Tour. Nevertheless France had dominated the race, sending two men on long solo escapades and then claiming two podium spots with Poulidor and Martinez. 'Under the leadership of the national director Richard Mariller and Jacques Anquetil, the French gave their opponents the example of a perfect collective organisation, of elaborate tactics and of an understanding which the Belgians and the Italians could only envy,'[143] reported Le Monde.

Perhaps the team had taken some inspiration from the women's race the previous day when, in a replay of the race in Gap two years previously,

Geneviève Gambillon took the final sprint by five lengths ahead of a Soviet, this time Bajba Tsaune. Britain's Beryl Burton finished fifth – the final placing in her illustrious world championship career. 'I think I should've attacked on the last hill,' she reflected. 'But at the same time I was hoping to do something in the final sprint. Still, it's a risk you take ... I wish somebody would hurry up and take over from me.'[144]

***

One week before the 1975 championships, held in Yvoir, Belgium, Merckx called a breakfast meeting for a Belgian team that would include Roger De Vlaeminck, Lucien Van Impe and Freddy Maertens. The team was so strong that Merckx wanted to discuss who would go for the win. On race day one-hundred thousand fans, in a frenzy of anticipation, came to watch their home team deliver what they were certain would be yet another rainbow jersey. 'The Belgian media presented their team as the most formidable machine of war imaginable,'[145] wrote Pierre Chany. But one man had apparently not read the script: Hennie Kuiper.

Kuiper was a twenty-six year old national champion of the Netherlands, a title he had secured a couple of months earlier, beating Joop Zoetemelk, his more fancied teammate, into third. Kuiper had also finished fifth and taken a stage at that year's Vuelta and then managed eleventh at the Tour.

So Kuiper was a rider who had had a decent season, but he was not the Dutch leader. That title was shared by Zoetemelk, who had taken fourth at the Tour, and Gerrie Knetemann, sixth at that year's Liège-Bastogne-Liège. But Kuiper developed a reputation throughout his career for racing tactically, best summarised by a famous quote attributed to him: 'Racing is licking your opponent's plate clean before starting on your own.' Those twelve words perhaps sum up the art of bicycle racing as well as any other attempt to analyse the sport.

On the penultimate lap, with around twenty riders at the head of the bunch and in contention, Kuiper attacked. 'I rode up to Joop [Zoetemelk] then and asked if I could try my luck and he agreed,'[146] he later said.

Behind, Moser and Merckx both led the pack but the chase was fragmented, compromised by the presence in the leading group of Zoetemelk and Knetemann, both ready to fight in a sprint if Kuiper was brought back by others. The Dutch had played the game perfectly – send a man up the road, hold back arguably your best two riders and allow them to sit on the wheels of others as they try to bring your man back. Kuiper held on to take a 17-second win over De Vlaeminck and the Frenchman Jean-Pierre Danguillaume.

For the Belgians, so strongly fancied in the build-up, there were recriminations. 'I could have brought Kuiper back on my own,' De Vlaeminck said later. 'But what was the point with Zoetemelk on my neck.'[147] He then said separately that with better help he could have joined and beaten Kuiper. That drew a stinging response from Merckx who had crashed early in the race before pledging support to De Vlaeminck: 'In truth, I made a monumental mistake by sacrificing my chances,' he said. 'No rider has ever helped me in a world championships like I did for De Vlaeminck.'[148]

Kuiper's win crowned an extraordinary Worlds for the Netherlands. The day before Andre Givers had won the men's amateur race while Tineke Fopma claimed the women's title in her first Worlds race. Twenty-two years old and without a major win to her name, Fopma jumped away with what she thought was just over a lap to go. But she had not heard the bell on the previous lap and, unbeknown to her, she was now leading the peloton with less than one kilometre left to race and her team's number-one rider, Keetie van Oosten-Hage, in the bunch behind. Fopma had no idea that she was about to ride into the rainbow jersey. 'I really did not know that we were on the last lap,' Fopma said afterwards. 'I thought we still had to go around again. When I saw people screaming I began to wonder ... My first time and immediately [I win] the rainbow jersey.'[149]

***

Keetie van Oosten-Hage, the 1968 champion, had finished third behind Fopma in Yvoir. Twelve months on and the race returned to Italy and a 36-kilometre circuit outside Ostuni. By now Van Oosten-Hage was an eight-times national champion who, since her debut in 1966, had stood on the podium of road cycling's world championships six times and taken one world title and six podium spots in the pursuit (she would go on to add another three titles to that haul). She knew what it took to be successful at the biggest event in the women's racing calendar yet since her win in 1968 the top step had eluded her. 'There would always be either a French girl, or a Belgian girl, or someone, who would beat me in the sprint,' she would tell me when reflecting on her career.

The race came down to a fourteen-strong sprint which included a familiar face – Yvonne Reynders. The Belgian legend was back, still angry at how she had felt compelled to leave the sport a decade earlier and determined to prove she still had good legs. In the end Reynders claimed third, an impressive performance given her time away from the sport. But Van Oosten-Hage was at the height of her powers and scorched ahead of the bunch to take the sprint, with Italy's Luigina Bissoli finishing second.

In the men's race the home favourite was Francesco Moser, part of a supremely drilled and well-cared-for Italian squad that started with ten riders, including 1973 champion Felice Gimondi. Belgium, meanwhile, had an embarrassment of riches, with their team including: Eddy Merckx, Joseph Bruyère, Marc Demeyer, Walter Godefroot, Walter Planckaert, Michel Pollentier, Lucien Van Impe and Freddy Maertens. Belgium could not find a place for the previous year's runner-up, Roger De Vlaeminck or for Rik Van Linden, a rider described by Pierre Chany as the 'fastest of them all.'[150] It was an unbelievably strong team, perhaps too strong some thought, too full of trade-team leaders who would struggle to work as one for the collective Belgian good.

The president of the Belgian Cycling Union, Van MosseVelde, came up with a plan to help engender unity and in the build-up to the race faced the team and tossed an envelope stuffed full of cash on to a table, saying: 'This money will be yours if one of you brings the rainbow jersey to Belgium. It is up to you to choose the best method [of doing so]. Sharing will be based on individual efforts.'[151]

Freddy Maertens told the team that if they assisted him he would give his share to them. 'All I needed to know [was] that they wouldn't ride against me,' Maertens later said. 'As it was, they all worked for me once I was away and for that I am very grateful.'[152]

With the favourites together at the head of the race on the final lap, Moser forcefully launched his bid, taking Joop Zoetemelk with him. Merckx and Bruyere led the chase before Maertens leapt away in pursuit of the two leaders, joined by Moser's teammate Costantino Conti. Eventually, with no help from Conti, Maertens made the catch. There were 16 kilometres to go.

Twice on the 7-kilometre descent from Cisternino, Moser tried to shake his fellow escapees. Twice he got a gap and twice Maertens, the man he was trying to distance, came back. 'When I couldn't get rid of him I knew I couldn't win the sprint,'[153] Moser later said.

He was right. In the final straight Maertens sat behind, waited for Moser to make his move and then came around the Italian to speed away with ease. Maertens had time to sit up, stop pedalling and raise both arms in the air 15 metres from the line and still win by a couple of lengths in front of a despairing Moser. At the finish line Gimondi was full of praise for Moser, his young teammate, saying: 'Francesco is a champion … If he did not win this year he will certainly be world champion next year.'[154]

***

Moser proved the wisdom of Gimondi's statement the following year in San Cristóbal, Venezuela. Three years earlier the UCI had confirmed at its Montreal congress that the event would be taken to South America for the first time. This was a considerable surprise because until the Venezuelan delegation arrived in Canada armed with an offer to build a new Olympic-standard velodrome and promising subsidised travel for the teams, no one had any idea they were remotely interested in the event. It transpired that the country's president Carlos Andrés Pérez wanted to see his nation become a world centre for the sport and pulled out all the stops to get the UCI's flagship event to Venezuela. In the men's race Moser won in a two-man escape ahead of Germany's Dietrich Thurau.

In contrast to Maertens' win in 1976 the Belgian team was now in disarray with Walter Godefroot's tenth place in Venezuela a poor return for the strength and depth the squad possessed. Years later Maertens said that

1976 was the only year Belgium had not ridden as individuals.[155] Part of the problem was that the Belgian team was being managed by Guillaume Driessens whose day job was managing the Flandria team – home to Maertens as well as Herman Beysens and Marc Demeyer, both of whom had joined Maertens in Belgian colours in Venezuela. That led to divisions within the Belgian team that came to prominence in Venezuela, with two of Maertens' Flandria teammates, Ireland's Sean Kelly and Sweden's Erich Loder, staying in the same hotel as the Belgian squad.

Pierre Chany wrote that on the evening of Moser's win Merckx told L'Equipe's Noël Couëdel of the issues within the team: 'Nothing is ever possible with Driessens!' Merckx said. 'Right here, he only dealt with his riders, I mean those of his trade team ... it was scandalous. When I talk about his riders I mean not only Maertens, Demeyer and Pollentier, but also the Swiss, Loder and the Irishman, Kelly. These two have lived here, with us, trained with us, they have used the masseur of our team. You find that normal? The other day, when [Joseph] Bruyere went down to lunch, Driessens was with Loder and Kelly and there was nothing left on the plates for Joseph ... You know the role of Kelly was to stick to my wheel and not move? He did that all day, and as he is very fast, I gave up.'[156] Maertens responded: 'Kelly is here to help me. And he did it very well. He is first my teammate and then Irish.'[157]

It is a peculiarity of the Worlds that while the race is contested in national teams, with the winner wearing the rainbow jersey the following season while riding for their trade team, the real beneficiaries of the jersey include not just the rider who wears it but also the trade team on which they ride. Trade team sponsors love nothing more than the attention the rainbow jersey brings to a team and the added exposure it gives whatever product or brand name they have plastered on the front. And team managements love the subsequent increased budgets team sponsors will offer as a result. National pride aside, it is perhaps unsurprising that while there is much history of national team discord and rivalry in the Worlds, equally there is a history of collusion between trade teammates who do not happen to ride on the same national team but ride together the rest of the year and stand to benefit by the presence of the jersey within the team. What happened in

Italian legend, Alfredo Binda, became the first professional road world champion in 1927. Binda broke away and won by more than seven minutes on the German Nürburgring motor-racing circuit.
© Offside/Farabolafoto

Ferdi Kübler of Switzerland crosses the line in Varese, Italy, ahead of a grimacing Fiorenzo Magni. It was a time of Swiss success in the world's biggest races and this 1951 win came just weeks after Kübler's compatriot Hugo Koblet won the Tour de France, echoing Kübler's own 1950 Tour win.
© Offside/L'Equipe

Fausto Coppi after his win in 1953 in Lugano, Switzerland. Giulia Locatelli, is looking on over Coppi's right shoulder. © *Offside/L'Equipe*

Belgium's Rik Van Steenbergen beats France's Louison Bobet in Waregem, Belgium, to take the 1957 title. It was Van Steenbergen's third win, adding to his 1949 and 1956 victories. © *Manuel Litran/Contributor/Getty*

Yvonne Reynders of Belgium stands on the podium in 1966 after claiming her fourth road race win. To her right is the Netherlands' Keetie Hage who was riding her first Worlds and two years later would win the first of her two titles. *Image courtesy of the UCI*

Luxembourg's Elsy Jacobs became the first official women's champion in 1958, winning by nearly three minutes in Reims, France. © *ZUMA Press, Inc./Alamy Stock Photo*

Belgian teammates Benoni Beheyt (left) and Rik Van Looy after the infamous 1963 race in Ronse, Belgium. © *Belga/PA Images*

Tom Simpson wearing his rainbow jersey before the opening stage of the 1966 Tour de France. Simpson won the jersey for Great Britain in Lasarte, Spain, ahead of Germany's Rudi Altig. © *Getty Images/Staff*

At the time of writing, Beryl Burton's two road world championship wins in 1960 and 1967 make her the only Briton to have won the elite road title more than once. © *Nationaal Archief*

Jean-Pierre 'Jempi' Monseré (22) rides fourth wheel in a small break driven by the Italian riders Gianni Motta (78) and Michele Dancelli (76) in Leicester, England. Monseré would go on to take a surprise win. Tragically, seven months later the Belgian died after colliding with a car during a *Kermesse*. © *Offside/L'Equipe*

Eddy Merckx crosses the line ahead of Italy's Felice Gimondi in Mendrisio, Switzerland, for his second world title in 1971. The Belgian giant of cycling would add a third in 1974. © Keystone/Staff/Getty

Bernard Hinault leads the way en-route to winning his 1980 rainbow jersey in Sallanches, France, on one of the toughest circuits in the Worlds' history. © Offside/L'Equipe

The USA's Greg LeMond after his second world championships victory in 1989 just weeks after winning the Tour in Paris. LeMond remains the last man to have won the Tour and the Worlds in the same year. © Ullstein bild/ Contributor/Getty

France's Jeannie Longo leads her teammate, 1990 world champion Catherine Marsal, during the 1995 race. Longo would win a record fifth title in Duitama, Colombia, while Marsal finished second. Earlier, Longo had claimed the first of a record four time trial titles. © *PASCAL PAVANI/Staff/Getty*

Spain's Oscar Freire won three world titles in the space of six years, equalling the record of Alfredo Binda, Rik Van Steenbergen and Eddy Merckx for most wins in the men's race. © *Frank Peters/Staff/Getty*

The Netherlands' Marianne Vos claims her first road world title in 2006 in Salzburg, Austria. Further wins in 2012 and 2013 would cement her place as the best female rider of her generation. © Bryn Lennon/Staff/ Getty

Six weeks after claiming Olympic gold in 2008, Great Britain's Nicole Cooke was back on the top of the podium wearing a rainbow jersey in Varese, Italy. Cooke was the first rider to win road Olympic and world titles in the same year. © Bryn Lennon/ Staff/Getty

Mark Cavendish celebrates the first win in the men's race for Great Britain since Tom Simpson's 1965 victory. Cavendish's 2011 win in Copenhagen, Denmark was the result of a three-year project implemented by British Cycling. © REUTERS/ Alamy Stock Photo

Great Britain's Lizzie Armitstead at the head of affairs in Richmond, USA. Armitstead would win the 2015 title ahead of the Netherlands' Anna van der Breggen after a small bunch sprint. © *Jonathan Devich/Contributor/Getty*

Peter Sagan of Slovakia crosses the line alone in 2015 in Richmond, USA. Sagan would defend his jersey the following year in Doha, Qatar, after a twenty-six strong bunch broke away in the desert. © *Bryn Lennon/Staff/Getty*

Venezuela within the Belgian team was the perfect example of the continued blurring of trade and national team loyalties.

***

Two wins for the Netherlands in the men's race brought the decade to a close, with Gerrie Knetemann winning a sprint ahead of Moser at the Nürburgring in 1978 and then Jan Raas prevailing at home on the tough Valkenburg circuit in 1979. In the women's races France's Josiane Bost (1977), Germany's Beate Habetz (1978) and the Netherlands' Petra De Bruin (1979) all claimed titles. Bost had thought a win for her was on the cards as soon as she was given her race number. 'Actually, I already knew in advance that it would go well,' she said. 'I come from the region of Bernard Thévenet and Michel Laurent. Thévenet won the Tour with number fifty-one. Laurent with the same number [won] Paris-Nice. Then here I was given the number fifty-one. I could not lose'.[158]

Bost's win was the third title for France in the women's race, but as the 1970s ended no French man had won the rainbow jersey since Jean Stablinski in 1962. It was time for that to change. It was time for *Le Blaireau*.

16

THE LEMOND
AND LONGO YEARS

By 1980 it had been eighteen years since a Frenchman had last pulled on the rainbow jersey. Four riders had come close – Jacques Anquetil, Raymond Poulidor, Cyrille Guimard and Jean-René Bernaudeau had all missed out in final sprints – but none had crossed the line first since 1962 and Jean Stablinski's terrific win in Salo, Italy.

The 1980 race was hosted by the Alpine town of Sallanches, on a course regarded as one of the hardest offered for a world championships road race, including twenty ascents of the Côte de Domancy, a climb with a maximum gradient of 16 per cent. The weather was miserable: damp and cold with the Alps cloaked with leaden skies. The riders were in for a terrible day.

The harder the ride, the more it suited Bernard Hinault. Earlier in the year the man nicknamed *Le Blaireau*, the Badger, had won Liège-Bastogne-Liège and the Giro before having his reign at the Tour temporarily interrupted because of an injured knee. Just six days before the Worlds he had abandoned the Tour du Limousin 30 kilometres from the finish of the second stage with abdominal pain. No one was sure of his condition, maybe not even Hinault himself. But if there was any doubt about how he was feeling, then that dissipated on the thirteenth lap when he split the field on the Domancy. Few could handle his pace. Next time round he did it again. And so, as the race entered its second half, the Badger was at the front of the race in a five-man breakaway. Then he really went to work.

One by one his fellow escapees faltered. First Belgium's Michel Pollentier, then Denmark's Jørgen Marcussen, then Britain's Robert Millar all fell by the wayside until, on the last lap, there was just one rider left alongside Hinault – Italy's Gianbattista Baronchelli.

'Et voilà! Now he attacks! Attack! Bernard Hinault!' yelled the TV commentator as the Frenchman pulled decisively away on the final climb of the Domancy. Baronchelli had no response. Soon Hinault was alone, left to ride himself into history. 'Hinault! Hinault! Hinault!' the crowds cried as he sped to the finish. 'Animated by the spirit which so characterises him, anxious to silence the rumours circulating concerning his possible decline … he struck strongly and gave us the image of a timely champion, one whose effort is meticulously planned,'[159] reported Le Monde.

Hinault finished just over one minute ahead of Baronchelli. On a brutal day of racing, out of 107 starters only fifteen made it to the finish, just 14 per cent of the starters, by far the lowest of any Worlds. Hinault's performance was Merckx-like in its strength and dominance and it prompted comparisons, with La Stampa running the headline 'Hinault: champion the old way.'[160] In the days that followed the paper imagined a world where Hinault and Merckx went head to head at the height of their respective powers. Merckx, meanwhile, lamented that their eras had not overlapped in any meaningful way. 'If I'd had a Hinault as an opponent, I probably would have given even more, I would have done even better,'[161] mused the Belgian. An ominous thought.

***

The day before Hinault's win the world's best women cyclists had faced four laps of the same Sallanches circuit. Seventy-three riders started, the largest field at that time for a women's world championship road race.

Cycling's editor, Ken Evans, reported that in ten years of covering the Worlds he had never seen a circuit so tough. 'For many girls the question was not whether they could get a medal, but whether they could even get round, such was the impact of the [Domancy] hill...'[162] he wrote. In fact sixty-one riders made it home, a far greater percentage than the men managed the following day.[163]

On the first climb of the Domancy a twenty-one-year-old local woman named Jeannie Longo attacked. Longo, already a two-times national champion, came from nearby Saint-Gervais and trained on the roads over which they were now racing. Her work prompted the decisive move but she fell away when she suffered a poor gear change and finished tenth. There would be much more to come from the Frenchwoman. The USA's Beth Heiden won the race, with a teenager from Rochdale – Mandy Jones – finishing third. It was Jones's first Worlds. Did she like her chances before the race? *Cycling* asked her afterwards. 'Did I heck,'[164] she said. Her Worlds story was just beginning.

***

After his 1976 Worlds triumph and collecting buckets full of stage wins at the Vuelta, Giro and Tour, including winning overall at the Vuelta in 1977, Freddy Maertens' career had hit a brick wall. After two years of injuries and problems, by the summer of 1981 the Belgian had returned to something a little like his former self, taking five stages and the green jersey at the Tour. Still, no one really had him earmarked for a serious shot at the rainbow jersey in Prague, with Italy's Giuseppe Saronni the fancied rider alongside the defending champion Hinault.

Italy controlled things in the run-in to the finish, ensuring the race would come down to the bunch sprint they wanted. With 200 metres to go, Saronni hit the front, peeling off the wheel of teammate Gianbattista Baronchelli. So far so predictable. But then, to Saronni's right, came a blur of whirling legs.

The blur was Freddy Maertens, turning back the years. Maertens had come off Saronni's wheel and blitzed past the Italian to snatch the rainbow jersey right out of his hands. Maertens' long and difficult climb back to the top of the world was complete. It would prove, however, to be the Belgian's final major win.

Once again there were bitter recriminations in Italy. How had the *squadra* contrived to throw away the win? They had placed eight riders in the crucial break and three riders in the top ten, but they had not got the only thing that mattered – the jersey. It was a result wholly indicative of a team not working together. The director, Alfredo Martini, had overestimated the difficulty of the course, said *La Stampa,* and then compounded it by choosing the wrong sprinter at the end. According to the paper, Martini should have gone with Pierino Gavazzi, 'who is, after all, our Maertens and had worked much less than Saronni.'[165] The same paper called the result an 'absolute condemnation of Italian cycling,'[166] and hit out at the rivalry between Saronni and Francesco Moser. 'Moser was supposed to pilot the sprint for his rival: he did not, because Beppe [Saronni] – who felt strong, indeed very strong – did not ask him ... Saronni did not want to "stoop" to ask a favour of Moser,'[167] wrote the paper's Marco Sannazaro. He concluded that Moser must have been happy not to have been asked, removing the need for him to choose between either helping his rival or refusing and then facing accusations of not working for the good of the team.

Germany's Ute Enzenauer, a future two-times national champion, claimed the women's race. Enzenauer was just sixteen years old and a shop assistant in a chemist shop in Freidrichshafen on the shore of Lake Constance in southern Germany. Her win made her cycling's youngest elite road world champion.

***

In 1980 Mandy Jones had announced herself to the world by taking an unexpected bronze medal in Sallanches. Two years on the Worlds were being hosted by Britain on the 15.2-kilometre Goodwood circuit in West Sussex.

Jones had long targeted these Worlds, tailoring her training and racing with the 1982 pursuit and road races in mind. She took the initiative early in the road race, first instigating a two-rider break with Mieke Havik of the Netherlands and then striking out alone at the end of the second lap. Her solo escapade did not last long. A flurry of counter-attacks out of the chasing bunch meant that after 20 kilometres at the head of the race Jones was back in the group.

When Sandra Schumacher of Germany shot clear with Italy's Maria Canins and Belgium's Gerda Sierens, Jones went with them. Over the top of the climb and down the other side she hit the front. Before she knew it she had a 20-second lead. Realising this was her moment and roared on by the crowd Jones ignored the pain cursing through her body to cling on to a slender lead and record a win that rewarded the years of effort and planning that had gone into preparing for the race. It was Britain's first Worlds win for fifteen years.

'It was just plan daft,' Jones said at the time. 'We were going downhill and I just rode past them. Just like that. Then I looked back and saw I had a gap, so I just kept going. It's a pretty strange way to win a world championship, I suppose.'[168]

***

The day after Jones' win, the USA's Greg LeMond had claimed the silver medal in the men's race after chasing down compatriot Jonathan Boyer in the final moments and effectively towing Italy's Giuseppe Saronni into a position where he could blitz past for the win. While the Italian press celebrated Saronni's win and the increasingly harmonious atmosphere in the Italian team after the controversies of the previous year, LeMond faced questions over his aggressive move when a fellow American was leading. 'We aren't on the same team and we are not friends,' LeMond said simply. 'I would not like to see him world champion.'[169] Twelve months later LeMond would trade silver for gold and the rainbow jersey.

LeMond had been awarded the junior title in 1979 after Kenny De Maerteleire, who had crossed the line first, was relegated for an irregular sprint that had forced LeMond into the tyres that flanked the circuit.

Now the American had his sights on the professional title.

The race was held in Switzerland on a circuit dominated by a 3-kilometre climb of the Wartensee that averaged 5.5 per cent. With four laps to go LeMond reacted to an effort by Britain's Robert Millar, followed by Spain's Faustino Rupérez and Italy's Moreno Argentin. The three quickly caught Serge Demierre, the Swiss rider who had been off at the front, and set about building a race-winning move.

LeMond took the first real opportunity he had on the final lap. With Argentin already distanced, the American dropped Rupérez on the first climb and struck out alone. Riding solo to a famous win, LeMond became the first American male to claim the rainbow jersey. Behind him Adri Van der Poel of the Netherlands won the sprint for silver with Stephen Roche taking third. Roche later said he had no idea he was in the hunt for a medal: 'I thought there were more ahead of us,' he said. 'I expected to be sixth or seventh.'[170]

LeMond had won the Critérium du Dauphiné earlier in the year but at the time this was by far his biggest win and put him on the path to cycling superstardom. 'You've got to take risks; in this sport, anybody who doesn't take them is certainly making a mistake,'[171] he reflected after the race.

After LeMond's first for the USA, over the course of the next three years wins followed a more traditional pattern, with Belgium, the Netherlands and Italy recording victories with Claude Criquielion (1984), Joop Zoetemelk (1985) and Moreno Argentin (1986) respectively. In the women's event meanwhile, following Marianne Berglund's 1983 win, a certain Frenchwoman was about to commence a remarkable run of four straight wins. Cycling history was about to be made.

***

In 1979 Jeannie Longo became the French road-race national champion. It was the first of some twenty titles over the course of a career that was remarkable both for its success and its longevity. Later that year she rode her first world championship, finishing eighth. Over the course of the next five years, while she ruled the domestic scene with an iron-fist (Longo was undefeated in the national championship road race throughout the 1980s), at the Worlds she would claim just one podium finish – second in 1981. Meanwhile, the Italian Maria Canins, the multiple Italian national champion and now into her thirties, was also trying to get her hands on the rainbow jersey – taking podium positions in 1982 and 1983.

With no women's Worlds race in 1984 because of the Olympic Games, all eyes were on Longo and Canins at the 1985 championships. The pair had crossed paths throughout the 1985 season with Canins beating the Frenchwoman at the Tour of Norway and, cruelly for Longo, the women's Tour de France earlier in the year. The 1985 Worlds were held in Montello, Italy. A Worlds on Italian roads seemed like the perfect place for Canins to at last take the jersey, or for Longo to exact her revenge.

It was a two-rider show as Longo and Canins went head to head. After their initial move was brought back Canins attacked again and Longo matched her. This time they were away for good. Canins forced Longo to the front in the closing moments for the sprint, her only hope that the advantage she would get from drafting would see her through, but Longo just steadily rode the Italian off her wheel. She did not win by much, a couple of lengths, but she probably had more to give if needed. It had been a long time coming, but now, at twenty-seven, Longo at last had the rainbow jersey. And now she had it she would not let go, holding the jersey through to the end of the 1980s. No other rider in history, male or female, had won more than two titles in a row before Longo and none has done so since.

Her domination was absolute. In 1986 she won the race in Colorado, described in the pages of *Cycling Weekly* as one of the 'shortest, severest, and certainly most dramatic races in the event's twenty-eight-year history',[172] after matching a fierce assault from the USA's Rebecca Whitehead in the final 5 kilometres and then riding on alone after Whitehead cruelly crashed on a slippery descent. Then she won again in 1987, attacking once, hard and definitively, on the final climb in Villach, Austria and riding alone to a 21-second win.

With no race in 1988 because of the Seoul Olympic Games, Longo had to wait until 1989 to equal Yvonne Reynders with a fourth title in the French Alps, attacking third time up the 2.4 kilometre long, 8 per cent steep Côte de Montagnole and dropping everybody except her old rival Maria Canins and French newcomer Catherine Marsal. With around one kilometre of the climb to go, Longo went again. This time even those two riders, one with a glorious past, one with a glorious future, could not match her. Longo was still at her best and simply rode away. Thirty-six kilometres later, when she crossed the finish line for the final time in front of an exuberant crowd, her lead had reached 04.05. It was the biggest winning margin in the history of the women's race and the third title of the week for Longo who had also claimed the pursuit and points race titles on the track. At the time it was thought to be her last season. 'She's incredible. The racing will be better when she has retired,' said Britain's Clare Greenwood who had come home thirty-second. 'Everyone will think they have a chance of winning and it will improve the competition.'[173]

One month after her win, Longo flew to Mexico City to tackle the women's hour record. In her sights was her own best mark of 44.933 kilometres set two years earlier, but also the mark set by another giant of cycling – Fausto Coppi. In 1942 Coppi had set a benchmark of 45.798 kilometres at the Vigorelli Velodrome in Milan, a record that stood for fourteen years until it was beaten by Jacques Anquetil. In Mexico Longo duly set the mark at 46.352 kilometres, bettering her own previous best for a woman by more than 1.4 kilometres and not only beating Coppi's record but also that of Anquetil.

***

If the first half of Stephen Roche's career had brought a number of good wins, including Paris-Nice, two Tour of Romandie titles and third overall at the Tour in 1985, nothing that had come before can really have prepared the world for what he achieved in 1987.

First of all, after a tumultuous three weeks during which the Irishman stirred the anger of his teammates, managers, Italian press and the *tifosi* by challenging the race lead of his team leader Roberto Visentini in the Dolomites, Roche emerged metaphorically battered and bruised but in pink as the first Irish winner of the Giro. A few weeks later he headed to France and went head to head at the Tour with Spain's Pedro Delgado, setting up an overall win in Paris with a courageous, race-saving ride to La Plagne that would enter Tour legend. He promptly collapsed on the finish line. Oxygen had to be given. Four days later he stood in yellow in Paris.

So by the time Roche stood on the start line of the 1987 worlds in Villach his season was already a huge success. The 11.7-kilometre circuit in Austria was thought to suit his teammate Sean Kelly better but as soon as Roche saw the course he thought otherwise, realising that the two climbs on the circuit were tougher than had been expected. He began to think the course could suit him, but still he was ready to work for Kelly.

With one kilometre left Roche found himself in a lead group of five. He was looking for Kelly but Kelly was a hundred metres or so behind being watched by Moreno Argentin. 'I saw that Argentin and Kelly were looking at each other,' Roche said after the race. 'I thought I would probably come fourth but then I thought I would give it a try. You have to take the bull by the horns if you want to win a world title.'[174]

Under a bridge and into the final 300 metres, Roche attacked through a narrow gap down the left-hand side of the road, nearly getting squeezed into the barriers as he did so. Had he made his move a split second later Roche's season could have ended very differently, but the Irishman made it through and hit the front rather than the barriers. Now he had clear road ahead. Behind, the chase group had caught the remnants of his small breakaway and the pursuit was in full swing. Roche just buried his head, dug deep and, with the final 100 metres of road gently rising, held on to take Ireland's first title.

One season; three jerseys: pink, yellow and rainbow. It was only the second time a rider had taken the Giro, Tour and Worlds in the same year – the triple crown of cycling. Roche had matched Eddy Merckx's 1974 feat. 'Merckx now wasn't a bad rider was he?'[175] Roche asked mischievously. Kelly, meanwhile, had finished fifth and immediately celebrated with his fellow countryman. The Italian press paid its dues to the performance of the Irish, described as coming from small country with no great cycling tradition. 'The Irish play football, rugby, the typical range of British [sic] sports ... are good in boxing ... practise traditional Celtic games ... And they have Roche and Kelly. Just one of these two cyclists would be enough to make the fortune of any nation on two wheels.'[176]

***

Inside the final kilometre of the 1988 race, and with more than seven hours on the clock, there were two riders ahead of a small chasing bunch: Italy's Maurizio Fondriest and Belgium's Claude Criquielion. All day, attacks and counter-attacks had flown in Ronse on one of the most difficult courses ever used for a Worlds, a course that included twenty climbs of the 12 per cent Kruisberg, a climb long featured in the Tour of Flanders and used here for a tough uphill finish.

Four years earlier Criquielion had won the Worlds in Barcelona. Now, in another Olympic year, he was again at the head of the race and this time he was at home and the crowds were cheering his name: 'Claudy, Claudy,' they cried. Then, weaving his way in and out of the motorcycles following the race, appeared a third rider, the Canadian Steve Bauer. With 700 metres to go two became three.

Criquielion looked at Fondriest, who looked at Bauer, who looked at Criquielion, who looked back. They all looked behind. Who would twitch first? With 200 metres to go, Bauer started his sprint. Straight on to his wheel was Criquielion. Fondriest sat third, resigned to bronze. Bauer and Criquielion were on the right-hand side of the road and Bauer was weaving a little from side to side. With 100 metres to go the Belgian had to choose which side to come off the Canadian's wheel. Left or right? He went right. It was the wrong decision. As Criquielion came off his wheel, so Bauer weaved back across to the right-hand side of the road leaving the Belgian nowhere to go. They touched. Criquielion was forced into the barriers, hitting a marshal and crashing down while Bauer's own speed was checked leaving a disbelieving Fondriest to come through for an uncontested win. Bauer rolled across in second while Criquielion was left to pick himself up, dust himself down, and walk to the line, wheeling his broken bike with him. To rub salt into a gaping wound, as he approached the line the small group from which he had earlier escaped passed by in the middle of their own sprint, forcing the Belgian further down the final classification. Boos rang out at the injustice of what has just happened to the home favourite.

The *commissaires* poured over the footage. Their conclusion: Fondriest was champion, Bauer was disqualified for coming off his line in the sprint. Martial Gayant, of France and Juan Fernández of Spain were awarded second and third. The next day the *Leidsch Dagblad* newspaper printed a picture of Criquielion walking his bike over the line with his hand in the air with the title 'Bauer robs Belgian of world title, Ronse is upside down'.[177] The UCI's President, Hein Verbruggen, likened the incident to a striker being brought down when clear through on goal only for the resulting penalty to then be missed. 'It's very annoying,' he said. 'But all the regulations can do is disqualify Bauer. No more.'[178]

***

Three years after his 1983 Worlds win, Greg LeMond had won his first Tour title. The scene seemed set for a period of American dominance but in the spring of 1987 he was accidentally shot in the back during a hunting trip. The American lost a lot of blood, suffered a collapsed lung and broken ribs and was in surgery for more than two hours. At the time LeMond's surgeon reported he would need a couple of months to get back to normal.[179] In the end the accident would cost LeMond two years of his career.

After a hard-fought recovery LeMond returned to France in 1989 to record his second Tour win, triumphing over the French favourite Laurent Fignon after a final-day time trial and the tightest ever finish to the Tour. It had been an incredible comeback but LeMond was far from done. A little more than one month later he was back in France for the Worlds and another face-off against Fignon. The result in Chambéry, after a day when thunder bounced across the Alps, would be the same: an exciting finale featuring both Fignon and LeMond attacking and countering each other during the final lap, with LeMond ultimately taking the jersey and Fignon missing out by seconds. The Frenchman, who had attacked on the final climb desperate to avoid a sprint, took sixth place just 3 seconds back, while LeMond held off a strong effort from Sean Kelly as the line approached. Kelly stopped pedalling just before the finish allowing the Soviet

Union's Dimitri Konyshev to flash by to steal the silver medal in the first Worlds in which a male Soviet rider had competed.

LeMond's win meant he became only the fourth rider in history to win the Tour and the world championships in the same year. No rider has matched that achievement since. 'This Greg is my *Bête Noire*,'[180] shrugged Fignon afterwards.

17

MANDY JONES (1982)

It is the morning of the 24 June 2016 and I'm bleary headed. Last night I stayed up late watching coverage of the UK's vote to leave the European Union. This morning, on my drive to the edge of the village of Littleborough, near Rochdale, just north of the Peak District National Park, I listened to the Prime Minister's resignation speech. So it is fair to say I am a little distracted when I turn into the driveway belonging to the winner of the women's 1982 world championship road race.

In her kitchen Mandy Bishop, née Jones, makes coffee and tells me a little about the lengthy renovation of the barn that is today the beautiful home she shares with her husband. We talk about the events of the night before and how we were both watching until the early hours. 'Shall we talk about cycling instead?' I ask Mandy. 'Good idea,' she agrees.

***

Mandy Jones:

My parents were cyclists. That was how they met – in cycling clubs in Manchester. I liked riding my bike and we had club runs every weekend, quite a lot of hostel weekends, traditional club riding. We used to go cyclo-touring – two weeks cycling and camping around the Lake District or the Wye valley or something. The first time my dad wanted me to ride a 10-mile time trial I didn't really want to do it. I was just nervous. I wasn't a particularly confident child. But once I started I enjoyed it. I liked the competition aspect really, seeing who you could beat. When I was a bit older, fifteen or sixteen, we'd do a club run of 100 miles or so at the weekends, with an 11am stop and a 2pm stop and then back for tea. That builds your strength even if you're not riding in the week. All the time you're just building and building your fitness until eventually, at sixteen, I started doing some ladies road races.

Jones's rise through the ranks was rapid. By 1980 she was at her first world championships in Sallanches, France where she came third.

I started training with Ian Greenhalgh who eventually became my coach. He was riding as a pro at the time and had been a very good amateur. I just went training every day with him, it was a simple as that. I didn't work so we didn't have much money. My parents used to drive me everywhere and usually my dad paid my entrance fees until I ended up living with Ian. I was eighteen when I moved in with him. From then on the training was literally full-time – he was training as a professional and I went with him.

I think other people saw potential in me more than I did. I didn't really understand things from that point of view, but others had been around a long time. Within a period of eighteen months I went from just starting to ride road races, to winning road races, to riding my first world championships in Sallanches.

MANDY JONES (1982)

It was nerve-racking – I mean we actually stayed in a hotel! British Cycling wasn't like it is now. It didn't have the funding, so you had to give the jerseys back – washed. The only thing I got to keep was my skinsuit. It was good being away with a team, you knew everybody but we'd supposedly gone from being rivals to riding as a team. Of course that didn't really happen – there was never any practice riding as a team.

Sallanches was an extremely hard circuit, very hilly. The circuit was basically a triangle and I didn't have low enough gears. In some of the pictures I have you can see me struggling. Beth Heiden won it. I could tell the other riders had lower gearing than me because they were attacking going up the climb while I just had to keep going at a steady pace. I just couldn't accelerate. It was such a steep climb, especially the bottom bit; it was so painful and I was glad we didn't have to go up more than three times. But I went into that race with no expectations at all. I'd gone from literally being a domestic rider who had gone and ridden in some 'fish 'n' chippers' in France, to suddenly riding the world championships with all these people and all this razzmatazz – look, there's a team and a mechanic and a manager! I was absolutely delighted in all honesty to get third place, I was just over the moon.

It gave me a massive amount of confidence. It's like anything you do. You ride a time trial and the next time you go a little bit faster and you realise, oh, I can go a bit faster. You ride a road race and you win – you get away on your own or whatever – and you know you can do that again because you've done it before. Then you come third in the world championships and you're thinking, 'God, I've got a bronze medal. A medal against all those women in my first year riding and I'm only eighteen.' It just gives you that much more confidence.

After coming third in Sallanches and then winning her first national title in 1981, Jones' focus turned to 1982 and the Worlds which were to be held in Britain, with the track events in Leicester and the road races at Goodwood.

We looked at the race programme for 1982 and planned the races I'd do bearing in mind I was riding the pursuit and then the road race one week later. We found a bit of road out towards Heywood. I'd go out in the morning and do two and a half hours and then in the afternoon, after we'd had a rest and some lunch, Ian would get the motorbike and we'd go out to Heywood. I'd ride behind the motorbike with him doing 30mph. Then, on a section of road we'd found which had a bit of a drop in it, we'd do a speed session at the top end, another one at the bottom and then two coming back. And we'd do it twice – so eight speed sessions. The idea was that I'd sit behind him and he'd build it up to 30mph and once we got to a certain lamppost I would have to come out from behind and ride at the side of the motorbike and try to maintain that position until we got to the next marker. Over the weeks it got to the point where I could actually pass the motorbike and get to the marker before he did. Then I'd go back behind him and do the next segment. We did that right up until the Wednesday before the pursuit on the Saturday! Of course, now I realise that we didn't do any tapering. You learn these things.

Earlier in the year, Jones had broken the world record for 5 kilometres on the same Leicester track that hosted the track world championships. But on the day of the pursuit she had nothing in the tank and posted a disappointing time, falling outside the medals.

I was so upset. I'd wanted to do so well at the pursuit I didn't speak to anybody. I remember riding round the centre of the track on my bike really, really fed up. It's a bit vague really but eventually I managed to get my head together by talking to my dad and Ian. I'd had so much pressure and expectation on me to do well in the pursuit, because of what I'd been doing in the build-up, I was so disappointed. I felt that I'd let people down. Then I just thought stuff it, I've got nothing to lose. I used to get very nervous. I learned to deal with my nerves over the years, but only by getting good at masking my nerves rather than actually not feeling nervous. But what happened at Leicester actually made me more relaxed. I felt like the pressure was off in some ways. Also, I'd finished that speed training on the Wednesday and other than the pursuit on the Saturday I'd actually had ten days' rest. That was my taper. It is only afterwards that you realise and think, 'Oh, yeah, I understand what happened now.'

So when it came to the road race I was flying. We stayed in Leicester a couple of days while the track was on and then went down to Goodwood. Because we were staying as a team at the hotel we went down there on the Wednesday to have a look at the circuit.

There was a discussion over tactics to decide that I was team leader but if somebody else ends up getting away then you support that person and be in the right place to be as much help as you can. The race was fast anyway, things were happening all the time. I went away with another rider – Mieke Havik – but we were caught on the climb. Then immediately three others escaped – Sandra Schumacher, Maria Canins and Gerda Sierens. Of course, I'd already been away so my legs were feeling it a bit but I thought, 'No, they're going and I need to go with them.' You can see me on the film gritting my teeth as I get back on the back of them. As we went up the climb I tried to recover and then I went past them again.

We were just going through and off to the next corner. I went round first and suddenly there was a big gap and I just went. I didn't intentionally go round that corner thinking I'm going to attack, but your head is working all the time and you are looking at what is happening in the race and you're feeling fit and everything is working out and you feel comfortable. I think it was just one of those times when it all came together. But I'm analysing this now years later. At the time it was just 'that's it, I'm going'. You make this split-second decision to take your opportunity.

So I'm on the motor-racing circuit and I can see them behind and I'm thinking get your head down and just keep going. Then I'm at the bottom of the climb again. It's one of those climbs that is really heavy on your legs, it just gradually drags up and then starts to climb and it was hurting, without a doubt it was bloody hurting, and I was thinking I just have to keep going, don't look back, just keep going. The motorbike came up with a board showing 30 seconds or whatever it was … and the crowd … as soon as I started climbing the crowd was just so loud, so many people cheering and shouting your name because they know who you are. It was brilliant. It carries you, it really does. And you're also listening for that shout that goes 'They're catching you … shit, hurry up!'

There was no easing up at the end. Those girls I got away with were only ten seconds behind me at the line.

And then, pandemonium.

You can't believe it, the people grabbing you and hugging you and whisking you off to be interviewed … yeah.

We did the podium presentation pretty quickly and I remember Hugh Porter interviewing me immediately afterwards. Part of the way through the interview my mum arrived at the barrier and she started going, 'Mandy! Mandy!' I went, 'Hiya Mum!' and carried on.

I was ecstatic, mind-blowingly so. It was too much of a whirlwind to think much about what it really meant to get the rainbow jersey. That feeling of total euphoria was also because the training had been so hard in the years leading up to the race but it had worked. It was the culmination of everything – my God, I'm here. I've done it. It worked. It was just unbelievable. It's not a feeling I've ever had since. It's hard to explain, everything just becomes … mad. Everyone is shouting and laughing and clapping and everybody has got smiles on their faces and they're crying – there's not a dry eye in the house … it's hard to take in.

The ladies race was in the morning on the Saturday and the amateur men raced in the afternoon. I was in with the press for hours and hours. The amateur's race had started and I was still in there, still in my gear … and the hotel we were staying in was just off the circuit, about two miles down the road. When I finally came out the only way back to the hotel was around the circuit. So I was riding back around the circuit, watching where the helicopter was to make sure I moved over if the men came by and as I'm going down the descent this bobby shouts, 'Stop! You can't ride down here!' All the people stood there watching went, 'Do you know who that is? 'She's just won the world championships!' 'Oh, oh I'm very sorry, congratulations, carry on!' It was so funny.

When I walked into the hotel everybody else had already been back and got changed and gone out to watch the men's race. I was starving as I'd not eaten and so I walked into the dining room and all the pros are sat round the table having just finished eating dinner. I got a really roaring reception as I knew them all because of Ian riding in the pros. They were there cheering me and shouting, 'Chef, get her some food, she needs some food!' I'm still wearing all my sweaty kit eating my dinner.

Then came the 1983 season ... the season after the season before.

We'd set a goal but we hadn't done any planning for what happened if I actually won. I did have a lot of difficulties with the constant pressure and the constant, really hard, training ... it got to me. In my head all I needed to do was win the Worlds and then I could go, 'Alright, that's it, I'm not riding my bike for a bit.' But of course you can't do that when you win the Worlds. When you win the Worlds you've got an obligation to ride the following year, you've got the jersey, you're an ambassador for your sport and that floored me. In the interview immediately after I won I said to Hugh Porter, 'I'm not riding next year, I'm having a year off. I'm definitely having a year off.' In my head I'd achieved my goal. Of course I couldn't do that so I actually found it very difficult. I didn't train as much. We opened a bike shop and I was also supposedly training but I was going out on my own and I couldn't be bothered. So I'd go and visit [fellow GB rider] Julie [Earnshaw] because she lived down the road. I'd go out for a ride, go for an hour and go spend an hour at Julie's, have tea and biscuits.

Even so, during the 1983 season Jones still managed to take her third straight national title and finish fourth at the Worlds in Switzerland.

At the Worlds I wasn't really as fit as I'd been the year before. I wish now things had been different. I was always hopeless at riding my bike on my own anyway because I like company. I found it really hard to go out on my own. I wish now I'd trained more – hindsight is a wonderful thing – because I got fourth in Switzerland and my chain came off at the bottom of the climb! I got back up and had I been as fit as I was the year before, and knowing what I was like once I'd caught people up following a puncture or whatever, I could have won it again. Without a doubt I could have won it again but I just wasn't fit enough. I had a year out the year after that.

Jones returned to racing in 1985 but a succession of injuries and difficult years hindered her return to the sport. It wasn't until the early 1990s that she began to feel something like her old self again.

I rode in Stuttgart in the Worlds in 1991, in the team time trial and the road race, and while I wasn't at full fitness I was feeling a lot better, a lot stronger. I'd been listed for the 1992 Olympics. I had a fantastic winter training locally and felt really strong, going out on the mountain bikes and out on the road bikes. I felt miles better. One day I was out on a mountain bike, on a dead easy ride, with a friend and my back just went. I crawled home. I had to crawl through the door and that was it. That was the end of my career. They sent me to Lilleshall and I spent two weeks there. I was in traction, having physio and all sorts of stuff trying to get back on the bike. But it was getting nearer and nearer to the Olympics and I said unless you can say to me, 'here you go, here's a miracle cure', I'm not going to be fit enough to go to the Olympics and I'm not going as a hanger-on. I'm going to try to win or I'm not going at all. And so I made the decision. I said this isn't getting any better so you need to find someone else to ride on the team.

That's a big black hole. I was really, really depressed. I think you could say pissed off. It took me months to get over it. Everything had been going so well. I was in a new relationship, the training had been going well, I felt really positive and I just thought I'd been kicked in the teeth. I didn't race after that. That was it.

I never felt that I met my full potential but I don't have any regrets about it. I did what I did at the end of the day. People say to me I don't make enough of my career because I've never been one to go, 'I was world champion.' It's just not me. When I do say people go, 'Oh, really? That's fantastic!' Yeah, I thought it was fantastic as well! I had a good life from it, not money-wise because you didn't win any money and there was no financial support, but from the confidence it gave me, from the people I met and the places I've been. And that comes from cycling as a whole, not just the racing. Cycling is such a social sport. You meet all sorts of people, all walks of life. It doesn't matter whether they are a lawyer or a bin man. That's not the thing is it? The thing is that they both ride a bike.

18

STEPHEN ROCHE (1987)

Stephen Roche walks across the bar of the Hotel Ponent Mar in Palmanova, Majorca towards my table. He looks fit and tanned in his cycling kit having just returned from escorting customers of his cycling holiday business on a ride. In his soft voice Roche introduces himself before disappearing for a shower but not before checking I am all right for a drink. Thirty minutes later we are sat in the office of his company on the first floor of the hotel, surrounded by cycling jerseys and books to talk about his 1987 world championship win in Austria: a win that crowned an unforgettable season for the man from Dublin.

That was the year that Roche won the Giro, Tour and the world championships. The holy trinity – the triple crown of cycling. Only one man had done it before – Eddy Merckx. Roche's 1986 season had been a disaster because of a knee injury sustained during the winter of 1985 after a crash at the Paris Six-Day track meeting. Two specialists had told the Irishman his career was over but an operation in late 1986 put him on the road to recovery and as the 1987 season appeared on the horizon Roche was training better than he ever had. That is where we pick up his story.

***

Stephen Roche:

My mind-set was quite simple going into 1987 because when I signed to Carrera after my third place at the Tour in 1985 I turned up as a podium rider, maybe even a potential Tour winner. So I was getting good money, but 1986 was a flop because of my knee problem and even though I rode the Giro and helped Roberto Visentini win, I didn't ride enough. I didn't ride half the races I should have ridden.

In the winter I got a call from the boss and he said, 'Stephen, you know, you're a nice guy but we're paying you good money and the returns aren't great, we have to renegotiate your contract.' I said, 'Whoa, whoa, here guys, no. When you get married it's for better or for worse. You've seen the worst hopefully, the best is to come. If I'd won everything this year would you have said, "Stephen here's a bonus, we haven't paid you enough?" I don't think so. So I propose that you leave me alone until next April. If by Easter I've got no results then I agree we can discuss and renegotiate my contract whichever way you want but I'm confident that I'll be having a good year next year.'

I had just met a new doctor in Germany – Dr Müller-Wohlfahrt – who had actually sorted my knee out. I was getting back to training normally and I had no more pain and so I was confident that I would have a good season, back to my normal self. But I could never have imagined what was going to happen. I had no thoughts at all about what was going to come, you know?

After winning the Tour of Valencia early in the season, at Paris-Nice Roche had a puncture on the penultimate stage while wearing the leader's jersey, losing the chance of winning overall. But he had ridden well. In the spring classics he then narrowly missed out on Liège-Bastogne-Liège when Moreno Argentin came back to Roche and Claude Criquielion in the closing metres while they engaged in a game of cat and mouse.

The night before Liège-Bastogne-Liège, in my room my *directeur sportif* was telling me how happy he was that my form had come back again. He told me I was too generous in my effort, that I rode too hard and that you had to be prepared to lose to win. That's why when I got into the break with Criquielion the following day, and Criquielion and I were the strongest in that race – we'd left Argentin far behind us – I knew that if I kept riding the way I would normally ride, Criquielion would win because he'd beat me in the sprint. And Criquielion thought the same. So we ended up doing a bit of cat and mouse and not thinking at all about Argentin or anybody else coming from behind. It was a big, big shock when Argentin came past me! But it was definitely the right advice – to be prepared to lose to win.

Roche then enjoyed an incredible summer. After winning his third Tour of Romandie, he went on to win the Giro amid a huge amount of team in-fighting with teammate Visentini and then won the Tour after a famous ride on La Plagne behind Spain's Pedro Delgado. Then came the Worlds.

There was a shorter gap back then between the Tour and the Worlds. We had the after-Tour criteriums – I was getting a lot of money in those days to ride them – so I rode two or three of them with my driver driving me around. I rode one in Belgium, eight or nine times up the Oude Kwaremont on the cobblestones. It was a bit humid and my wheel slipped … aahh … I hurt my leg. That was a sign of fatigue so I cancelled all the rest of my criteriums and went down to my wife's parents' holiday home and avoided everything. I had a few days total rest, I went fishing and just relaxed a little bit. Then, slowly but surely, I started getting back into it, leaving very early in the morning and going out on long and hot rides. The leg was OK, everything was great. I felt good enough then for some of the end-of-season races – the San Sebastián Classic and some criteriums in Ireland – the Kellogg's Series.

That was very important for the Worlds. I was there, Sean Kelly … Martin Earley … Paul Kimmage. We all thought it would be nice if I could win in Dublin being it was my home crowd. So we approached some of the elite

British pros and said, 'OK, maybe we can do a deal here, maybe we can make our group a little bigger and try to make it so I could win.' So rather than sixty individual riders just racing for the win we would have a pool of seven or eight riders on my 'team' trying to fight off all the other guys and try to get me in a position where I can win. But the British pros didn't really want to entertain our plan. They thought Stephen's won the Tour. If he wants to win here then that's his problem, you know?

That kind of got the adrenaline flowing. It brought myself, Sean, Paul and Martin together. We started off with the bit between our teeth to make sure we were going to win. I got away a few times and I won. It was great, I won! We went from there down to Wexford for the next one. Some of the British professionals came along and asked if we could ride together. No. We rode rings around them in Wexford and Sean won. We were so motivated after those races. We didn't go to a restaurant but had fish and chips and beer and just sat in the corridor of the hotel. For me that was a very important part of building for the Worlds. It was a big bonding experience. We were in there and we were beating these guys who really didn't want us to win, but we're going to beat you anyway, you know?

The next race at Cork was the same again, take no prisoners. We knew that everyone was waiting for Sean for the final corner and the final 200 metres. He came out of the corner with a 10-metre lead and that was it. By the time the guys realised what was going on they had 20 metres to catch up on Sean, which was impossible. They started coming by me and one guy's handlebars touched mine and we brought down twenty-five guys. It was a big pile-up. Some of the guys said it was my fault and that I had brought them down deliberately so Sean would win, I mean totally ridiculous. Some were even having a go at me while I was on the floor. My brother-in-law was there and he jumped over the fence to pull them off me. But once again we had won. We left Ireland then for the Worlds.

Roche had injured himself during that fall in Cork and had to nurse himself through to the Worlds, held in Villach, Austria.

What saved me the day of the Worlds was the weather. If it had been warm the pain would definitely have been alive but because it was cold and damp it acted as an anaesthetic on my knee, which meant it helped me get through it, but once I'd finished I couldn't even walk.

The race was on the Sunday and we arrived on the Friday. I was thinking of the Worlds as a race where I would be helping Sean because everybody had said that it was definitely a sprinters' race. So that was me ruled out.

So I was going there with good form and hoping that I would be able to help Sean. Sean had form at the Tour but had broken his collarbone and he had got good form again so I felt he was back now, back in the saddle again, and it's a good sprinters' circuit so I can help him … great.

On the Friday we went on to the circuit. It was a really hot day. I rode around the circuit once and thought, 'Wow, this isn't for a sprinter. Twenty-two times around this circuit with two steep climbs at the end?' Four or five times around, yes, but twenty-two times? No, it's impossible for a sprinter. Only then, for the first time was I thinking, hmm, maybe. I didn't ride selfishly on the day. I knew it was a really good circuit for me and I knew it wasn't going to be a pure sprinters' race, but then Sean wasn't a pure sprinter; he was the kind of guy who could get over that circuit. So for me it was a circuit that suited both of us, definitely Sean and definitely me. The plan was for me to be there at the finish to lead out Sean and then you never know.

On the morning of the race I pulled the curtains back and saw the rain coming down. I said to myself that this was definitely my day, not necessarily for winning it but my day for going well. I was really tired after my season and if it had been hot that day I think it would have been a totally different story, I would have felt fatigued a lot more. But because it was raining and cold it was like a breath of fresh air. The rain was a blessing in disguise for me.

After breakfast a friend of mine from Paris rang me. He used to ring me up before any big occasion. He was one of the first to say to me, 'Stephen you know if you win today you will equal Eddy Merckx and win the triple.' It was the first time I thought about it. You know, the number 13 was very prominent for me in everything I did in my career. So I'm on the phone in the reception of this old-style hotel. There are no electronic key fobs, just big, old keys on keyrings. My friend is saying to me: 'You know Merckx is the only one who has done the triple before and if you win today … it's raining, it's going to be good for you today. Don't throw your chances away, today can be your day.' So I say, 'Yeah, yeah, OK, listen Angelo I'll call you afterwards.' I put the phone down and realised I had something in my hand. I looked down and found I was holding the key to number 13.

Before the race the team talked tactics.

It wasn't like a PowerPoint presentation, this wasn't like a Sky-type marginal gains briefing! It was basically like, listen guys, Martin and Paul: any breaks that go early on try to cover them and if a group of good riders go then try to close them down. Then I'd look after Sean at the end, as late as I could – look after him at the end.

A breakaway got away for a while and Martin and Paul chased it down. They were instrumental in bringing it back, some other teams helped as well because we only had a small team. It was good to have our guys up there riding to bring it back, doing our share of the work. It was brought back and in the final three laps we took over – that was an amazing three laps.

On the final lap a break had got away with twelve riders. Myself and Sean weren't in it. As we crossed the start/finish line and went up the first climb for the final time I attacked and Sean came with me. We both got across to make a group of fourteen. When we got across we went straight to the front and Marc Madiot got dropped. We were thirteen in the break! I rode at the front the whole way up the climb, right to the top and round to the second climb on the far side of the circuit. I tried attacking on the final climb, thinking that if I get away Sean gets a handy ride behind me and if I stay away, I stay away.

They caught me very quickly and I went right to the back and rested a bit so I could ride for Sean in the final 3 or 4 kilometres. As I went to the back an attack went away. I thought, 'Well what do I do now? I need to chase this down.'

So I tore past the others and up to the back of the group. I looked around and there was nobody there. So I was sort of half happy and half not happy because there I was in this group and there were four or five of us there but how was Sean going to win if the guys behind didn't ride because they knew they would be bringing Sean across? I was in a group with Rolf Sørensen, Teun Van Vliet and Rolf Gölz, those three alone were much faster than me in a sprint. I hadn't done all that to finish third or fourth.

We decide to watch the video of the final kilometres.

So I'm waiting ... waiting ... waiting. You can see we are all watching each other. I'm thinking, shit, hoping that it's going to come back for Sean. I keep looking back thinking I'm just going to hang in here.

After a few minutes on the back of the group my idea was to attack with one kilometre to go, before the final corner. I'm going and going and going but they come across so I can't pass. Going into the final corner, with Van Vliet and Gölz, I knew I could beat them. I knew there was a lot of friction between Van Vliet and Gölz. I know those two are fighting each other ... you can see them watching each other. If I attacked I knew that they wouldn't come straight away because Gölz knew that if he came around with Van Vliet that early he's not going to win and vice versa. So I knew I could gain a bit of time on these guys, but I had to get Guido Winterberg off my wheel. If I went on the right, into the wind, he would follow me, but if I went to the left, while it was tight to the barriers, if I managed to get through he might just back off and I might get 5 or 10 metres or something and that would be it. That was my plan.

The amazing thing about cycling and bike racing is those things go through your head in seconds. It has to come naturally. The guys today, because of radios, don't really have to develop that instinct whereas when I came around the final corner straightaway, my brain was working.

It was very tight, even looking at it now you've got to say, 'Well Stephen it was a bit dodgy going through that gap by the barriers. Dangerous even.' But the brain does wonders and that was it. I was using my knowledge of the surroundings, my knowledge of the peloton and my knowledge of the relationships between riders.

Roche got away in the final 500 metres and held off a fast-approaching group for the win. Kelly celebrated as he rolled across the line in fifth and went straight up to Roche to congratulate him.

Sean threw his arms up in the air, you know? For me you can talk about friendship or team work or loyalty and for many years I'd help Sean in races unofficially. Sean was a friend and while certain people and journalists in Ireland would have liked to have had myself and Sean against each other because it would have made for better stories, we were always good friends. Even to this day.

Sean sprinting for second place and throwing his arms into the air. That was spontaneous, that wasn't staged for a photograph. That was, 'Ah he's won!' He was happy for me. We don't see many images like that. There are two images that stand out in my mind from my career. One was that image of Sean and the other was when I beat Delgado in the final time trial in Dijon at the Tour in 1987. We went to a television show together. He was already on the set when I arrived and he stood up, came over and threw his arms around me and said, 'Well done Stephen.' The TV presenter says,

'But Pedro, this guy has just taken your yellow jersey and you're giving him a hug?' 'Yes, but we've spent 4,000 kilometres fighting each other. We've 100 kilometres left tomorrow into Paris … it's been a great fight.' That's a bloody good reaction.

It's not about having grudges or fighting or verbally abusing each other; it's about fighting each other and at the end the best man wins, or being happy for someone who has put in a great performance. Pedro Delgado recognised it and Sean recognised it.

We're watching the chaos that ensued right after the race. Kelly has his arms around Roche as the photographers gather. A man in a green beret arrives, hugs Kelly and then grabs Roche and gives him a kiss.

That's Herman! Herman Nijs was the guy that Sean lived with throughout his early years in Belgium. Herman was Belgian but in many ways he was more Irish. Sean lived with Herman and his wife Elise for years. Every year at the Worlds, Elise would sit down and sew our race numbers on to our jerseys. It was a ritual. Every world championships. They cooked all the food and everything for us. They were a great family. Herman was a very important man in Sean's career.

Roche's win meant he was only the second man in history to have won cycling's triple crown. To date no one has matched that achievement.

It is impossible for me to separate those three wins. The Giro was incredible because of the way I won it, with Visentini, with the problems, with the *tifosi*. The journalists were asking when I was going to go home. I said, 'Do what you want. I ain't going home.' If you were to describe that scenario to me before that race and asked me how I'd react, I would've said I'd be on the first plane home. But when I was actually in that scenario, when it was a real-life experience, I'm there saying do what you want I'm not going home. I spent sixteen days being escorted back to my room every night, bodyguard on the door, my masseur making my food, my mechanic looking after my bike, being escorted down to the start line, at the finish line being escorted back to the hotel. It was amazing, you know?

For me that was a huge achievement. So to then come out of it and go to the Tour … and then the stage La Plagne where I buried myself. When I try to tell people today how damaging race radios are I offer them that experience to highlight how radios could have changed history. I didn't really know where Delgado was, I just knew he had been a minute and a half up. I didn't know where he was, the crowd was shouting, I had no idea. I buried myself the last 4 kilometres: ride, ride, ride. With about 500 metres to go I went from the small ring to big ring … I got out of the saddle, dropped Denis Roux who had been with me, go round the corner and Delgado's there! It didn't register because for me Delgado is still well ahead, you know? I see the cars and I just think, 'Oh,' you know? Then of course I collapsed, the journalists all want to know where I came from…

If race radio had have been there that day, and my DS had told me when I was at 30 seconds, I would have backed off probably because I knew I could probably win by one minute in the time trial. So while I was killing myself on La Plagne I could have backed off. But because I didn't know … history was made because everything was just so natural, we did what we did with what was available to us, just pure strength and willpower. Radios have changed a lot in my opinion.

The triple could happen again. It's not that the calibre of riders aren't there or are not capable of doing it. There are a couple of factors, for example if you win a Giro or a Tour then you are a stage-race rider. If you then get a flat world championships there is little chance of you winning it unless you are a guy like Bernard Hinault or Laurent Fignon who also has a very good sprint. You are not going to see a Contador or a Froome go out and win a flat world championships.

But if there was a world championships that was hard enough for these guys to win then it is possible to do it. Also the rider who wins the Giro and the Tour knows that he has spent a lot of energy, but his career doesn't end there. There is next year as well. So if he keeps going to the Worlds six weeks later you're into October. So when is he going to recover from the Giro and the Tour and prepare for next year? They are more inclined to say, 'Well I've done all this, I've done my thing. I'm totally wasted so I better rest up and bring my season to a close in preparation for next year.' So there are lots of aspects there that make it difficult for a rider to do it but it is definitely possible.

In a way I was lucky to win the Worlds that I won, the way that I won it. But I went after it. I didn't wait for the race to come to me. I took the race on and went and won it.

19

SPAIN'S WAIT FINALLY ENDS

For five years, from 1991 until 1995, one man ruled the biggest bike race in the world. Spain's Miguel Indurain was unbeatable at the Tour, becoming the first rider to win five straight editions of the race. For good measure he had also added back-to-back wins at the Giro in 1992 and 1993, the only rider to record successive Giro/Tour doubles. Before Indurain had come Pedro Delgado who recorded three straight podiums at the Tour for Spain between 1987 and 1989, standing on the top step in 1988. But while Spain was a force to be reckoned with in stage racing, in the Monuments it was a different story. The country had only recorded two wins and they had come in the 1950s when Miguel Poblet won two editions of Milan-Sanremo. At the Worlds it had been a similar story. By 1995, as the world's best cyclists flew to Colombia for the sixty-second championships, Spain's best returns had been silver medals for Luciano Montero in 1935 and Indurain in 1993. Meanwhile, in the women's race no Spanish rider had ever made the podium. As Oscar Freire told me, at the time the mentality in Spain was not geared towards one-day racing.

The Colombian circuit was brutal, effectively a 9-kilometre climb topping out at just over 2,850 metres before a precipitous fall back into the city of Duitama for the finish straight. It was a circuit suited to climbers and surely presented a great opportunity for the Spanish to break their Worlds duck.

Such had been Indurain's success in the early 1990s that in Colombia the commonly held belief was that if anyone was going to win for Spain it would surely be 'Big Mig'. As it turned out Indurain would ride strongly and figure prominently in a race where Spain finally took the jersey – but it wouldn't be on his shoulders. Instead his teammate Abraham Olano returned home with the rainbow jersey in his suitcase while his more celebrated teammate had to be content with another second place.

The Spanish team worked hard throughout the second part of the race, managing the attacks of the Colombians, Italians and French. As the final lap started, Olano was up the road alone with a full and difficult lap to go. Behind there was hesitation. Everyone looked to Indurain to pick up the pace. Indurain looked back as if to say, 'What are you looking at me for?' He faked a couple of moves but Olano was his teammate and Spain had been working as a team all day. Indurain was not going to chase one of his compatriots. So he slowed and watched the others.

Olano had 20 seconds at the bell and 46 seconds at the foot of the climb. This was the decisive moment; could the Spaniard keep his lead when behind him the likes of Italy's Marco Pantani and France's Richard Virenque were stirring?

Spain had played a tactical blinder. Their number-one cyclist could now just sit in and see what happened. If the others managed to drag Olano back, Indurain was in the perfect spot to benefit from their work – if not then Olano would be the rider to bring home Spain's first rainbow jersey.

In the closing moments Olano's rear tyre punctured. There was no chance to change it. 'I didn't really think about it,' Olano later reflected. '[I] just concentrated on finishing as quickly as I could. I knew that if I hesitated I might be caught.'[181] All riders need a little luck if they are to win the biggest races and Olano was no different. Fortunately for the Spaniard the tyre held out and Olano crossed the line with a timid raise of the arm. Thirty-five seconds behind him Pantani led the sprint for second only for Indurain to come around him as the line approached to make it a one-two for Spain. Indurain had sat out the Vuelta in favour of preparing for the Worlds, training for a month in Colorado,[182] but when the time came he had played the ultimate team role, refusing to go for personal glory. 'The five-time champion of the Tour gave a lesson of sportsmanship and companionship in favour of Olano's victory,'[183] reported the Spanish daily *ABC*.

Earlier in the week Indurain had taken gold in the time trial with Olano taking silver. In Colombia Spain had been unbeatable with two rainbow jerseys and four medals across two disciplines shared by two riders. Spain had at last arrived at the Worlds.

***

Throughout its sixty-three year existence, the UCI had taken its flagship event outside Europe only three times: North America (1974 and 1986) and South America (1977). In the 1980s riders from outside Europe had made their marks on some of cycling's biggest races. American cyclists had won the Tour and the Worlds (Greg LeMond), and the Giro (Andy Hampsten) and riders from Colombia had made the podium and won stages at the Tour (Luis Herrera and Fabio Parra). No non-European had yet triumphed in any of cycling's Classics, but Australia's Phil Anderson and LeMond had come close, taking second and third respectively in the 1984 edition of Liège-Bastogne-Liège. At the Worlds, Australia had been the first non-European nation to send a team in 1935 with Hubert Opperman taking eighth. The USA followed in 1936, and Argentina became the first South American representative in 1958. Three years later Japan sent Yasumitsu Nakano to Bern, the first of the Asian nations to appear. Professional cycle sport was slowly beginning to spread around the world.

It was to Japan that the UCI looked when it took another leap towards further globalisation of sport by taking the event to Asia for the first time in 1990. Utsunomiya, a city around 125 kilometres north of Tokyo, was the host with a 14.5-kilometre circuit and a climb that rose nearly 150 metres in a couple of kilometres at gradients that reached a maximum of 9 per cent.

Maybe it was the sun and the 30-degree heat or maybe it was the jet-lag that affected the men's peloton. Whatever the cause it was a huge mistake by the favourites to let a twenty-strong break go early in the race and leave them to build a lead of over six minutes. In the break was Dirk De Wolf, a Belgian rider who had finished second in Paris-Roubaix and eighth at the Tour of Flanders the previous year, results that proved his strength as a rider. He was still at the front of the race as the final lap started, joined by teammate Rudy Dhaenens, France's Martial Gayant and Spain's Alberto Leanizbarrutia.

Dhaenens had also stood on the podium of Paris-Roubaix, taking second in 1986 and third in 1987. Now the two Belgian teammates went to work – the Belgian in-fighting of previous decades past consigned to history. With 10 kilometres to go the two Belgian jerseys were out in front. Behind the chase was in full swing and gaining. With De Wolf now exhausted, the question was what the pair would see first – the line or the bunch?

The answer was the line as De Wolf sat up and Dhaenens went through for the win. The two Belgians had worked perfectly together over the closing kilometres and had closed out the perfect race. The day before Eddy Merckx, now manager of the Belgian team, had warned the world that Dhaenens was very strong. 'All I could think of when the others were coming was, ride, ride, ride! It's wonderful,' said Dhaenens. 'I didn't fully realise what was happening when I crossed the line. It's only when I braked a little further on that it began to sink in.' [184]

**

The women's world championships of the mid- to late-1980s had been dominated by France. To be more exact they had been dominated by Jeannie Longo. But now she was absent, enjoying what would turn out to be a temporary retirement from road racing, and the women's peloton was primed, ready to race a world's road race without a Frenchwoman dominating things. Unfortunately for everyone other than the French, what transpired in Japan was all too familiar, even if it was a different face at the front.

Catherine Marsal was just nineteen years old. She was France's national champion and the previous year had had finished second behind Longo in the Chambéry Worlds while still officially a junior. In Japan Marsal pulled away on the first climb. She was caught before the end of the lap but already knew the title was hers. 'The first time … when I looked round and saw how far I was ahead, I knew I would win the race,' she said later. 'When I was caught I wasn't worried.'[185]

On the next lap Marsal established a gap again. This time she would keep it. No one could match her that day and as the bell rang she had a lead of over four minutes. She eased up over the final kilometres, careful not to take any risks on the descent down into Utsunomiya, but her winning margin was still 03.24. Marsal had destroyed the field in a performance reminiscent of the Longo win a year earlier – a solo parade to the pinnacle of the sport. It was the cue for relentless comparisons between the French veteran and the newcomer. 'Now I think that the transfer of power is done,' Marsal said. 'I had a thought for her in the morning, it was she who taught me to ride, to attack, to dare, to win, that's what to do.'[186]

In the space of four years Marsal had won the junior Worlds, finished second in her first elite Worlds, even though she was still a junior, and then won in her first year as an elite rider. Longo was seven years older than Marsal was she won her first elite worlds and the scene seemed set for another French rider to dominate. *Plus ça change…*

But it did not work out that way. Marsal struggled with the attention and it would be another five years before she stood on the road-race podium again.

There were notable differences to the way each team approached the task of a Worlds in Asia, with some arriving a week or more in advance and others waiting until the day before to arrive. Dhaenens and Marsal had been there for five days or so before the race. The event was a success, attendance was good (around 120,000 bought tickets), the organisers offered financial support to riders and teams, and both the main races were entertaining. 'Japan, Land of the Rising Sun, Samurai warriors, Sake and Sushi, was a most gracious and courteous host,'[187] wrote *Cycling*'s John Wilkinson. It had taken some work to get the circuit right, with the UCI reporting in a pre-event inspection that the descent off the main climb was too narrow and dangerous and noting some twenty-one sharp bends needed to be reworked. 'They did everything they were told was needed,'[188] UCI representative Arthur Campbell told Wilkinson.

Yet it would still be twenty-six years before the event returned to Asia. The race was notable as the last time that East and West Germany would compete as separate nations.

***

Third behind Dhaenens and De Wolf in Japan, had been Italy's Gianni Bugno. One year on, the newly crowned national champion entered the 1991 Worlds in Stuttgart as one of the men to watch.

The Stuttgart course was dominated by a single major climb to the top of the Hoher Bopser, 6.2 kilometres long and averaging 4.2 per cent, but with stretches at 8 per cent near its summit. Then followed a 5-kilometre descent, 4 kilometres of flat and then back on to the climb. Italy's team manager Alfredo Martini said that opportunities for recovery were limited. 'What does it mean?' he said. 'It means that at the end of the sixteen laps legs will be broken.' And as for Bugno's chances? 'Don't wait until the end, escape first.' Was he being pessimistic? 'No, it's just a technical report.'[189]

Bugno had ridden solo to a Milan-Sanremo win and then dominated the Giro the year before. After years of threatening to break through he had finally managed to secure his first major race wins, taking the season-long UCI World Cup competition in the process. At the Giro he had proved himself by far the strongest rider, holding the pink jersey from start to finish – only the fourth rider to do so, following Costante Girardengo, Alfredo Binda and Eddy Merckx. He won two time trials, a mountain stage and claimed the points' classification for good measure.

If his 1991 results had not quite lived up to his previous season, Bugno had still won the Clásica de San Sebastián and the national title as well as taking stages at the Giro and the Tour – including a second successive win on the fabled Alpe d'Huez. And the Stuttgart course was thought to suit him.

The Italians rode strongly all day and on the final climb of Hoher

Bopser, Bugno attacked, prompting the final selection. The Netherlands' Steven Rooks and Spain's Miguel Indurain went with him and eventually Colombia's Alvaro Mejia joined to make a final four as they headed down the descent towards the finish line.

With 500 metres to go the four were still together. Rooks and Bugno were the strongest sprinters. The Italian bided his time. He sat behind Meija and waited. When the time was right he opened up his sprint, chased by Indurain and then Rooks. Bugno was looking left and right as he sprinted to the line. After one last look left he was happy neither were coming back. With the line approaching, he sat up, clapped his hands and threw his arms above his head. At the same time Rooks was throwing his bike across the line. It was close, closer than it should have been, but Bugno had done enough. 'It was important to me to have my arms in the air at the finish,'[190] Bugno said. 'I saw 5 kilometres from the finish that the world title could not escape me.'[191] Rooks, meanwhile, reflected that if Bugno had sat up one metre earlier he would have caught him.

Bugno had finished second to Indurain at the Tour earlier in the year, now Indurain had been beaten into third by the Italian. If some saw that as revenge Bugno viewed it differently, casting the two jerseys in very different lights: 'To feel complete, to be able to say to myself, now you have accomplished what you wanted to achieve, I have to win the Tour,' he said. 'The world championship is one thing and the Tour another. Two different goals. I have dreamed of a rematch. But I make a promise: sooner or later, and hopefully sooner rather than later, I want to take the Tour.'[192]

The following year Bugno won another jersey – but it was not yellow. Instead he would take a second straight rainbow jersey, claimed in a bunch sprint in Benidorm after taking third at the Tour, again behind Indurain. It was the first time for thirty years that a rider had defended the title in the men's race and it left the Spanish fans, who had turned out en masse to watch Indurain, distraught. Indurain had been the favourite after winning the first of his Giro/Tour doubles, but was cautious even before the race. 'You have to keep in mind that there are people who can cover their season winning this race,' [193] he said in the build-up.

***

In 1991 and 1993 the women's title was won by the young Dutch rider Leontien van Moorsel (there was no race in 1992 because of the Olympic Games). A twenty-one-year-old Van Moorsel dominated in Stuttgart, in what Dutch daily *De Telegraaf* called 'a phenomenal one-woman show'.[194] She had dedicated herself to the race, training five hours a day, taking in strength and conditioning work and reducing her weight by 15 kilos. She described her reward of a gold medal and the rainbow jersey as 'the jewels'. Two years later Van Moorsel claimed her jewels again, out-sprinting Longo, who had come out of retirement the previous year, in Oslo. In addition to those road-race wins, Van Moorsel ended her career with two time trial world titles, four track world titles, four Olympic gold medals (three on the road, one on the track) and a host of other major wins.

***

A couple of months or so before Van Moorsel's win in Oslo, a twenty-one-year-old American had made his Tour debut riding for the Motorola team. The young man from Texas wasted little time in announcing his presence at the race, winning the stage-eight sprint into Verdun. While he would abandon the race a few days later, saying the Alps were 'too long and too cold',[195] it was the first act in Lance Armstrong's Tour story.

Two months on Armstrong was in Oslo for his second world championships. He had not made it to the finish the previous year in the heat of Benidorm, but now it would be a very different story.

The day dawned with heavy rain which did not relent throughout the race, making for one of the most crash-strewn Worlds for years, with riders careering over walls and being carried off on stretchers or taken away in ambulances. One rider who crashed more than once was Armstrong, but his tumbles on to the wet Oslo roads did not prevent him being with the lead group, chasing a three-rider breakaway on the final lap.

On the climb of the 2.5-kilometre Ryenberg, Armstrong attacked out of the group. First he caught the remnants of an earlier breakaway and then set off in search of the race leader, Norway's Dag-Otto Lauritzen, with the Netherlands' Frans Maassen on his wheel. They caught the Norwegian on the descent. Then, as the road began to tip upwards again, Armstrong found himself with a few lengths' lead. He had been warned by his Motorola director Jim Ochowicz not too attack too early after a race in Zurich in which Armstrong had been feeling strong but ultimately finished outside the top twenty having ridden too hard too early. Now he was at the head of the race with just one climb of the 1.6-kilometre Ekeberg and a 10-kilometre largely downhill run left to the finish.

Armstrong stood up, stamped on his pedals and was gone. His lead at the top of the climb was just seven seconds but on the descent, with the very real danger of sliding off the road and into an ambulance ever-present, Armstrong dragged his lead out and by the time he was back on the flat, powering towards the finish line, he had 18 seconds and the jersey was as good as his.

On the run-in Armstrong looked back and saw the size of the gap he had. Panic set in. He was convinced that something was wrong, that there was actually another lap to go, that again he had gone too early. He double-checked his bike-mounted computer. It confirmed there were only a few kilometres to go. He relaxed a little; he had in fact timed his effort perfectly.

Into the final straight and with a few cautious looks behind to make sure no one was coming back, the Texan sat up. He waved left and right, he blew kisses, he saluted the crowd and pumped his fists and shook his head as he crossed the line. Nineteen seconds later, Indurain, who for the second year running was targeting a triple crown, won the sprint for second. 'It's always difficult to get away,' the Spaniard reflected. 'There is always someone who will follow.'[196]

It was Armstrong's first major title. What happened in later years is well known and the subject of countless books and articles. Suffice to say that, following his lifetime suspension in 2012 and the stripping of all results from August 1998 until 2010, for large-scale anti-doping violations, the Texan's 1993 Worlds win remains the only major win with which he is today still credited.

One year later France's Luc Leblanc and Norway's Monica Valen took titles in Sicily, Italy. Leblanc's win was the first for France since Hinault's triumph in Sallanches fourteen years earlier while Valen's came after Longo chased back a break containing two of her teammates, including Marsal, and set up a sprint that the Norwegian won, claiming her country's first title at the Worlds. Longo had stayed separately from the French team, choosing to sleep in a different hotel and making her own travel arrangements. 'I can't understand why she didn't play the game,' said Marsal afterwards. 'As soon as I saw her I knew it was over for us. I was going to attack on the climb … then I saw Longo come up.'[197] *Le Monde's* damning verdict:

> [Longo's] ninth place finish only confirmed that she has lost some of her past talent, but that she has kept her divisive capabilities intact.[198]

Twelve months on Longo made amends. In Colombia, the day before Olano's first victory for Spain, she sealed her place in the Worlds' record books by finally breaking Yvonne Reynders' twenty-nine year record for most wins. Longo crashed on the second lap of the 88.5-kilometre race but picked herself up to ride solo to the win ahead of Marsal. On the podium there were tears in her eyes and a gash on her leg while in the pits her bike had a buckled wheel. 'I was going to stop at the pits,' Longo later said. 'But I was encouraged to carry on. My husband was in the pits and looked at my leg and said "It's nothing." When you have been racing mountain bikes you learn to recover from crashes.'[199]

Earlier in the week Longo had won the time trial, the first of four victories in that event. Another record.

***

On the day of the 1996 Worlds, the Belgian rider Johan Museeuw turned thirty-one. He had enjoyed a terrific career. Already twice a Tour of Flanders champion, he had taken his first Paris-Roubaix title earlier in the year, famously and improbably leading home a Mapei team one-two-three. Now he was in Lugano, Switzerland for a shot at the world title.

In early October, after finishing twentieth during Paris-Tours, Museeuw suddenly announced he had lost all enthusiasm for his sport. He was still leading the 1996 edition of the season-long World Cup but he was tired. 'Suddenly everything can be too much,' he said. 'It's too much for me to always fight for the World Cup.'[200]

He threatened to retire and announced he would not ride in Switzerland. But one week and a change of heart later, he was in Lugano. 'I'm going to start because I promised. I will not withdraw. I have promised and I am a person of my word,'[201] he said. For him and for Belgium, it was a good thing he did.

With two laps to go Museeuw was in a small leading group. He had already tried to escape earlier on the 9 per cent Crespera climb but too many riders went with him. Now, on the penultimate 2-kilometre climb of the Comano, he tried again.

Museeuw established a gap but he was still more than 30 kilometres and three climbs from the finish. He needed help. He looked behind and saw that Swiss rider Mauro Gianetti was trying to get across. Gianetti was riding on home roads and was motivated to make the break work, but crucially he was weaker in a sprint than the Belgian. He was the perfect companion. Museeuw knew that if the two could work together to keep ahead, and if he could stick with the Swiss over the course of the final lap, he had a great shot at grabbing the rainbow jersey.

Several times on the final climb Gianetti stood up on the pedals in a bid to get away from Museeuw but the Belgian sat on his wheel untroubled. Once they went over the top of the Crespera for the final time together the race was as good as Museeuw's. With a little more than one kilometre to go the pair slowed and talked. Museeuw led throughout that final kilometre as the pair played the ultimate, track-style, waiting game. Finally, Gianetti broke from behind and hit the front. But it was fruitless. Museeuw, by far the better fast-man, immediately came around the Swiss and won the final sprint with ease. Suddenly Museeuw's enthusiasm for cycling was rekindled.

'I've won a lot of big races, but this is special,' Museeuw said. 'This is something that stays with you for a whole year ... I wasn't the strongest rider out there today, Mauro was. But I was the smarter. In cycling, it's important to use your head ... You can celebrate your birthday with a meal and champagne, and you can also celebrate it by becoming world champion. Tonight, I'll have both.'[202]

Museeuw would ride for another eight years, adding further wins at the Tour of Flanders and Paris-Roubaix. In 2007 he confessed to not being 100 per cent honest during his career and in 2015 spoke about his career to the Belgian newspaper *De Zondag*: 'Let me say that in my time, maybe two per cent took no EPO,' he said. 'It was inevitable in that period. I am only sorry that not everyone confesses. I understand that people were disappointed. Fortunately, they also realise today that everyone then fought with equal resources and they see me as the champion of my generation.'[203]

***

As the end of the decade neared, Switzerland's Barbara Heeb (1996), Italy's Alessandra Cappellotto (1997) and the Lithuanian duo of Diana Ziliute (1998) and Edita Pucinskaite (1999) took wins in the women's races while France's Laurent Brochard (1997) and Switzerland's Oskar Camenzind (1998) claimed rainbow jerseys in the men's races. Before the end of the 1990s there remained one more race in Verona and the emergence of a young unknown Spanish rider who was just about to explode into the top-flight of cycling.

Oscar Freire was twenty-three and had spent the previous two seasons riding for Vitalicio Seguros. He had endured an injury-hit season and did not yet have a contract for the following season, but his life was about to change. 'The silence in the finishing straight was deafening when the little-know Spaniard Oscar Freire seized his opportunity to win the world title in front of a disbelieving Italian public,'[204] reported *Cycling Weekly* after the race.

With about 500 metres to go Freire had broken out of a leading group of nine that included Germany's Jan Ullrich, Belgium's Frank Vandenbroucke, Italian favourite Francesco Casagrande and the Swiss pair of Oskar Camenzind and Markus Zberg.

Reflecting on his win 17 years later, Freire explained how the make-up of that group was key to his next move. 'The only team that had two riders was the Swiss team and Camenzind was dead,' Freire said. 'So I thought I'd try. When I was separated, 20 or 30 metres, I knew it was too complicated for the group to try to follow.

Freire seized his moment and struck out for the line. Behind no one reacted, wary of towing a rival to the win. Freire had caught them all napping. By the time the rest understood that they needed to chase, it was all over and the Spaniard was completing a famous, if surprising, win. 'This was the first time that I was at the front in a big race and so I knew the other riders didn't expect me to win,' he said afterwards. 'I think that helped me.'[205] Oscar Freire's Worlds' story had just begun.

20

CATHERINE MARSAL (1990)

In 1990 France's Catherine Marsal won the rainbow jersey in Utsunomiya, Japan. Marsal had finished second the year before behind Jeannie Longo, who did not race in Japan. Marsal's win was the fifth in five straight championships for the French, and the comparisons to Longo flowed. Marsal would stand on the podium on a further two occasions but would never again win the jersey. Today she lives in Copenhagen and is the coach of the Danish women's cycling team, helping to guide Amalie Dideriksen to the country's first win in 2016.

***

Catherine Marsal:

My father was a farmer in eastern France. We were a family of eight kids, I was number six and the first girl. It was my eldest brother that started cycling first and he gave the bug to all of us. I can't say my brothers were very tender with me. They teased me a little bit as I was the first girl, so I had to fight a little bit to find my place amongst them. They gave me some hard times but in the end it was for the best.

At the age of ten, I was like, 'OK, I want to start cycling.' My mum was a little bit against it because she thought it was not a girl's sport. But I insisted, saying it is either that or soccer! So she said, 'OK, well, go ahead.'

When you are at that age you are riding with the boys, there is no girls category. There was this guy winning all the time. I watched him racing and he was winning every Sunday ... I remember saying to my brothers when I start racing I'll beat that guy. They were like, 'Yeah, yeah, sure, go home ... blah, blah, blah.' Then I started to race and came up against him. I beat him at my first, second, third race ... I think he couldn't believe he was beaten by a girl. He actually ended up quitting cycling not long after.

In 1987 Marsal won the junior world title in Bergamo, Italy. Her win catapulted her into the spotlight in France.

I remember the day I won the junior Worlds very well. I was in the breakaway with the Russian girl Aiga Zagorska who was climbing well. I was thinking, 'Oh my God, I'm second at the world championships, this is awesome.' I was already very happy to come second, I wasn't expecting to win, but I managed to beat her in the breakaway and I became champion. It was a complete surprise for me because I had never raced at that level. From there everything went very fast.

The expectation got more and more from the federation, more and more from the media. I was presented as the next Jeannie Longo. It was my first world championships but I was pushed very fast into the elite world and to succeed there at a young age.

That was really hard for me. My parents ... my dad was a farmer ... my mum looked after the house and eight kids. Neither of my parents had the time to take care of us in a way that ... I mean, we never wanted for anything at home but there were so many of us that my parents didn't have the time to look after our emotional state. So you had to sort of find your own way. We were not very good at communicating. When I was home and I was training I never expressed any sort of emotions or discussed my feelings. It was not in my instinct. So when I became junior world champion, and then again when I became world champion in the elites, everything went way above what a girl of nineteen could handle on her own. The expectations of the media became very difficult. To become elite world champion at nineteen ... it was way too early, I was never ready for that kind of attention and media coverage – it hadn't been explained to me.

We talk about this gap between junior and elite riders but for me I didn't feel it. I was training-mad, I mean I was training *a lot* and also I ... would you call it an eating disorder now? I don't know. But I was really searching to get skinnier and skinnier and skinnier and I touched the line where you can talk about, you know ... anorexia in sport. I was kind of stuck into my sort of eating disorder and the desire of success and the media pressure ... all this ... everything became too much and my body just went, 'Arghh, stop.'

I had been warned by people, you know. You need to eat, you're too skinny or you are training too much. But I was a hard-case. I'd say to people, 'What are you talking about, I'm world champion. It's working.' I sort of had to experience things for myself, to make my own mistakes. My best friends, my teammates ... they all said you have to be careful, you have to eat. But I didn't want to listen to them ... I couldn't deal with it. It was a difficult time in my life.

In 1989 Marsal rode her first Worlds as an elite rider. She finished second behind Longo.

In 1989 the desire of Jeannie to be world champion again was very clear. It was really Jeannie and then the rest of the team. She wasn't in the hotel with us, she was doing her own thing. It was pretty obvious early on that Jeannie would ride her own race and I would ride mine. I know that the same thoughts were in the heads of all my teammates. She was invincible that day. She was so strong on the climb. So really my getting second place was a surprise to everyone, for myself as well. I remember at some point, maybe the second-last lap, I was alone with Jeannie on that climb in Chambéry and she dropped me. I mean it was *mano a mano* – it was a little bit like the situation later in 1995 in Colombia, in Duitama, when Jeannie and I found ourselves on the last lap alone. But, you know, certainly it was a big surprise that somebody like me came second at those world championships. But I had the freedom to race against her.

Jeannie and I had a friendship where we loved each other, then we hated each other, then we loved each other. The competition between us all the time dominated our relationship. I mean I won only when I was performing at my best. She beat me more than I beat her. And of course when I did beat her it was even sweeter because she was a monument of world cycling, she was really, really strong in the mid-1980s and early 90s. The media always played with us: Longo, Marsal, Longo, Marsal, Longo, Marsal. It was difficult for me, at nineteen, to be called the next Jeannie Longo when I was battling for my own identity, for my own sake, for my own personal life. So to be called in the media the next Jeannie Longo … I remember saying, 'No, I'm not Jeannie Longo, I'm Catherine Marsal.' Sometimes it could sound arrogant but I was really fighting for my own identity. It was enormous to be compared to her at that time but I really wanted to be recognised for myself.

In 1990 Marsal won the Worlds in style, finishing more than three minutes in front of second-placed Ruthie Matthes of the USA. Earlier in the season Marsal had won the French national championship, the Tour de l'Aude and the Giro.

CATHERINE MARSAL (1990)

I remember the 1990 season as being a season where everything was calm. At that time all the international races were ridden in the national team and we had an extensive programme where we went to the Tour of Texas, the Tour of Norway ... Tour of Italy ... and I won them all. Not by much ... at the Giro, against Maria Canins ... I remember almost fainting at the side of the road because it was so hard to break Canins. It was always a very tough fight to win those stage races.

In Japan we had four or five days to prepare. I remember feeling really anxious on the start line. I watched a video of the race and at the start you can see all the other girls chatting amongst themselves, but on that video I am silent, in my bubble, focused, not moving an inch. In the days before the race and on the day itself I just focused and focused and focused. I am protecting myself from the rest of the girls, everyone, even my teammates. I was just trying to keep everything under control ... not letting anyone in. That's how I was. I was very introverted, very hard to reach. Very few people knew the real me. It was a way of managing a race and a big event like the world championships, but on the other hand it was very dangerous because I wouldn't let the outside world in.

When we started to race we went up this climb that was so hard. I wasn't attacking, I was just riding my own tempo. I remember even at that pace no one could follow me so I went on my own. At the end of that first lap they caught me on the start/finish line and one of my teammates said, 'No one can touch you today.' I asked her what she meant and she said, 'You will do what you want today, no one can follow you.'

On the next time up the climb I attacked and went on my own and I rode to become world champion by over three minutes. When I was on my own and in my own zone it was really hard, I was concentrating so hard. I weighed only 47kg then ... of course when you are only 47kg you might not have the highest power in the world but because of your weight you are so much stronger than all of the other girls, your power/weight ratio is so much better than anyone else's. All race long I was focusing on only one thing: crossing the line first. Now, when I sometimes look at pictures from the race, I think, 'Oh my God, there were people on the side of the road.' I can't even remember them cheering for me.

The reaction to my win was unbelievable. I went back to my parents and to my normal life to go training. All of sudden all these photographers appeared without even setting appointments. I remember one morning: ding-dong, the bell rang and it was a photographic agency saying they had come to take pictures of me. I said, 'What do you mean, you've come to take pictures of me?' They just said you have to let us. You're the world champion, you have to have pictures taken. Without me knowing it my parents had signed a contract with those guys and it was an exclusive contract. My parents thought they were just signing like a consent agreement to say they could use a picture of their daughter but it was actually a contract of exclusivity. Then came another company taking the same amount of pictures … we made a lot of mistakes like that … we had no idea what this business was like. In retrospect it would've been good to have had a manager before that, or at least someone who could explain things like that. We got ourselves into trouble at first. We were like, 'What? Really? We did that? OK, sorry!' It wasn't on purpose but it was very difficult for all the family, everyone suffered.

Then they wanted you to defend that jersey, to perform even better. How can you want to perform even better than that season? It's impossible. You sort of have to come down from that situation and accept that you can come second or third and so on. When I was second at Tour de l'Aude in 1991 I remember it was immediately, 'Marsal Second!' I mean, what? I was only twenty but people accepted that a race could be defined as, 'Marsal Second! Marsal Defeated!' If I'm second it's not bad, it's not a terrible result. It's OK to say that now but back then the difference between first place and second place was very difficult to accept. That created a lot of doubt in myself and a lot of stress. It pushed me to lose even more weight and to train even more. It fed my desire … it pushed me deeper and deeper and deeper and also made it difficult for me to be at home.

CATHERINE MARSAL (1990)

I remember the end of 1991 when I had to defend my title in Stuttgart. I was almost relieved to lose the jersey [Marsal finished 27th]. Ahhh, now I can breathe again. It feels kind of incredible to say that now. Later in my career, in 1997, when I went for the jersey again in San Sebastián, I remember feeling I was ready to be world champion and have the jersey on my shoulders again. I ended up third but I remember the feeling that I would like to have the jersey again, that I would like it again to appreciate it.

That jersey weighed heavy on me. I was not equipped to deal with it. Not in my family, not me … all the media around me … I was not ready. Absolutely not ready.

After her 1990 win Marsal endured a few tough seasons where she struggled to regain her previous form.

I'd had these nice high seasons when I won the juniors and then the elite world titles and then I had a few years down, when I was going through my [hard] times when I had to figure out how to become good again. So I mean 1992, 1993, 1994 were difficult. A big turning point in my career was 1995, when I attempted the world hour record. Corima [the French bike maker] wanted me to try this record that hadn't been beaten for six years. The challenge sounded good to me but my God, really this was a mountain, something very serious that requires preparation. But I threw myself into it and I beat Jeannie's record when no one, absolutely no one, except one of my best friends, believed that I could do it. Even the guy who was doing my training said to Corima the day before the ride, 'I want to prepare you, she is not going to beat it.' But I did beat it. I didn't have the odds on my side but the magical day happened. That was the turning point of my career. All of a sudden things were possible again. That record is the thing I'm most proud of because I started from a very bad place.

It taught me things that I still use in my professional life today. To focus on the hour was a learning process on understanding where your limits are, how much further you can go, how you can trick the mind to go through periods of discomfort. I remember I was very good at time rials after that hour record because it is only mental, accepting the pain and getting through it. You unplug your brain from that feeling of pain and then you can go to another zone and that zone is what pushes you further. I think that is sometimes what makes the difference between two riders with equal abilities, if one rider is able to mentally accept that position, of being in pain, and to let it go … that's the thing.

Ten years after her hour record Marsal moved to Denmark. By 2016 she was the coach of Denmark's women when Amalie Dideriksen claimed the world title.

I came to Denmark in 2005 and I didn't know how long I would stay, but it turns out here I am more than ten years later. In 2015 we started a programme for women's cycling. Amalie has only just become an elite rider. She has her coach who has looked after her since she was sixteen, he is also one of the national coaches in Denmark. So her physical level has been taken care of for a long time. The way I played it with Amalie was to build a team around her and create a team spirit. These girls are used to racing against each other on trade teams all the time and they are competing at the national championship – they are always racing against each other. Then you take them with the national team and you have to say, 'Hey guys, you need to focus for one rider, Amalie is the leader and you have to help her to try to win the Worlds.' That's where I have a role to play to create this team spirit and to choose the right girls to support Amalie and devote themselves 100 per cent to her.

We do it by talking and explaining that by sacrificing yourself for your leader and getting the world championship title, even though you are not the one who is going to carry the jersey, you are promoting your image. If someone is driving the race for themselves and trying to make their own place it is going to show to the world that the team spirit is not there. It is not in the interest of anyone to play that game. The beauty of this sport is that today you are working for Amalie but maybe in two years' time Amalie is going to sacrifice herself for another person who is stronger than her and help that person go on to victory. And that person might be you. So you have to have long talks, take notice of the personalities of everyone and give them opportunity to express themselves. Give attention to everyone but, when it comes to a race like the Worlds, then have the respect and the authority to enforce your strategy.

The experience of the world championships in Doha was unbelievable for Amalie, and for her teammates Julie [Leith] and Cecilie [Uttrup Ludwig] together. I really felt as happy as if I had won myself and had a strong sense of pride which I still feel. It's not that people were convinced of the potential of Danish women's cycling, but I kept pushing it and then all of a sudden comes this kind of result and it's sort of a relief because it means the decisions you made for two years were right. The world championship jersey always represents tremendously the pinnacle of what a rider or a national coach can achieve. It's an honour.

21

THE LION KING ROARS

If Oscar Freire was a virtual unknown when he grabbed his first rainbow jersey in Verona, by the time of his follow-up win everybody knew him. In 2000 he joined Mapei, perhaps the biggest team in the world, to race alongside the likes of Michele Bartoli, Andrea Tafi and Johan Museeuw, each one a Monument winner.

Freire was the world champion and in that company the pressure to deliver was immediate. But deliver the Spaniard did. He won his first race for the team, the Trofeo Mallorca, and performed well throughout the season, taking third in Milan-Sanremo and scoring stage wins at Tirreno-Adriatico and at the Vuelta. Freire had felt huge pressure moving to Mapei but with those results he relaxed. At the 2000 Worlds in Plouay he had finished third, beaten in a twenty-five-rider sprint by Latvia's Romans Vainsteins and Poland's Zbigniew Spruch. That result sealed a victorious championships for former Soviet states with Zinaida Stahurskaya winning the women's race for Belarus.

Rasa Polikeviciute of Lithuania won the 2001 women's race in Lisbon and the day after her win Freire took to the start line of the men's race. The course had been billed as the hardest for five years with twenty-one laps of a 12.1-kilometre circuit in the hills above the city, climbing the Alto da Serafina and the Alto d'Alvito, with gradients touching 9 per cent. Neither were particularly long but the short circuit meant the climbs came rapidly – forty-two times the peloton would have to head upwards – with more than a fifth of the 254-kilometre race spent climbing.

An aggressive race with a win from a small final selection of riders was predicted. France's Richard Virenque, fresh from a Paris-Tours win a week earlier, was expected to shine, as was Germany's Jan Ullrich, who had taken the time trial crown a few days earlier and then said that all his preparation had been for the road race not the time trial.[206]

Despite the tough circuit and the high pace – only two elite world championship races had been ridden faster – the forecast split did not happen. Masterful riding by the Dutch and Spanish teams meant that as the race entered its final 5 kilometres there were still forty-five riders in with a shout. Once the sprint was on, Oscar Freire took the wheel of German Erik Zabel, who himself was looking for someone to lead him out. With the line approaching, Freire flirted with disaster, squeezing through a narrow gap between the Netherlands' Erik Dekker and the road-side barriers, but survived to take his second world title in three years.

There had been no shortage of riders trying to get away in the preceding 250 kilometres. Virenque, Ullrich and Italy's Gilberto Simoni all tried during the final laps, all were brought back – Simoni by a peloton led by his compatriot Paolo Lanfranchi, making for the curious sight of one Italian being chased by another. It was yet another case of an Italian team seemingly riding to different agendas. Lanfranchi later said he thought Simoni had already been brought back into the fold while Paolo Bettini, who missed out on the jersey by centimetres in the final dash to the line, complained of being hampered in the sprint by teammate Bartoli. 'If you look at the video, it seems impossible that Freire won it and that I have not found the space,' he said. 'Cursed 15 centimetres! Someone could have given me space, the orders were clear … the dream vanished two metres from the line.'[207]

Bartoli refused to accept the Italian team failed to work well together: 'It is not so,' he said. 'So much so that on the last lap I had yelled at Simoni to get away because he seemed the best of all of us.'[208]

Also riding in Lisbon was a young Welsh woman called Nicole Cooke. The year before she had taken Britain's first gold medal at the Worlds for eighteen years, winning the junior road race. It was no fluke. Even though she was only seventeen, Cooke was already gaining a reputation for attention to detail and had visited the Plouay course twelve months earlier in preparation. In Lisbon, Cooke followed that win with the double, becoming only the second junior rider to take the road race and the time trial at the same championships, matching Canada's Geneviève Jeanson's 1999 wins.

Cooke was up against far stronger teams but dominated the race. 'The rest of the field followed her like sheep as she dictated the race from the front'[209] reported *Cycling Weekly*. Just one month earlier Cooke had won the junior rainbow jersey at the mountain bike cross-county Worlds in Colorado. Four world titles in little more than twelve months was the start of a remarkable career.

***

If Italy left the 2001 Worlds as a team only in the loosest sense of the word, in 2002 they were a picture of perfect harmony, even if Bettini, the man who had so narrowly missed out in Lisbon, was still talking about what had happened in that dash to the line. 'Last year, in Lisbon, at the end we had ten *azzurri* out of forty riders but only Nardello gave me a hand and so I ended second,' he told *La Stampa*. 'Over the past few years something strange has always happened in the national team, but the episode in Lisbon was really something.'[210]

Zolder in 2002 brought a course as flat as a Worlds was ever likely to see. The 12.8-kilometre course was for large parts held on the Belgian motor circuit. The two hills, the Bolderberg and the Pitshelling, were neither long enough nor steep enough to be anything other than a minor inconvenience to the professional peloton. This was a Worlds circuit for a sprinter if there ever was one.

Mario Cipollini, aka the Lion King, was Italy's main man and a sprinter par excellence, The thirty-five-year-old from Lucca was no stranger to attention, in fact he lived for it. The Italian had a reputation for enjoying the high life, playing up to his playboy image and perfectly sculpted physique by turning up to the sport's biggest races dressed as Julius Caesar or in animal-print skinsuits and riding a bike with images of model Pamela Anderson adorning the handlebars. Cipollini liked to turn heads and to shock, but even a cycling world accustomed to such stunts could not quite believe it when 'Super Mario' announced in mid-2002 that he was retiring from the sport.

Cipollini had won Milan-Sanremo earlier in the year, his first (and only) Monument. He had just taken six stages and the points jersey at the Giro and everything seemed to be gearing up nicely towards the Worlds – the first time he would pull on the blue jersey of the national team at the event. But then his Acqua & Sapone team did not secure a wildcard invite to the Tour and on 9 July the Italian issued a statement saying he was through with the sport: '[The] disappointment at not being able to compete for victories in the Tour de France, and the disappointment that the main sponsor of my team has not recognised the value of my sacrifice ... has forced me to take the drastic decision to say enough with cycling. In the next few days, I will explain the motives of this choice,'[211] Cipollini said in a statement.

At a press conference a few days later he complained of the atmosphere within his team and the lack of sponsors willing to invest in him. Cipollini was walking through cycling's exit door but he was not quite locking it behind him. 'For the moment this is my decision. Maybe in two weeks I will wake up and think of those who have followed me throughout all these years and decide to come back,'[212] he concluded.

In fact it would be a little over three weeks before it was confirmed that Cipollini was returning after the briefest of retirements, that is if he had ever truly been away. Just days after Cipollini's press conference Italian national team coach, Franco Ballerini, had told reporters he knew 'Cipo' was training with his lead out man Giovanni Lombardi and said he had two weeks to make up his mind if he still wanted to be considered for the Worlds. Now Cipollini's mind was made up. He was back. Cipollini went to the

Vuelta, won three of the first seven stages and then abandoned the race to focus on Zolder.

Apart from a dramatic crash in the final few kilometres bringing down or impeding all but the leading thirty-five or so riders, the 2002 race played out as many had thought it would. A couple of breaks formed and built a decent lead only to be brought back when the right time came. On the final lap the Italian team who had controlled the race superbly all day were all massed at the front – eleven blue jerseys perfectly placed, and in amongst them was Super Mario.

It was coming down to a mass sprint and everyone knew whose wheel they needed to be on if they were to have any chance – Cipollini's. Behind the Italian a battle royal was raging between Australia's Robbie McEwen and Germany's Erik Zabel for that prime spot.

One by one Italy peeled off, working for their man. Into the final kilometre Alessandro Petacchi did a huge turn before giving way to Lombardi, the man with whom Cipollini had been training with during his 'retirement'. Lombardi guided Super Mario to the 200-metre mark before leaving it to his leader. Cipollini hit the front and that was that. It never really looked like McEwen or Zabel could do anything to prevent Cipollini from winning. Cipollini still had 100 metres to sprint when first Bettini and then Lombardi both raised their arms in victory behind him. It had been a textbook display of team riding by the Italians who had given the Lion King the perfect lead out. The team had been unified all day, no better illustrated than by the spontaneous celebrations behind Cipollini as he crossed the line. 'I couldn't afford to make mistakes after everything my team had done for me,'[213] Cipollini said afterwards.

It was the fastest world championships in history – the average speed was 46.538 km/h, more than 3.5 km/h faster than the previous record set two years previously in Plouay. Cipollini, buoyed by the thought of wearing the rainbow jersey quickly put all thoughts of 'retirement' behind him. He spoke of winning a second Milan-Sanremo and beating Alfredo Binda's seventy-year record of forty-one Giro stages (he had forty at the time) while wearing the rainbow bands. He would miss out on the former, coming fourth behind Bettini, but achieve the latter, before finally retiring in 2005 and staging a brief comeback in 2008. In 2012 he hosted a party in a nightclub to mark the tenth anniversary of his win, with members of the team celebrating with him. 'We were all world champions that day and showed how to race as a national team,'[214] he said.

Some eleven years after Cipollini's win, *La Gazzetta dello Sport* published a front-page story that perhaps shed a little more light on that short summer 'retirement' in 2002. 'Operacion Puerto – Here are the cards that accuse Cipollini,' ran the headline on Saturday 9 February 2013. The story alleged that a doping programme had been faxed to a number allegedly linked to Cipollini that detailed a range of prohibited products and practices to be taken and followed throughout the year, including a course of detectable anabolics during the period of his brief retirement.[215] Cipollini issued a fierce denial through his lawyer and the Italian Olympic Committee (CONI) announced an investigation. Then, nothing. Later Cipollini's lawyer, Giuseppe Napoleone, told *Procycling* that a file was never opened.[216]

With barely a rise of note, and with wide and well-surfaced roads and long straights punctuating the technical corners, the Zolder course and the final bunch sprint had perfectly suited Cipollini. The day before, however, the women's peloton had delivered a very different race, even if it was equally fast. Sweden's Susanne Ljungskog took her country's second rainbow jersey, nineteen years after Marianne Berglund had claimed its first, in a crash-hit race. Ljungskog prevailed from a four-rider breakaway after averaging 42.840 km/h, by far the fastest women's world championship road race at the time. The following year Ljungskog defended her title in Canada while Igor Astarloa took the biggest win of his career in the men's race. It was Spain's third win in five years.

***

'So was this really a man worthy of the title champion of the world? Only time will tell whether Freire lives up to this win,'[217] *Cycling Weekly* had said at the time of Freire's first win in 1999. Five years later we had our answer. Freire was one of the most feared fast-men in the peloton, a marked man and a rider others looked towards. He was the leader of the Spanish team and since that win, aside from 2002, he had never finished an elite Worlds outside of the top ten. In the spring of 2004 Freire had claimed his first Monument, winning Milan-Sanremo. Now he would cement his place in Worlds history with a record-equalling three wins in six editions.

In 2004 the event returned to Verona, scene of Freire's first triumph. This time the course was different – a little shorter but with more climbs of the tough 3.5-kilometre Torricelle thrown in. Again Italy and Spain dominated the pre-race talk, with Paolo Bettini, Freire and Alejandro Valverde all cited as favourites. Italy's 'Little Prince', Damiano Cunego, who had won the Giro earlier in the year at twenty-two years old and would go on to take the Tour of Lombardy two weeks after these Worlds, was also primed. 'Bettini is the captain but I am ready,' Cunego told *La Stampa* on the eve of the race. 'The roles are clear and the team is very united and competitive, with excellent *gregari*. A nice group, in which everyone will be important.'[218]

While the first half of the race was animated by a two-man break that established a lead of more than seven minutes, the real drama was unfolding behind. Bettini suffered a couple of mechanical problems and during one wheel change badly banged his knee on the open door of his support car. He was suffering, his knee causing him great pain. Team members dropped back to try to nurse him through the worst of it but it was no good. With just over 60 kilometres to ride Bettini was talking with Ballerini. He abandoned the race. Now all of Italy looked to the Little Prince.

While Italy was dealing with the change in strategy, Spain were calm. For them, the race was going exactly to plan. 'The team knew that if we rode like that [as a team] we could win more world championships,' Freire said when looking back on the race.

With less than 45 kilometres remaining Spain became more active. Freire was their leader and the team were working only to ensure the race came down to a sprint so their man could deliver the goods. On the final lap, following a strong move from Italy's Ivan Basso, a group of twenty-five formed at the front of the race. Remarkably a fifth of them were Spanish and they took to the front, closely followed by Italy, including Cunego.

Under the *flamme rouge* Freire still had three riders in complete control. The only tense moment came when Germany's Danilo Hondo hit the front trying to lead out Zabel, but his teammate was not on his wheel, Valverde was. And behind Valverde was Freire. With around 200 metres to go Hondo swung off and looked to his left, only to see Valverde power through. Then, with Valverde's turn done, Freire took over to blast over the line and claim his third title in five years, beating Zabel by one length and joining Alfredo Binda, Rik Van Steenbergen and Eddy Merckx as the only men to claim three elite road-race world titles.

'I preferred to follow the wheel of Valverde,' Freire explained afterwards. 'I knew that we were going to have a difficult sprint with Zabel and O'Grady. But I had confidence ... I was sure that Alejandro would allow me to pitch things perfectly. He also showed that he could win. I owe him a lot.'[219] After decades without success, Spain had claimed five world championship titles in the space of nine years, three of them courtesy of Freire. It was a golden period for the country but one that would end in Verona.

In the women's race Germany's Judith Arndt rode solo to a ten-second win ahead of Italy's Tatiana Guderzo. Arndt had won silver in the road race at the Athens Olympics earlier in the year, flicking a middle-finger salute that was caught on camera as she crossed the line in protest at the non-selection of her partner, Petra Rossner. In Verona Arndt recorded Germany's first title in more than twenty years. 'I'm not sad or angry anymore,'[220] she said.

***

In 2005 a twenty-four-year-old Tom Boonen exploded into the very top echelons of the sport. First he won the Tour of Flanders, attacking with nine kilometres to go and staying away to win by thirty-five seconds, and then claimed Paris-Roubaix in a three-rider sprint in the famous old velodrome. Belgium's new favourite son, Boonen had achieved a rare double, something that only eight riders had done before him and that the likes of Eddy Merckx and Johan Museeuw never managed in their own stellar careers. Then, in September, at the Worlds in Madrid, his season got better still.

Dominating the build-up was again the issue of national versus trade team alliances. Australia's Robbie McEwen rode for the Belgian team Davitamon-Lotto and three of his Belgian teammates were also riding for Belgium in Madrid. Who would they support? Their own national teammates, who they raced against for the rest of the season, or their trade teammate McEwen? Even the riders became involved in the debate. After Peter Van Petegem, one of the Belgian Davitamon riders in contention for a start in Madrid, had led McEwen to victory in Paris-Brussels the Australian quipped, 'If the Belgian national coach watched the race today, he'll know he has to take more of our team to Madrid. They know better than anyone else how to guide a sprinter to the finish line.'[221]

Then there were the Italians who rode for the Belgian Quick Step team. Would they work for Fassa Bortolo's Alessandro Petacchi or would they be swayed by the opportunity to secure the jersey for Boonen? Petacchi had long been targeting the race. 'For months, we have prepared for this day,' wrote La Stampa on the eve of the race. 'He [Petacchi] was the only one to twice inspect the parcours while his opponents were riding the Tour or elsewhere. And he is the only one who has already mastered it, a few weeks ago winning the stage of the Vuelta which ended in the exact spot where, we hope, he will unleash his cry, in front of the Bernabeu that still resounds with the shouts of Tardelli,'[222] a reference to the famous goal celebration of Italian footballer Marco Tardelli after he scored in the 1982 World Cup final. Petacchi also seemed in form – he had won five stages at the Vuelta – while Boonen had abandoned both the Tour and the Vuelta after his impressive spring.

Italy, Belgium and Spain were all active during the race, placing riders in the break, with Bettini looking strong. Behind, Australia was leading the chase while the leaders began to launch wave upon wave of attacks, all trying to get away alone. Curiously, despite team tactics being laid down for the six-strong team to ride for Roger Hammond, the early stages of the race brought the British riders Tom Southam and Charly Wegelius to the fore. 'I don't know why they took the initiative to ride,' Hammond said after the race. 'It wasn't our team plan and I still don't think it was up to us to do that. We didn't have enough riders as it was, and I don't know … we will find out later on.'[223]

After a split of six riders went off the front of the break, Belgium ratcheted up the chase and as the leaders swept into the final 500 metres twenty or so riders were closing fast. Boonen's teammates had been instrumental in closing the gap but Petacchi had missed the split and was caught in the second-chase group. His chances were over. Belgium had done all they could for their young leader, now it was up to Boonen. With 200 metres to go he hit the front of the race for the first time and stayed there, recording Belgium's first win since Museeuw's in 1996.

The result left the Italian press angered, saying that a team that was supposed to dominate the race had been nothing but flops. Petacchi said he did not have the legs by the end leaving Bettini, who finished thirteenth as the top-placed Italian, to say it would have been more beneficial to him to have known that earlier than 8 kilometres from the finish. Ballerini, the national team coach, insisted that the Italians had ridden the race correctly: 'The strategy was right,' he said. 'We had Bettini in an important break and it forced a sprint, as we predicted.'[224] Unfortunately for them, Italy's sprinter just was not there when it mattered.

In Britain, meanwhile, the race brought severe repercussions. It later emerged that the early work of Southam and Wegelius, who rode for the Italian trade team Liquigas, had been as a result of an agreement to assist the Italian team in controlling the first half of the race before abandoning. They paid for the decision with their British Cycling careers. Team boss John Herety also tendered his resignation. 'I regret what happened,' Wegelius told *Cycling Weekly* in 2011. 'I wish it hadn't happened like that, I underestimated how much people care about those things and also the power of live television.'[225]

In the women's race Regina Schleicher made it two wins in successive years for Germany, winning a thirty-three rider sprint. Britain's Nicole Cooke took second with Australia's Oenone Wood third. Afterwards Cooke was in tears after taking her second podium spot in three years but again missing out on the jersey. 'Now it's another twelve months I have to watch another rider race in the rainbow jersey,'[226] she reflected. In 2006 Cooke would again have to watch as another rider beat her to the title she so badly wanted.

***

Two years after taking the junior world title in Verona, the Netherlands' Marianne Vos was on the start line of her first elite Worlds road race in Salzburg. It had already been a tremendous season for the nineteen-year-old. Nine months earlier she had taken her first elite level rainbow jersey by winning the cyclo-cross title and then, five months later, claimed her first road national title. Now Vos was about to take on the best the world could throw at her.

In some ways Vos was an unknown quantity. Yes, she was young, yes it was her first senior Worlds, and yes there were far more experienced and battle-scarred rivals around her, some with the bit well and truly between the teeth having come close to the jersey before. But Vos had already won races against many of the same women in the months building up to the race and everyone in the peloton already knew what she was capable of, including her more experienced teammates. The only question was whether she was ready to deliver on the biggest stage.

On the penultimate lap Cooke attacked. Cooke was the world's number-one ranked rider and two weeks earlier had been crowned the winner of the World Cup. Recounting her preparation for these Worlds in her 2014 autobiography, *The Breakaway*, Cooke writes that her move had been planned well in advance as she hoped to create a small break of talented climbers.[227]

Only Switzerland's Nicole Brändli and Vos could match Cooke, but ultimately the move faltered and after a flurry of attacks and counter-attacks when the same three broke away only to be brought back again, the race came down to a sprint.

In the blur of a bunch sprint, split-second decisions can make the difference between a gold medal, the jersey and hearing your own national anthem, or a medal of a different colour or, worse, a lonely and sad trudge back to the team bus. As the sprint started Vos was in sixth spot, behind Germany's Trixi Worrack. Cooke was fourth, on Oenone Wood's wheel. Vos went left, Cooke went right. The Dutchwoman would later tell me that she knew Worrack and Cooke were the riders to watch out for and that she wanted the left-hand side of the road because it was the shortest way around the final bend. Vos powered towards the line with Worrack in her wake to take second while Cooke, tiring as the line approached, narrowly held on to third ahead of Italy's Noemi Cantele. Both Vos and Worrack had teammates in that final selection that had worked to set up the finale they wanted, while Cooke had to do her work herself. But Vos was by far the strongest in the sprint and Cooke was generous in her praise afterwards, saying, 'She was doing her fair share of work in the break and she was strongest in the sprint, so she's a just winner.'[228]

'Marianne Vos surprised herself and the world,' ran the headline in the Dutch newspaper *NRC Handelsblad*. Vos told the paper how she quickly looked back with 50 metres to go. 'I saw no one. It can't be true, I thought. I'm surprised if I win a criterium, can you imagine how I feel now' she said. Meanwhile the national team coach, Johan Lammerts, simply said: 'Physically and mentally. She's a killer.'[229]

***

Going into those 2006 world championships, Italy's Paolo Bettini was a man with little to prove. The thirty-two-year-old had won a handful of Monuments, taken stages at all three Grand Tours, won the points jersey twice at the Giro, claimed Olympic gold in Athens and been crowned winner of the season-long World Cup three seasons in a row – 2002 to 2004. But the rainbow jersey was missing.

At the Vuelta, a week or two before the Worlds, Bettini was asked by *VeloNews* what still motivated him after such a successful career. 'I have to say the world championships,' he replied. 'This is the only thing I need to win to make a perfect career, even though I have to say I am very content to have won what I have already ... The world title by far is the most important one.'[230]

With a couple of climbs punctuating the 22-kilometre circuit, Italy's coach Franco Ballerini selected Bettini as the team's leader before saying that the route would only prove to be selective if raced hard.[231] Sure enough Italy were busy all day, present in every meaningful break and initiating many themselves. On the final climb Bettini attacked but could not establish a decisive gap and was caught on the fall back down towards Salzburg.

With one kilometre to go it looked like Italy's efforts might have been in vain. Despite their work a fifty-strong bunch sprint was on the cards. Then Spain's Samuel Sánchez went to the front just before a tight right-hand bend, taking Alejandro Valverde with him, followed by Germany's Erik Zabel. Bettini was fourth wheel going into that bend, alongside Spain's Xavier Florencio who slowed down those behind. Round the next corner and the four were away. Spain may have initiated the move but it had played out perfectly for Bettini. With 500 metres to ride, the decisive blow had been struck.

Bettini claimed his rainbow jersey by half a length. A life in cycling that had begun with a bike built from parts found lying about by his father that was handed to him when he was seven had finally delivered one of cycling's most coveted jerseys. After the controversy of the previous year it was a welcome boost to national coach Ballerini. 'When, on the last climb, about 10 kilometres from the end, I saw the Norwegian [Thor] Hushovd literally planted on the pedals ... Then I realised that we had worked well,'[232] Ballerini reflected. 'Thank you to everyone,' Bettini said. 'My career is now perfect.'[233]

**

The following year Bettini became the first man in fifteen years to defend his title, winning from a small bunch sprint and crowning a golden weekend for Italy in the German city of Stuttgart after twenty-year-old Marta Bastianelli had taken Italy's first women's title in ten years. Arguably Bettini's biggest challenge in Stuttgart was getting to the start line. The organisers had negotiated an arrangement with the UCI that meant they would not accept any rider at the start who had not signed an anti-doping pledge. Bettini disliked some of the clauses and refused to sign. The UCI said the issue was a moral one and that it could not legally prevent a rider's entry just because they had not signed the agreement. Bettini reportedly signed a modified version but the organisers remained dissatisfied and they launched a court injunction attempting to block the Italian's participation. The courts found in Bettini's favour.

While Bettini, who during his twelve-year career never recorded an anti-doping violation, celebrated his win others threw their arms in the air in frustration. With cycling embroiled in a series of doping controversies, and with a number of riders embattled in various doping-related stories, the sport was reeling. In *The Daily Telegraph* Daniel Freibe described the 2007 championships as having, 'all the dignity and splendour of a Britney Spears night on the town.'[234]

As he crossed the line Bettini had mimed the shooting of a gun. 'It's been a week shooting at me, but the gesture was not directed at anyone in particular,' he said. 'But if someone felt targeted, it means that he had good reason to fear my shots.'[235]

22

OSCAR FREIRE
(1999, 2001, 2004)

No man has won more world championship road races than the Spaniard Oscar Freire. He shares his record of three titles with Alfredo Binda, Rik Van Steenbergen and Eddy Merckx. Freire rode his first senior Worlds in 1998, finishing seventeenth, before taking his first rainbow jersey twelve months later. Further wins followed in 2001 and 2004. A three-time winner of Milan-Sanremo, Freire won stages at the Vuelta and the Tour and took the green jersey at the latter in 2008. By Freire's own admission he was not a prolific winner, particularly when compared with rivals such as Erik Zabel or Robbie McEwen, but instead he targeted major races. Freire retired in 2012 after a fifteen-year career and now lives in northern Spain.

***

Oscar Freire:

I have three brothers and I am the youngest. I started playing football in the beginning but only for one or two months. A small cycling club was close to my home so I said, 'OK, maybe I'll go cycling with them.' I don't know why I started but at first it was only as a hobby. I was very young.

I was cycling for two or three years and I started winning but still it was really only a hobby. I didn't have any idols at that time, I wasn't watching cycling on TV or anything. Then, as the years went by, cycling got better and better for me. When I was a junior I rode some very good races and was winning and so I thought I'd try to continue. I passed into the under-23s and I rode the Tour of the Basque Country – in my region in Spain. My region is not the most important region in cycling but the Tour of the Basque Country is a very important race in Spain, so all the good riders were racing there and I was racing with them and doing well.

When I was an amateur I only did two international races. I did the European Championships where I finished in fifth place and then I did the world championships as an under-23 rider [Freire came second]. For Spanish people to ride an international race was unusual; now they ride a lot outside of Spain but before, when I was an amateur, nobody was riding international races. So I rode only two races but they were two important races and I got very good results. Before I came second in those under-23 world championships I had signed for a professional team [for the next season] so it was perfect for me.

In 1999 Freire took his first world championship win in Verona. He was just twenty-three and it was only his second season as a professional, riding for the Vitalicio Seguros team. At the time of his win Freire had not secured a contract for the following year.

It was at that moment my most important victory for sure. I was injured in my second year as a professional and I didn't race much. It was the most complicated year of my career because I had this injury and it was only my second year as a professional and I didn't have a contract for the next season. I didn't have a lot of races from when I was injury-free until the end of the year but I was really focused and had a lot of energy, so I thought I'd try to do something. I said, 'Now I'm feeling good so I have to train hard, I have to focus.' But I never expected to win the world championships.

I thought I had to be at the front because it is a one-day race. I had experience in that kind of race, not in the world championships maybe but on that type of *parcours*. I felt good. I'd done a lot of training and I thought I had to try to be at the front and then see what happens. I never really expected to be in the group of favourites but then, when I was there, I thought now I have the chance to win.

Each lap there were fewer and fewer riders, the climbing was not so steep so it was good for me. I told myself that my finish was the top of the final climb and that if I passed that climb in the front group then I had a good chance to finish well. When I was in that front group it was a perfect situation for me, nobody knew me. I was really clever and really smart when I was racing, I did a lot of races that had that kind of situation, not as a professional perhaps but before ... in my region, in my country, in the Tour of the Basque Country. Those races normally finished with a small group. We didn't have big bunch sprints in the amateurs and we were always racing in small groups in similar situations to that world championship. So I thought, 'Nobody knows me so now I have to take this chance ... now is the moment to win, why not?'

When Oskar Camenzind attacked in the final kilometres I followed but nobody asked me to pull. Sometimes I passed the attacking rider and helped a little bit, but not much. They were pulling like crazy because they thought who is this guy? He can't win the world championships so why should he pull? I didn't expend a lot of energy before the sprint, I was following the attacking riders but I arrived with good legs. When we turned the last corner I worried the finish line was too far but I thought maybe I should try to attack and if somebody follows me then I'll stop immediately but if not I'll continue. At that moment Camenzind was pulling, I remember, but he was also empty, so I said this is the moment to attack. I attacked and looked behind and no one was following so I thought now I have to keep going.

I knew in that situation that any riders who pulled to get across to me for sure they would not be the world champion. So nobody was trying to pull at that time. It was definitely the most critical moment of the race because if somebody had followed me I would have stopped, but then that person would not have won either. If there are two or three riders from the same national team in a break then it is really complicated to do something like that. But the only team that had two riders was the Swiss team and Camenzind was dead. When I had 20 or 30 metres I knew it was too complicated for the group to try to follow.

I remember Markus Zberg was second. He was really angry because he was thinking we would arrive all together and so he would be world champion. The following year, when he saw me at different races and where I was also winning the sprints, he said he was more relaxed because even if we had arrived all together in those Worlds maybe he still would have been second. But back then nobody knew me. Nobody knew I was a sprinter. Not even me.

It changed everything in my life. In my career and in my private life that moment changed a lot. I was a normal person. Everybody was thinking who is this guy? Not only the Spanish people, but the cycling community around Europe. Everybody was looking for information because, while in my team a lot of riders were saying he is a champion, he is a good rider, nobody expected that victory. For me it was difficult because I was really young and I'd had a very bad year so I didn't know what to do. I remember for one week I didn't sleep, I was really nervous, I had a lot of pressure. At that moment I didn't have a contract for the next year. It was a nice situation, but a complicated situation as well.

OSCAR FREIRE (1999, 2001, 2004)

Following his win, Freire signed for the Italian-registered Mapei team, one of the biggest teams in cycling.

I never expected to race in an Italian team. Until then I had raced in Spain and in my region and when I passed into the professionals it was with a Spanish team. Then I go to being in the best team in the world at that time – Mapei. When I arrived there I was with good riders like Johan Museeuw, like Michele Bartoli, like Paolo Bettini ... big names ... really big names. At the first race they said: 'Now we have to work for Oscar,' so it was a lot of pressure at twenty-three. It was not like it is now. Now, in my opinion, riders are more professional in their approach before they turn professional. When I was an amateur, I was an *amateur*. Now, when the riders move to being a professional the change is not so great. The change in their life, in their training is not so different.

You have to have a really good mentality and for me that was the most difficult thing. In that first year with Mapei I won nine or ten races and I said now for me to win in small races is not important. I was not like a lot of riders who won small races so that when they finished their career they'd won a lot but not always the big, important races. I didn't win as many races because I was not focused on those small races. When it was an important race I was more focused, more concentrated. I remember one year with Rabobank, when the season finished they said to me, 'You didn't do so well this season because you won seven races but they were not important races.' So that is the difference between a good rider and a champion rider. A champion rider must win important races.

The following year, in Plouay, Freire came third at the Worlds, smacking his handlebars in frustration after having to check his sprint to avoid a collision. Without that incident Freire says it could have been an easy win for him such was his shape and condition. He was now well known as one of the fastest men in the peloton and in 2001 entered the Worlds in Lisbon as a marked rider.

Lisbon was the opposite of Plouay. In Lisbon I was really lucky to find the speed at the most important moment. I was not really strong that year, I was riding good sprints but I didn't think I could win that time because I didn't feel so good. In the final moments I found a good place behind Erik Zabel and I didn't have any problems during the sprint. In the last 100 metres or so I just came out from behind and I had a very nice sprint.

Normally the result of the sprint depends 80 per cent on your position and 20 per cent on your condition. It depends on things like if there is a headwind and how much energy you have to expend before the sprint. Most of the time when I won it was because there were many riders who were in a similar situation to me without a teammate. In other situations, when I didn't win, it was against riders who had a very good team and so they didn't expend a lot of energy until the last 200 metres when for me it had been totally different – having to expend 99 per cent of my energy beforehand.

How did the two wins compare? The situation was different. After being a world champion everybody knows you and I'd had some very good results afterwards. When I went to the world championships [in 2001] the Spanish national team was working for me, they built a team for me. I was really focused on the world championships. I thought now I've shown the people that I am a good rider so I know I can figure in these Worlds. The pressure was different. I had already won many races … I just had to win in the first part of the season after my first world championships; after that everybody knew me, everybody had confidence in me, the national team was built for me … I was really focused … it was a totally different situation.

Three years later the Worlds returned to Verona, the scene of Freire's first win. Earlier in the season Freire had won Milan-Sanremo for the first time, pipping an already celebrating Zabel to the win by throwing his bike across the line.

It was a little bit different to the 1999 route. It was shorter but harder. It was the race before which I felt the most pressure on me in my life. Before the race I knew the circuit was perfect for me and when I was training beforehand I knew I was in really, really good form. I knew I had never been that good before in my life. Before the world championships I always trained on the same route at home and I was taking the times, recording my speed and everything, and at that time I said to myself, 'Whoa! I have never been like I am now.' So it was the perfect race for me and I had a strong national team … I said to myself, 'I cannot lose this time, I have to take this moment.'

In the last two laps I spoke with Alejandro Valverde and I said to him, 'If you are feeling really good you could attack now because I also feel good.' He said, 'No, no, I'll stay with you, I'll work for you and then if you are good, we can win the world championships.'

He did the perfect sprint lead-out for me because I didn't have any problems before my sprint … I didn't expend a lot of energy. I think I was in my best moment but also I was with the best team. To win that race … it was not easy, but it was easier than the others before.

The route was really hard. It was a leading group of fifteen or twenty riders maximum. Of those twenty riders, ten were empty, they were really bad. The best riders had no teammates so nobody put in an attack. Everybody was thinking now we have to beat Oscar Freire in the sprint and they were fighting for the position behind me. It had happened to me many times before, the same situation, finding somebody behind the leading rider. So to have a team in the final part of a race like that is the most important thing, even more so when you are feeling good. You cannot lose a race like that.

When I won I said now I can relax and I can enjoy this. My first title I didn't really enjoy it much because I never expected to be world champion … 2004 was the nicest race of my life.

Freire's win took him level with Binda, Van Steenbergen and Merckx with three world championship titles.

You cannot compare yourself with other riders or with other eras. It is nice when they compare you to Eddy Merckx, when you do something like him – of course not in all the other races that he won, but in this one race. Then everybody told me I had to win again to be the only one with four wins. I said many times, 'OK, but it is really difficult to be just a one-time world champion.' If they'd said to me before I turned professional that I could sign now to be a world champion, one time, I'd have signed for sure. So for me it was not so important. Maybe it was for the media, for TV, for the people, but not for me.

Just to be the world champion again in itself was the most important thing for me. You wear the rainbow jersey, the only one in the peloton and it is really special. In a race, in all races, you are a different rider, that is the most important thing. You are not thinking about if you have won it two or three times … you are thinking now, in this moment, in this race, I am a different rider because I am wearing this jersey. That was the most important thing for me.

23

THE RAINBOW STRIPES
AND THE OLYMPIC RINGS

By 2008 Nicole Cooke had been Britain's premier cyclist for a number of years. From her first national title in 1999, won at the tender age of sixteen after outperforming women on British Cycling's World Class Performance Programme, to 2008 the Welshwoman had won every major race on the calendar apart from the Olympic Games and the Worlds. In 2008 she set about putting that right.

For Cooke the 2008 season was all about the Olympic Games in Beijing. In late 2007 she had signed for a new Halfords-backed team, comprising solely of British riders and supported by British Cycling, thinking it would provide the perfect backing heading into the Games. While attending the launch Cooke presented herself as if everything was on track for Beijing when in reality it would be March before she would even start a race and a further two months after that before she'd take her first win of the season – claiming the first stage of the Tour de l'Aude.

Despite a number of issues with her team Cooke set about applying her customary attention to detail. The Beijing course was hilly and defined by a steep uphill finish. At home Cooke practised on a hill that shared similar characteristics to that final haul up to the line and in Beijing she visited the circuit before the official training day, making the most of every opportunity to see the course. All her preparation paid off. In August 2008 she became the first (and to date only) British Olympic road-race champion, timing her effort perfectly and outsprinting Sweden's Emma Johansson and Italy's Tatiana Guderzo in that tough grind to the line. A lifetime's ambition was fulfilled. But still there remained the small matter of the world championships to be held the following month, once again in Verona, Italy.

Cooke had performed well in previous championships but had never quite made the top step. Three podium spots in five years had left their mark and Cooke was disappointed with her returns. It was on the podium in Beijing that Cooke decided that a unique double was now on. No rider, man or woman, had followed road-race Olympic gold with the Worlds. And so Cooke reset her target to the rainbow jersey.

Cooke's previous attempts at the Worlds had been hampered by a lack of strong teammates to help her. Now things were different and with Cooke on the start line were riders of the quality of Emma Pooley, Sharon Laws and Lizzie Armitstead. Armitstead got into the early break, meaning the pressure was off Cooke; other teams would now be forced to work to pull the break back, particularly as one of the teams to have missed it was the Dutch team of Marianne Vos.

By the time the bell rang that group had been caught and a single rider, Nikki Egyed of Australia, was in the lead. On the climb of the Salita di via Montello, Vos attacked. Five went with her: Judith Arndt and Trixi Worrack of Germany, Emma Johansson and Susanne Ljungskog of Sweden, and Cooke.

Ljungskog suffered a puncture, ruling her out, and then Vos went for a solo win on the final climb. For a while it looked like a good move but the four she left behind worked to bring her back. In the closing kilometres the five leaders had a gap of more than 55 seconds. Now there were definitely only five left in with a shout. Worrack tried to get away; Cooke tried to get away; Johansson tried to get away. The Swede's bid looked to be the one with the most potential to succeed with all the riders behind reluctant to be the first to chase her down. In previous years this was just the sort of move Cooke might have chased, but now she just sat and looked at the others having learned the hard way that if she chased she would only be towing someone else to the win. Eventually Worrack, who had momentarily been distanced by the group, launched a pursuit.

Johansson was caught inside the last 500 metres. With 200 metres to go Vos came around on the outside and Cooke jumped straight on to her wheel. In the final 50 metres of the 138-kilometre race, Cooke came on the inside to grab the win on the line, adding the rainbow to her gold in one of the most exciting finales to a world championship race. A season that had started full of doubt and frustration for Cooke had ended with the two titles she most coveted and the record of becoming the first rider to win the Olympic and world road-race titles in the same year.

***

As Cooke was riding to victory, Paolo Bettini, the double-defending champion, had called a press conference. 'I will be very brief because tomorrow there is an engagement,' Bettini said after kissing his wife and taking to the stage. 'In recent months several things have happened and during the last week, [the week] of the worlds that has become my race for a couple of years, the idea has grown to end my career ... I thought about it so much and I have not found any drawbacks to choosing this race, my race, to attach a last number to my jersey.'[236]

Bettini spoke fondly of the national team and the special sensation of representing your country. He said he could not have asked for anything else from his teammates who had sacrificed their own chances for him before assuring reporters that his motivation for winning in Varese was undiminished. No man had ever won three titles in a row. 'If Italy wins with me, it would mean rewriting the history of the cycling world,'[237] he said. Bettini left the stage to applause.

In the end it was his compatriot Alessandro Ballan who inherited the jersey from Bettini in Verona. Bettini had been heavily marked all day and so remained in the peloton, unable to escape its clutches. Ballan escaped from a twelve-rider breakaway around 2 kilometres from the finish and won alone with Italian hands applauding his every pedal stroke. When news filtered back to the peloton that Ballan had won, Bettini grinned and punched the air in celebration. It was just the fourth time that the same country had recorded three wins in succession in the men's race: Italy 1930–1932, Belgium 1948–1950 and Belgium 1955–1957.

'He [Bettini] let us go,' Ballan said. 'It was a great act. We have huge admiration for him.'[238] It was the fourth victory for the Italian team under the guidance of national coach Franco Ballerini and for Bettini it was as sweet a way to end a career as possible without donning the jersey himself. He was touched by the fond farewell messages he received from the peloton in the closing kilometres. 'I'm leaving the rainbow jersey in good hands,'[239] he said.

***

Fifteen days before the 2009 world championships in Switzerland, Australia's Cadel Evans was riding the thirteenth stage of the Vuelta. He was lying in second place, just seven seconds off the leader, Spain's Alejandro Valverde. Stage 13 was a 175-kilometre monster, with barely any flat and taking in five classified climbs as well as any number of ascents that the organisers had not bothered to categorise.

Near the top of the penultimate classified climb of the day, Evans was sitting comfortably alongside Valverde in a small group of favourites when disaster struck. A puncture. Evans raised his hand to summon the neutral support vehicle, which arrived after a short delay. But they could not change the wheel. Evans was stranded, looking in desperation down the mountain for his team car which was held up in the crowds of motorcycles and cars making their way up the sinuous climb. Eventually they arrived. A bike change got him going again. Now he was on a new bike and while they were within the final 15 kilometres, the severity of the final climb meant there was still nearly 45 minutes of riding left. Given the bike change Evans now did not have a bottle. So he took another, even though it was prohibited to do so in the final kilometres of a stage. It had taken one minute and 23 seconds to get the bike change and then the organisers docked him a further ten seconds for illegally taking a bottle. Evans was furious.

'I don't deserve this,' he said after the stage. 'I do everything right in the f***ing sport and I don't deserve this shit.'[240] In total that incident cost Evans 01.33. Just over one week later he stood in Madrid on the third step of the final podium. Valverde was receiving the jersey of overall winner. Evans had missed out. The margin? One minute and 32 seconds. 'Obviously, there's something that doesn't quite add up,'[241] Evans would later say.

Third in the Vuelta was Evans best result of the season. After picking up his third second place in a row at the Dauphiné Libéré, his Tour was disastrous. In 2007 and 2008 Evans had finished runner-up in the world's biggest bike race and in 2009 he was expected to feature again. This was one of his two targets for the season but he did not have it in the legs. At the start of the final week his gap to leader Alberto Contador was three minutes and on the stage to Verbier he lost another 01.26. His race was now well and truly over. 'At that point I was like, shit, I'm just not good; I'm bad,'[242] he later said.

Evans' main target for the season had gone. But also in his mind had been the Worlds. As soon as he had seen that the Mendrisio course brought two tough climbs with little opportunity to rest between, he had thought it could suit him. Evans fought hard to secure the race itinerary he thought best suited his chances at the Tour and the Worlds, and his subsequent poor showing at the Tour meant the pressure was now on. He had to salvage his season.

Evans' European home was right by the circuit and so he knew the roads well but no one was talking up his chances. Evans was thought of as a stage-race man, not a one-day racer. Yes, the Mendrisio circuit was hilly but it was riders such as Italy's Damiano Cunego, Spain's Alejandro Valverde and Luxembourg's Andy Schleck who were thought of as likely winners while Swiss eyes were on home favourite Fabian Cancellara. Even the Australian team did not overly rate Evans' chances – their leader for the day was Simon Gerrans.

With just over 9 kilometres to go a lead group of eight riders had formed including Gerrans, with Evans five seconds back. Evans worked hard to get across to the final break just as Gerrans fell away. Eight kilometres to go.

Then a gap appeared in the group. Spain's Joaquim Rodríguez attacked down the left-hand side of the road and Evans and Russia's Alexandr Kolobnev followed. Suddenly three were at the front of the race. Behind, the chase was disorganised. Spain, who had managed to get three riders into that nine-man selection, were happy because Rodríguez was up the road. The rest were reluctant to chase because that would just tow the other Spaniards to the line. Evans, by following that move quickly had played a tactical blinder.

Then Evans flew. Behind, no one reacted. The Australian now faced a 5-kilometre time trial to the finish. On he went, up the final climb over the top and down the other side, pulling out time all the way, driving the bike forward with every pedal stroke, driving a large gear.

Cadel Evans crossed the line in Mendrisio 27 seconds ahead of Kolobnev. His first major one-day win had brought Australia's first Worlds title. History had been made. 'If a GC guy is going to win a one-day race, it might as well be the big one,'[243] wrote Rob Arnold in Australia's *RIDE Cycling Review*. Meanwhile the *Sydney Morning Herald* described Evans as a 'rainbow warrior.' 'It's an answer to those criticisms that I've had, saying I never attack,' Evans said. 'The world's been telling me for years I can't win big races, can't win one day races, because my job is to win stage races, and then today I come out and win the world championship, I don't quite believe it.' [244]

***

After Cooke's 2008 win, Italy took three titles in a row in the women's race with wins for Tatiana Guderzo in 2009 and back-to-back victories for Giorgia Bronzini in 2010 and 2011. Bronzini's 2010 win was particularly poignant, coming at a difficult time for Italian cycling following the death of Franco Ballerini, the director of the Italian national team, after crashing while navigating for rally driver Alessandro Ciardi in the Rally Ronde di Larciano. The man who had twice won Paris-Roubaix and, in his role as director, had guided the men's squad to four world championship wins and

Olympic gold in the space of seven years, died of his injuries. He was just forty-five. Five thousand mourners attended his funeral.

The 2010 men's race was won by Norway's Thor Hushovd when the rider nicknamed the God of Thunder prevailed in a sprint in Melbourne by a length from Denmark's Matti Breschel. Hushovd finished with a huge grin etched on his face while Breschel banged his handlebars in frustration.

***

With 100 metres to go in the 2011 men's road race, Great Britain's Mark Cavendish looked to his left to see who was still alongside him. There was no one. Sure, Switzerland's Fabian Cancellara was only a bike length back and behind he had Australia's Matthew Goss fighting to stay with him, but three years of preparation by British Cycling was culminating in exactly the scenario they had planned: Britain's number-one sprinter with an empty road ahead of him at the head of a mass dash to the line with less than 100 metres to go. There had been a few bumps along the way, a few moments of fortune and good luck, but now everything had come together for the perfect ending. A few seconds later the best sprinter in the world crossed the line as world champion.

Since Tom Simpson's 1965 win Britain's women had managed to deliver three world titles to add to Beryl Burton's 1960 win. Despite often ramshackle organisation, lack of strength in depth and limited resources, Burton (1967), Mandy Jones (1982) and Nicole Cooke (2008) had all brought the rainbow jersey back to Britain's shores in the forty-six years since Simpson's victory. In that time the best Britain's men had managed in the professional road race was one fourth place courtesy of Les West in 1970. It was a poor return for a nation that was again beginning to make its mark in the cycling world, particularly in the velodrome, and in 2008 a plan was hatched.

British Cycling had established an under-23 academy under the direction of Rod Ellingworth in 2003. Cavendish was among the first intake of riders. Five years on from establishing that academy, and with Britain finally possessing a sprinter that could match the best of the world in Cavendish, Ellingworth set about ensuring everything was in place to give the rider nicknamed the Manx Missile the best opportunity to compete for the rainbow jersey within three years. As early as December 2008 *Cycling Weekly* ran an article on the project. 'We need to start thinking about it now,' British Cycling's performance director Dave Brailsford told the magazine. 'What riders do you need, how are they going to work? You can't just rock up two weeks before, select the best riders and hope we can get Cavendish a lead-out train.'[245]

Over the intervening years *Project Rainbow Jersey* as it became known left little to chance. The routes of world championship races were visited and filmed, kit was carefully assessed and provided early to make sure riders were used to it, care was taken over season-long results to ensure the team amassed enough ranking points to field as complete a team as possible and riders' roles and responsibilities were clearly laid out and defined. All the resources of the federation were put to work. While books and articles were later written on the project, in reality little about it can be said to be truly revolutionary. It was simply good preparation. Nicole Cooke had done many of the same things herself years before: visiting courses years in advance, filming them and then training on similar terrain and being meticulous over the kit she used. The difference was that Cooke often had to rely on her own resources and even fight against her own federation to try to do what had now become, for the men, a specific project.

In early 2009 Ellingworth set goals for the next three world championships: 2009 – top twenty; 2010 – top ten; 2011 – first.[246] As it turned out those first two targets would be missed by some distance. In 2009, out of nine starters, Britain managed only two finishers with Stephen Cummings the top-placed rider in fifty-second; meanwhile, in 2010 Britain only qualified three starters, including Cavendish, none of whom finished. In his book *At Speed*, Cavendish writes that the events of 2010 taught him how to manage his form. 'Essentially, in Melbourne, I'd had to learn to lose the worlds in order to understand how I was going to win it,'[247] he wrote.

Cavendish's run-in to the 2011 in Copenhagen event was less than perfect. He fell ill at the Vuelta and abandoned the race in the early stages. Concerned, he went to Girona to train with teammates David Millar and Jeremy Hunt. While he recovered and started training well, the team was worried. A month without a race in the legs was not good preparation for the Worlds. The Vuelta was still running and rules forbade the abandoning of one race and then starting another before the first had finished. Special dispensation was applied for and received from the UCI for Cavendish to ride in the Tour of Britain and so Cavendish went to Britain, lasted the seven-day race and won two stages. His form was back.

The Copenhagen race was 266 kilometres, with a run from the Danish capital to the finishing circuit in Rudersdal, where the peloton would face seventeen laps of a 14.3-kilometre circuit with a couple of small hills and a drag up to the finish. The British team was at the front of the peloton all day, monitoring the breaks and in the closing laps keeping the pace high in a bid to stave off attacks. In short, the team rode perfectly.

With one lap to go, after David Millar, Chris Froome, Jeremy Hunt and Steve Cummings had done huge amounts of work, a three-rider break was up the road and Bradley Wiggins was on the front of the peloton bringing them back. Behind Wiggins was Ian Stannard, behind Stannard was Geraint Thomas, behind Thomas was Cavendish. With 5 kilometres left the order at the head of the peloton was exactly the same. But now the break had been caught. Now Wiggins was not just at the head of the peloton but at the head of the race.

Wiggins peeled away, job done. Immediately the other nations started to assemble their sprint trains. Italy appeared, Australia appeared, Spain appeared. A team can lay the groundwork and prepare for their own race as much as they like but one thing they cannot do is completely influence what other teams are doing and now, having let the British control the entire race, the other nations were naturally intent on spoiling Britain's day.

Australia were now setting the pace with four men working for their man, Matthew Goss. Stannard and Thomas were riding to keep Cavendish in touch, close to the Australians. Then the US team made their way forward, followed by the Germans working for André Greipel. For the first time in more than five and a half hours the British weren't in control. But Cavendish stayed calm.

With around 1.5 kilometres to go, Stannard and Thomas brought Cavendish up on the right-hand side, the British sprinter nearly coming to grief on the barriers at the side of the road. While he squeezed through unscathed, he could not follow Thomas to the front. Cavendish had lost his lead out but now he was on the Australian train and he was happy. Thomas looked left and right, searching for his man. In *At Speed* Cavendish recalls the closing moments and shouting over to Thomas not to worry: 'Gee, I'm OK!'[248] he yelled.

As Heinrich Haussler led out for Australia, Cavendish, now on the right-hand side of the road, waited for a gap to appear as the race drifted left. When the gap came, so Cavendish went, a little earlier than perhaps he would have liked, but, wary of the threat of Fabian Cancellara, he had little option. It meant that Goss came back at him over the final 50 metres but the line came just in time. Project Rainbow Jersey had been a success.

'We knew three years ago when this course was announced, that it could be good for us,' Cavendish said. 'We put a plan together to come with the best group of guys to this race and to come away from it with the rainbow jersey. It's been three years in the making ... I feel so, so proud.'[249] At last, Britain's men had a second world champion.

***

In 2012 the world championships returned to Valkenburg, in the Netherlands for the fifth time for another shot at the infamous Cauberg. It was a race for classics riders and in 2012 one of the best was Belgium's Philippe Gilbert, who in 2011 became the first Belgian and only the second man in history to win the three Ardennes Classics (Amstel Gold, La Flèche Wallonne and Liège-Bastogne-Liège) in the same season. If the Copenhagen Worlds course had not been suited to his strengths, the 2012 route certainly was and while Gilbert's early- to mid-season form paled in comparison to his 2011 season, his eyes were firmly on the rainbow jersey. It had been a long-held dream for the Belgian and just as late summer arrived in northern Europe, so did Gilbert's form, with two stage wins at the Vuelta indicating his season was in many ways just about to begin.

Gilbert attacked on the final time up the Cauberg after Italy had led the peloton on to the climb. It was the right move at the right time. Paolo

Bettini, now the Italian coach, would later lament his team's relative lack of experience, saying they should not have been on the front so early. 'We should have kept [Vincenzo] Nibali well placed but he shouldn't have attacked before Gilbert did,' [250] Bettini said.

Gilbert's attack was as decisive as it was fierce. In front of the baying crowds on the Cauberg, with flares lit and flags waving, he roared up the road. Norway's Edvald Boasson Hagen, Russia's Alexandr Kolobnev and Spain's Alejandro Valverde tried to hunt him down quickly but they could not. The Belgian had disappeared over the top and was riding to a memorable win.

It had been six years since Tom Boonen's last win for Belgium. With 400 metres to go Gilbert looked round and saw his chasers safely behind. He grinned and clenched his fist in triumph before letting out a primeval roar of celebration.

'I don't know what this jersey means yet,'[251] he said. He would soon find out. From his triumph in Valkenburg through to the world championships the following year, Gilbert won just one race – a single stage of the Vuelta. 'It's not a cursed jersey,' Gilbert told *L'Equipe* in September 2013. 'But the problem is that it doesn't pass unnoticed in a peloton where everybody is looking at it. In the finale of a race, nine times out of ten, there'll be someone on your wheel when you attack … This jersey is a symbol unto itself. I didn't think it would be such a burden to wear it. Obviously, I'm the last person to complain about it, because it was a dream, but it has an incredible influence on your style of riding.'[252]

***

By the summer of 2012 Marianne Vos was widely recognised as one of the best and most versatile cyclists ever to have turned a pedal. The 2006 champion, still only twenty-five years old, had won world title in cyclo-cross and track and was an Olympic gold medallist, having claimed the points' race in 2008. She had twice won the Giro (she would win a third title in 2014) as well as La Flèche Wallonne four times (a fifth came in 2013). In short she was the woman everyone looked for in the peloton. If you wanted to be in with a chance of winning, you needed to pay close attention to whatever Vos was doing.

She also had an extraordinary record at the world championships. From her win in 2006 she had never come away with anything worse than a silver medal but being second was getting old news. Given her achievements it seems ridiculous, but questions were being raised. In 2012 Vos needed to win another rainbow jersey.

It was an Olympic year and so Vos had the chance to replicate Nicole Cooke's achievement of four years earlier – the Olympic and world road race double. 'Am I stronger than ever?' Vos said in the build-up to the London Olympic Games. 'Yes, I think I can say that.'[253]

Sure enough Vos beat Lizzie Armitstead in a three-way sprint on a rain-soaked Mall and then completed her double on home roads. Despite her record of five straight silvers, despite her status as overwhelming favourite, and despite the Valkenburg course being to her liking, Vos's Olympic win had relieved little of the pressure on the Netherlands' number one rider. 'After London, I felt OK, I achieved my big dream,' Vos later told the magazine *Peloton*. 'Now it would be extra to win in Valkenburg. Of course, I was a little nervous, but actually I was pretty relaxed for a world championships.'[254]

Vos predictably forged her win last time up the Cauberg. Everyone knew it was coming but that did not mean they could do anything to stop it. Darting over to the left-hand side of the road she left everyone standing. In that crucial moment the world championships was sealed.

With 200 metres to go and with an unassailable lead Vos veered sharply to her right to collect the Dutch flag. She had time to take it in both hands and raise it high above her head as she crossed the line. At last, six years after her first, Vos had won another rainbow jersey on the road.

***

Vos defended her jersey in Tuscany in 2013, again riding solo to the win but this time ignoring the offers of flags held out for her, while in the men's race Rui Costa took a first win for Portugal from a final four-rider break that contained two Spanish riders. The following year Michal Kwiatkowski recorded Poland's first win while France's Pauline Ferrand-Prevot took her country's first title for nineteen years. Ferrand-Prevot would go on to win the cyclo-cross and mountain bike world titles in January and September 2015 respectively, meaning that for a short while she held rainbow jerseys in three different cycling disciplines, a unique achievement.

***

Before 2015, Lizzie Armitstead's best placing at a world championships had been seventh – once in 2011 and then again in 2014. On both occasions she had said the opportunity for a podium finish had been taken from her by circumstances outside her control, first questioning whether teammate Nicole Cooke had followed team orders in the closing moments of the 2011 race and then publicly wondering why Emma Johansson and Marianne Vos had not contributed to the breakaway they had formed in the final kilometres of the 2014 event.

Before the 2015 race Armitstead sealed the defence of her World Cup title. Her preparation had been perfect and she was confident of her chances of getting a good result. Could the twenty-six-year-old land the biggest prize in women's cycling?

The 16.2-kilometre circuit in Richmond, Virginia featured three stiff climbs, including a cobblestoned ascent of Libby Hill. With just 8 kilometres left to race, two riders, Australia's Lauren Kitchen and Italy's Valentina Scandolara, jumped off the front of the leading group but as they turned on to Libby Hill for the final time, so the peloton came into view and they would soon be caught.

Into the closing straight Armitstead found herself at the front of the small group. It was the last place she wanted to be and so she waited. The line was approaching but still she waited for someone else to twitch. Eventually Anna Van der Breggen came through. Armitstead had played the game perfectly, she jumped straight onto the Dutchwoman's wheel, enjoyed a brief tow and then came out of the slipstream to become the fourth British woman to pull on the rainbow jersey.

If it seemed everything had gone exactly to plan in Richmond then eighteen months later Armitstead would paint a somewhat different picture.

Throughout 2016 and 2017 British Cycling was rocked by a series of reviews into its culture and governance, including allegations of bullying and sexism. In March 2017 during an interview with *The Guardian* Armitstead, now taking her married name Deignan, revealed that as she rode to glory British Cycling's team manager and her national coach, Brian Stephens, was not present because he had prioritised the junior men's race run earlier in the day. Remember that she was the World Cup winner and one of the fancied riders going into that race. 'I'd done everything right going into that competition and I just needed them to get it right for me on the day,' she told Simon Hattenstone. 'And they didn't ... they let me down big time.'[255]

The following year Deignan would finish fourth in Doha as the twenty-year-old Dane Amalie Dideriksen rode a perfect sprint, claiming Denmark's first elite Worlds win after enjoying a free ride from a Dutch sprint train that had seven riders at the head of the race with just 5 kilometres to go. The Dane sat on the Netherlands' Kirsten Wild's back, only putting herself into the wind just as the line approached. It needed a photo-finish but Dideriksen had taken it by half a wheel. 'I wanted to be in that [Wild's] wheel so badly,' the newly crowned champion said. 'It was a hard fight for that wheel with the other girls.'[256]

***

And so to the phenomenon that is Slovakia's Peter Sagan, perhaps the biggest star in cycling today, a supreme talent and a rider who ignites races and has enjoyed great success despite his sometimes unconventional approach – Sagan once won a junior national event after borrowing an old bike from his sister after his sponsored machine failed to arrive on time.[257]

After a year with the third-tier Dukla Trencin team in 2010 Sagan signed with Liquigas. Over the course of the next three years the Sagan story moved on apace. Stages and green jersey wins at the Tour de France, podium finishes in a couple of Monuments and wins in a shortened Gent-Wevelgem, where he wheelied over the line, and in the E3 Prijs Harelbeke propelled him towards the top of the sport. But a win in one of the top one-day races – the Monuments or the world championships – eluded him. Questions were being asked. 'At only twenty-five years of age, the Classics are already becoming an albatross around the Slovakian's neck,'[258] wrote James Witts for *Cyclist* magazine in April 2015

At the Worlds Sagan's name had often been bandied around as being among the favourites and in 2015 he was again in the frame. His season had been a curious mixture of success and disappointment, no better illustrated than at the Tour where he ran away with the green jersey competition but did not win a stage. Sagan had a problem. Such was his profile and strength that his presence in any group made others wary and unwilling to work with him. That had the potential of being a real issue in Richmond given the uphill nature of a finish that was considered ideal for Sagan.

On Libby Hill for the final time the Czech Republic's Zdeněk Štybar launched a move closely marked by Germany's John Degenkolb, Belgium's Greg Van Avermaet and Norway's Edvald Boasson Hagen. Over the top and the bunch was strung out by the fearsome pace being set at the head of the group. Sagan was there, in touch and waiting for the right time to strike.

Van Avermaet led into the second-last climb, gaining ten bike lengths or so. Then, a rider emerged, sprinting across the gap. Sagan. He blasted around the Belgian and led him up the climb. Behind, the peloton was ripped to pieces. On the descent Sagan adopted an aero-tuck position, perched on the top-tube with his head as low over the handlebars as possible, dropping as fast as he could to pull out a gap. There were 2.5 kilometres to go.

But Sagan was tiring and was not riding smoothly. Into the final kilometre his right shoe came unclipped as behind Colombia's Rigoburto Uran tried to make a break out of the bunch. The finish was taking an age to come. With 200 metres left Sagan stood up on his pedals, one last injection of effort. He looked back and finally knew that they were not going to get to him. At last he was about to win the biggest one-day race in cycling. He knew that he was about to become world champion. Behind there was a frantic twenty-four-rider sprint for silver, won by Australia's Michael Matthews.

'I was waiting for this moment,' Sagan said. 'On the last cobblestoned climb I said I'm going to try. After I arrived alone at the top I said I have to go full-gas. It's very strange. All the things happened very fast … boom … boom … boom … and after, I am here.' [259]

Twelve months on Sagan repeated his win in a very different race in Doha. Sagan had enjoyed his 2016 season, representing the rainbow jersey with aplomb and winning his first Monument – the Tour of Flanders in the spring. 'I think if I only win this race, it's a very good year,'[260] he told *Rouleur*. Then he went to the Tour, won three stages, wore the yellow jersey for three days and claimed the green jersey for the fifth year in a row.

The 257-kilometre route in was pan-flat and took the riders out of the city and into the desert before two 90-degree corners turned the bunch back towards Doha and seven laps of a 15.2-kilometre finishing circuit. When the day dawned with flags billowing, everyone knew where the crucial point of the race was going to be: those turns in the desert. Sure enough it was there that the race split with twenty-six riders making the break. Sagan was the last man to make the split at that corner. 'That was the first victory of the day,'[261] he later reflected. Belgium, with six riders present, then went to work with the Italians. More than 175 kilometres to go and the race was already done for nearly 90 per cent of the peloton. Under the leadership of the Belgians, the break would not be seen again.

Sagan rode his sprint perfectly, squeezing through on the right-hand side, dicing with danger alongside the barriers. 'I played just one card,' Sagan said. 'And that was the sprint.' He had had Cavendish on his wheel but at the last moment the Briton opted to go left instead of faithfully following the Slovak, got caught in traffic and finished a frustrated second. Belgium's Tom Boonen took third, his first Worlds medal for eleven years. Sagan; Cavendish; Boonen; One, Two, Three – the first time former champions had graced all three steps of the men's podium.

And as Sagan later said. 'Everybody was happy again.'[262]

24

NICOLE COOKE (2008)

In 2008 Nicole Cooke became world champion in Varese, winning from a five-rider breakaway. Cooke's win came after a run of three podium places in five years and added the rainbow jersey to an Olympic gold medal, won just six weeks earlier, and an already impressive *palmares* that included the Giro d'Italia (2004), the Tour de France (2006, 2007), La Flèche Wallonne (2003, 2005, 2006) and the Tour of Flanders (2007). Cooke was the first rider to win the Olympic and world championships road races in the same year.

A ten-times national champion, Cooke was easily Britain's best road-racer of her era, arguably of any era. No other rider of any nationality has enjoyed a career in which they won the Giro, the Tour, Olympic Games, world championships and the two biggest women's classics, a feat that now cannot be challenged given the sad absence of an equivalent of the Tour de France on the women's race calendar.

Cooke endured an uneasy relationship with her national governing body British Cycling throughout her career. She was determined and meticulous in her preparation, focused on giving herself the very best opportunity to be successful. The stories she recounts in her 2014 autobiography *The Breakaway* paint a picture of that success often coming in spite of, rather than because of, the approach of her national federation. That includes poor organisation during her first junior Worlds' win in 2000.

I met Cooke under the shadow of St Paul's Cathedral. We started by talking about her preparation for those Worlds in Plouay, France and her first junior world title.

***

Nicole Cooke:

To prepare for those world championships I went out to Brittany the year before. I rode the course and just started to get to know the event, the venue, what it was likely to entail. Even the year before there was already Plouay 2000 memorabilia on sale so everything about it was gearing up. They were building a new road where the finish was going to be and you couldn't avoid it going round the town. Even the supermarkets had memorabilia out on sale already.

At that time my main support network was my family, and visiting courses was our normal approach to preparing for races if they were big. It was always very important to have thorough preparation and yes, it was potentially novel to British Cycling at the time but from my point of view it was just so useful to know the course. It takes away a lot of uncertainties – you can plan your training around knowing what the course is like. It was a very normal way in how I approached things. Even using a skinsuit to win those world championships in 2000 was common sense. It wasn't anything particularly hi-tech or radical.

Going away as part of the Great Britain team at the time was very different to my normal preparation for races and there were a lot of things in the way that the Great Britain management was set up at the time which were absolutely ridiculous. We were doing ridiculous things in training and going on the course at silly times. It was one debacle after another. It was hugely frustrating for me because I knew that these were things that shouldn't happen and every time I made a good suggestion I was just totally ignored. It was very draining trying to get ready for the biggest race of the year and having what seemed like obstacles put in my way. It was absolutely possible to organise things so much better. Everything should be relaxed and straightforward.

The internal drive and motivation was always there – it was hugely frustrating at times but I just had to move on and concentrate on what I could still control and what could still make the difference to my race. I just had to continue to go through all my preparation, planning what tactics to use in the race and everything else, so at least when I did start I was as good as I could be given the circumstances.

After Plouay, and at other times, I provided very in-depth feedback to British Cycling about how things could be run much better. Some things got taken on board, some things are everyday standard practice today, marginal gains etc … which is great to see but it shouldn't have been as hard as it was.

In the closing moments of the Plouay race Cooke worked to ensure the rotation in the breakaway was such that her biggest rival was furthest away from her when they reached the part of the course where she wanted to attack. It was an early demonstration of her tactical acumen.

A lot of my tactical development happened in Holland. My dad, from his own racing experiences, knew how important tactics were in road races. British youth racing, and we're talking the mid-1990s, was very thin and so most road races and bunch races were actually just time trials. There wasn't a lot of tactical racing going on and so my dad found out about some races that were happening in Holland. The British Schools Cycling Association took trips to these races every summer and so we got involved in those and I raced in Holland for the first time when I was twelve. In the younger age categories in Holland they race the girls down a category, so I'd be a twelve-year-old girl racing eleven-year-old boys. We'd race on restricted gears and everyone was sort of maxed out at the cadence which meant the races were bunch races and tactics then became the way of making the difference. Racing fiercely and competitively against the boys, who won't give an inch, certainly honed your tactical thinking.

By the time I was fifteen or sixteen I had a very developed tactical sense and, yes, it is about lots of subtle moves. I think I was always ready to put the hard work in, to drag the break along and do my fair share of the work and then, when it came to setting up an attack, obviously I would want to set things up nicely. You knew the strongest person who was a threat and I wanted them in the wrong position to be able to chase me down. Things like that were always in my mind.

Plouay was a fantastic victory. Both the fact that amongst my peers I was the world champion which was great – but also that tactical nous. That was really good to show in a junior women's world championships where I was racing against people I had never raced against before. You can search for results on the internet but there was only so much intelligence you could gather beforehand then, and so it was very pleasing to go into a major race against people essentially I didn't know that well and still tactically make some very good decisions.

In 2001 Cooke followed a junior mountain bike world championship win by winning the junior time trial and soloing to a second road race title in Lisbon. She has previously said she felt under a huge amount of pressure before that race. On her return, Cooke's home village of Wick turned out in force to celebrate her achievement.

I think for everything to remain on track it was very important to do the double as a junior and build upon what I did in 2000. Personally that was huge and it was something that I really wanted to do. At Plouay we were four riders for Great Britain, in Lisbon there was just one teammate and I knew that from the important part of the race she wasn't going to be able to support me. It was also the pressure of knowing that, for the teams with lots of very good riders, like Holland or Italy, or for teams that are very well drilled, like Germany, it would be very easy for them to come up with a strategy to cancel me out; to eventually use their numerical advantage to beat me. That was the bit which was the hardest to approach in terms of what am I going to do here?

It was an amazing race actually. Yes, the pressure was really high and I was really feeling it going into the race, but once it started it was a matter of, OK, I have a proactive race plan, let's get a break away, let's see what happens. This I did and we stayed away for a long time. But then we were caught towards the end of the race. I think it was that resilience of character to attack again once the first break was caught and to take away another group of riders, and then go again on the second hill before the end and solo to the finish. Again, we had restricted gears and I remember there was one part downhill … when you ride on restricted gears what do you do on the downhill? You just sprint, tuck, sprint, tuck. Every part of that course I knew how to play it to my advantage.

It was really nice to have those celebrations, obviously, with the people who had supported me over the long term but also the wider cycling community. Everyone talks about 2008 being the great emergence of cycling here, but in the 1990s Britain was still known as being quite rubbish at cycling and for me to win in 2000/2001 … OK it was a *junior* world championships, but it was actually showing that someone from Britain can come up and with a good approach – racing abroad in Holland, going out and finding the competition and racing and learning – they actually can be competitive. I think it was huge for the cycling community in south Wales. There were people from all the Cardiff cycling clubs that came to that welcome home party, people like Geraint [Thomas] and the Rowe brothers [Luke and Matthew] were there. They could see that: Yeah we know Nicole, we train on the same roads, and we can do this too. It was obviously really nice for me but I think it was also really important for the cycling community to share in that and inspire some other riders as well.

By the start of the 2008 season Cooke was one of the best cyclists in the world with a string of major wins and world championship podium finishes behind her. In late 2007, with eyes on the Beijing Olympic Games, she had signed for a new team sponsored by the British retail company Halfords, supported by British Cycling and comprising solely of British riders. Cooke was the team's star rider but her preparation for the season had been hit by a knee injury sustained the previous season. In the summer of 2008, Cooke was told the team would not be riding in the Tour de France, a key race in her Olympic preparation and where she was defending champion. The result was that Cooke had to take it upon herself to find a team at short-notice for the race so as not to derail her season. In the end she rode for the Swift Racing team as a guest rider, finishing third overall.

I never gave up on that Olympic dream or that world championship dream, but I knew that I hadn't done my basic training in the winter and I knew that it meant I was going to be working really, really hard, which I was fine about. But it was very frustrating when there was still this uncertainty: When could I actually start training? What is it going to take to get over this injury?

I still had races I wanted to win. I wanted to win a world championship. It's hard to say you want to win the Olympics because there are so many factors that go into it and it is only once every four years, so saying you want to win an Olympics is potentially going to lead to disappointment because of the stakes and the things that can happen in what essentially are three races in a career. The world championships was always a must do on my list and obviously the Olympics were right up there. An Olympic medal ... any colour ... would be brilliant.

I was absolutely furious with the decision to miss the Tour. I was riding for Halfords, a team that was meant to build its calendar around the optimum plans for the Olympics, so that I could remove all the uncertainties that come with riding for a professional team that potentially has other commitments and other things it has to do. So having made the decision to go with the Halfords set-up and then to be told within a few weeks of the start of the race that they've just decided we're not going was … I was absolutely livid and it did just totally sum up British Cycling in my career up to that point. I could complain, 'This was in the plan, why aren't we sticking with it', but they could just ignore me. They knew there was nobody to hold them to account properly.

The benchmark that I got by going to the Tour in 2008 and coming third was that I actually needed to change my focus for the last six weeks before the Games because the training that I'd been doing up to that point still wasn't giving me that competitiveness that I needed. One factor was that I was still on a sort of upward trajectory anyway, having started the season's preparation later, but it was that reference point that I needed, to really focus on the areas that I had to work on for those last six weeks.

Following a visit to the Beijing course the year before, Cooke set about preparing for the race. She found a hill near her home that shared the same characteristics as the crucial climb in Beijing to train on and then later, whilst in China, took every opportunity to prepare on the actual course. Prior to departure, at a team meeting in Manchester, the coaching staff laid out a plan for Emma Pooley to be Britain's medal prospect in the race, by using Cooke, who would be marked, as a decoy, whilst Pooley broke away to win alone. Cooke disagreed with the strategy, thinking Pooley would not be allowed to break away but would be marked. During the race, just after a break featuring Pooley had been caught, Cooke got into the crucial five-rider break and took Britain's first Olympic road race gold medal.

That was the call that was being made by Shane [Sutton], again with no discussion, it was just sort of taken. With full respect to Emma this was an Olympic race. People knew Emma's tactics of attacking and being very strong alone. She was going to be marked and so other teams would have to either chase her down or put another rider with her who probably would have beaten her at the finish. It was not a strategy that was going to lead to a gold medal for Britain.

It was extremely frustrating not to have the backing from the British Cycling coaching staff. I'd proven that I was capable of winning a gold medal and to not get the full backing, or to go for a strategy that wasn't going to result in a gold, was really frustrating.

I thought through the scenarios before the race: What's my worst-case scenario? What's the worst thing that can happen in terms of the race tactics? Having a plan for every scenario that I could think of, knowing who you are definitely going to chase, who you are going to give a bit more space, things like that, just help in those tactical moments when you do have to make a split-second decision.

But I just love the racing so I was just absolutely focused on what I could do to put myself in the best position of winning. That was what I was going through, processing all the time: OK, this is happening, what do I need to do? Do I need to be following someone else in particular? What should I be looking out for? What attacks are likely to happen at this stage of the race? Those are the things that just come … I suppose intuitively, or automatically through racing experience.

With a lifetime's ambition met Cooke had to refocus sharply on the Worlds which were starting five weeks later in Varese, close to her home. In preparation Cooke videoed the route and sent it to her teammates. Despite her own efforts and preparation, in the run-up to the race the newly crowned Olympic champion still had to deal with issues regarding her equipment and clothing. First she was told a new part was unavailable to repair the headset on her bike and then on the eve of the race she was told she couldn't wear a skinsuit because there wasn't one with the logo of British Cycling's new sponsor on it.

I'd had some very frustrating senior world championships. I'd had silvers and bronzes but they were very disappointing because I was probably one of the strongest in those races but didn't have the luxury of a strong team to support my challenge, like Germany or Italy for example. I was in effect a lone rider in a team sport.

It was when I was on the podium in Beijing that I thought: OK, I can actually do this double even if it does mean pretty much doing it myself. I can do it, I really want that rainbow jersey. This time it would be different because I had absolutely nothing to lose. I'd proven myself – I'd won my Olympics and I saw it as I've got great form and I've got that little bit of extra confidence going into the world championships. When I purchased my apartment I knew it was just 30 kilometres away from the 2008 world championships and I wasn't not going to go. It was really just, 'Wow, this is a great opportunity – what a way to go into a world championships.' That was how I saw it.

By that point I knew that if I wanted something doing it would be much more relaxing and stress-free to just do it, so I videoed the course myself. It was time very well spent, even just driving it. I was just happily getting on with preparing for a world championships and I enjoyed it. Yes I made the video and sent copies round to all the other girls and to the team manager. It was all about sharing this intelligence so the others could practise for it as well, but it was definitely also a case of who else was going to do it?

Some people had the full backing of whatever they wanted … we saw that in Beijing with the track team and some others, but going to the world championships was almost like a bit of an afterthought for a lot of people. We didn't have a full team in terms of staff or riders, although they did send a full team for the men's race on the next day … The approach to fixing the headset was very unprofessional. Yes, it was a minor thing but it was symptomatic of the attitude – 'Oh, it is too hard' – no, come on, get it done. Up until then at every world championships I'd raced for Britain I'd raced in a skinsuit; it was a standard request from me and this time they didn't supply one. Then, at the last minute Sky came on board as the GB sponsor. Well, so what? I'm not getting anything from Sky and I've got a world championships to win so I'm going to wear the best racing kit I've got. It wasn't my fault they didn't sort one out, so I'm not going to reduce my chances just because of someone else's mess. It was farcical. Dave Brailsford insisted I could not ride in kit without the logo and I was insisting I was not going to ride in kit that disadvantaged me. Eventually my teammate Emma [Pooley] suggested cutting out the logo from the new kit and sewing it on the skinsuit I had brought to the championships … Emma getting her sewing kit out and sewing on a Sky logo … I didn't care, I just wanted to race.

I was extremely excited. Nervous? Yes, but more really in that this is a great opportunity. Just the excitement of knowing I'm in good form and that I know the course. I love the world championships and the race lap format, where you start off slow and it builds. It's a race of attrition, the pace builds up and then it just all sort of accumulates in the last couple of laps, which are always the action-packed part, with everything kicking off.

The race went very well in terms of our tactics. Lizzie Armitstead got in the early break. She was in there covering that for us, she just had to sit in and not contribute to the work, which was really good, and then I was just waiting for it all to come back together. As a team we did what we could but the bottom line was at the finale I was alone. I was in the breakaway from which the winner would come with two Germans [Judith Arndt and Trixi Worrack], two Swedes [Emma Johansson and Susanne Ljungskog] and Marianne [Vos].

Cooke later described the run-in to the finish as the most exciting finale to a race she had ever been involved in. In the past Cooke had been very active in the closing laps of world championship races and had on occasion narrowly missed out on the top step perhaps because of those efforts. This time she waited to see the final moments play out and timed her sprint well to win from a five-rider break after refusing to chase down a last-gasp effort from Johansson.

It was brilliant. Did I enjoy it? Yes! It's just the thrill of competition that I love. It's the whole thing of working out what's going on and thinking how can I slightly change things and influence things to turn this from a potentially winning situation to a real win?

I think those past performances in the Worlds have to be put in the context of having no teammates, where, if you just do nothing other teams will go into the last stages with more riders and therefore more options. Either way, neither working to reduce the group or leaving it to others and therefore possibly having a larger group at the finish are best-case scenarios. At the time, after those earlier Worlds I was very disappointed, but then writing my book and looking back at those races, I actually think that given my lack of effective teammates, I rode extremely well.

Did I feel the strongest? In terms of form, yes. But when you and your rivals are all at such a close level in terms of performance you've never got lots to play with physically. It's about managing everything on the day and not wasting energy. In the last kilometre with Emma Johansson alone in the lead, I was quite happy to see the race play out because so close to the finish I knew that I wasn't going to win if I chased Emma. That's the situation. Chasing her won't help so I'm not going to. I mean, it was quite a logical approach.

If you're about to win a race, normally at some point before the finish line you know you're going to win. As I came past Vos I knew, so for the last ten, fifteen metres, I know I'm going to win. And it's amazing. In terms of the enormity, I knew it beforehand. I definitely knew that if I won the Worlds after the Olympics it would be a dream come true.

Further down the line, when you reflect at the end of the year, it's then you fully realise what you've done. I think that because I was so into the race-day build-up and tactics … it's clear that these things just didn't happen by accident. I know exactly what went into setting up that finish to give me that springboard to launch the sprint and win. I get all of that in terms of the mechanics of winning immediately, but the reflection on it being an amazing year comes much later, during the winter.

At thirteen or fourteen, as things started getting a bit more serious for me in cycling, winning the senior world road race championship was what I wanted and at that point in my career it was the last thing that I hadn't done. That added to the moment as well, knowing that I had completed the full set. I was just wanting to savour every moment of it. At the junior world championships I was still on a journey to a career as a senior and many other things, whereas I think at Varese I was on top of the podium of my cycling-life goals and … I don't think any of my other senior world championship podiums were pleasurable experiences, they were extremely upsetting, and so to actually have that rainbow jersey after some very close calls was incredible.

Living close to Varese and going out training all that winter, all that season was wonderful. Even going training in the rainbow jersey is amazing. Those are the things that stay with you when you're going up some hill and it's raining and it's cold and you've still got hours of training to do and you think, why am I doing this? It's because one day I'm going to ride in the rainbow jersey. Things like that were inspirational for me. I wanted to earn the right to wear the rainbow jersey and enjoy what came with it. Winning in the rainbow jersey is … well everything is just better in the rainbow jersey! It was really nice to enjoy wearing it; it is a very visible symbol of fifteen years of hard work and everything that went into winning it.

In every world championships I did, I raced with absolutely everything I had. Looking back at all those years I'm really proud of my record in world championships. They really were some of the best races of the season in terms of everything being on the line, racing for the jersey, the atmosphere, the scale of the event. It is on a different level to all the other races in the season. And the format: the laps, the building up, building up, building up, to that crescendo, the last few seconds of a very long race are terrific to be part of whether you win or lose.

In all my races I always gave it my very best. I think I always rode passionately and some say, courageously; I hope that is how I ride. That was how I liked to race and it is something I'm very proud of.

25

CADEL EVANS (2009)

In 2009 Australia's Cadel Evans won the rainbow jersey in Mendrisio, Switzerland. Despite recording top-five placings in both Liège-Bastogne-Liège and the Tour of Lombardy in the years leading up to 2009, Evans was considered more of a stage-race specialist than a one-day rider. Consequently he was not thought of as a favourite for the win in Switzerland, but he rode away from the decisive small group in the final kilometres and rode solo to the jersey.

Evans retired in 2015 after becoming the first Australian to have won either the world championship or the Tour.

***

Cadel Evans:

My first elite Worlds was in Portugal, in 2001. It wasn't by any means a hard Worlds but then there was this downhill sprint where it was so fast it was a little bit strange. You came out into the wind to move up and lost places. The end of that was very odd because the Italians were all following each other. It was a strange world championships on reflection.

The next one was Madrid, which was all about positioning. I wasn't well prepared for that actually and I didn't finish. Then in Verona, when Oscar Freire won in 2004 and Stuart O'Grady finished fourth – I rode that one working for Stuey. That was my first taste of how hard the Worlds can be and then Stuttgart in 2007 was my first good one. [Evans finished fifth.]

I don't think I was ever really much looked on as a rider to win the Worlds. I rode the one-day races but as a road rider I was really pretty much exclusively focusing on stage races. I'd always go to the one-day races but I was never actually that well prepared for them – I'd prepare for time trials and the Commonwealth Games or something like that, but the 2009 Worlds in Mendrisio was the first year I actually had a good opportunity to really fully focus and prepare for a one-day race.

In Stuttgart I'd certainly learned about the Worlds. By that time I was getting … not that I was looked on as a rider for the Worlds … but I was sort of thinking I could get a result there. That year I was going for the ProTour [the season-long competition, now the WorldTour] as well and you got ProTour points for the Worlds.

In Stuttgart, Evans hit the front with one kilometre to go but couldn't get away and was left poorly positioned, leading the five-strong group to the line.

Neil Stephens was my director and he was yelling at me to go away in the last kilometre but I was like, 'No, no, I'm going to wait because it was an uphill finish.' I still regret to this day that I listened to him and followed his orders. But that's all part of the learning experience – things I took from races to prepare me for future years.

CADEL EVANS (2009)

*Two years later the Worlds were hosted in Switzerland, close to Evans'
European home.*

From when they announced the course I realised it could be good for me.
The two climbs weren't super-hard but they were quite close together,
so I knew the normal riders that could climb were going to have trouble
recovering between them. For me to be good over that sort of distance I
was almost always better when I had a Grand Tour in my legs, so going to
the Vuelta was important for me in getting ready for the Worlds that year.

I was having a few difficulties with the team ... a lot of difficulties actually.
I had to fight pretty hard just to get a start in the Vuelta strangely enough
when you think I led it for a while. In the back of my mind I was always
thinking about the Worlds between all the problems with the team and
so on. My performance in the Tour [28th] was below what I wanted. It was
actually by my standards, and by the team's standards, my worst year. I'd
won one race, a stage of Coppi e Bartali ... I had quite a few second places
that year, at the Dauphiné Libéré and so on, but of course they aren't wins.
Then coming up to the Worlds ... it's the one race outside of the Tour that
can turn a bad year into a good year.

I was the second rider on the team, the second choice. Simon Gerrans
was the leader. A big break went early and Michael Rogers was in that
early break so I was just staying calm, we had a good rider there, so that
was fine. Everyone stayed calm and then it really wound up towards the
end ... of course I was hoping to be able to do something. Then, when the
selections started being made, I realised what a good day I was on. Then
backing the final move, I think assessing that and reading that move fairly
cleverly brought about the result.

Simon Clarke was my guy, the guy who was with me throughout the
whole race, from start to finish, putting me in the right positions and so
on until then the selection started to be made. I ended up being in
the group of nine or ten at the end with Simon Gerrans, three Spanish

riders and Alexandr Kolobnev, Fabian Cancellara and Damiano Cunego.

Gerrans had actually made it into the decisive break, being driven by Cancellara and Belgium's Philippe Gilbert, before Evans. Evans then had to work hard to get over by himself.

Because Simon Gerrans was there I had to wait for a moment when I could go across alone without bringing anyone else up. When I went straight across a couple of guys were getting shelled out the back. Gerrans was one of them.

Because there were three Spanish guys there I was thinking that if a Spanish guy goes he's probably going to stay away. It was Joaquim Rodríguez who attacked. There were these small traffic islands on the descent with a small gap and he went through it. Because I knew the roads so well I was sort of waiting for someone to do something like that – that was my experience from Salzburg in 2006 – back then it was heading to a final sprint and it went under a bridge, someone left a little gap and that cost Australia the chance to try to go for the win [Robbie McEwen and Stuart O'Grady finished fifth and sixth that day]. That's racing, you learn about these things and learn to watch for them. So I was watching and waiting, waiting … it was something that I noted to myself to be careful of in the race, in the end it became the instigator for the winning move.

So I followed that move along with Kolobnev. With the three of us in front Kolobnev and Rodríguez were watching each other and left a little gap for me. That was when I put everything down and gave it everything I could to the finish.

I attacked a little bit before the final climb. It was on the flat that I went away, about 6 kilometres from the finish. I live right there but I don't think I've ever ridden along that road because it's in the middle of an industrial zone, it's not really a nice part of the town. When I went away there I gave it everything knowing it was all or nothing from that point onwards.

Once I had gone clear over the top … I couldn't quite believe it actually. From when I hit the climb … a road I actually rode back from training nearly every day … I was like here I am riding up here as I have so many times before, but now there are thousands of people at the side of the road. There were a lot of Italian and Spanish fans on that climb. Funnily enough, eerily enough, they were silent when I came along, unlike all the previous laps! Of course I'm just giving it everything, I had to increase the gap and get to the finish line solo.

It was a real feeling of disbelief, for a few reasons. I'd had the worst year ever, my trade team had lost a lot of faith in me, I wasn't even the leader of the Australian team, and here I was riding down this road that I ride home on. That finishing straight there is about 6 kilometres from where I lived – and I live only about 3 kilometres from there still today. It really just turned my year around. I'd had a year of people just doubting my ability as a bike rider and here I was riding towards the finish line and a rainbow jersey.

Evans won by nearly 30 seconds but with no outward celebration.

I'd had so much doubt in me and I was thinking of the people who I needed to greet. You know, my Australian team hadn't expressed a lot of confidence in me and my own trade team hadn't expressed a lot of confidence in me for that whole year, but the people from the town where I lived, from near Mendrisio, well they had expressed a confidence in me. It was very emotional.

In mountain bike and road Worlds I think I'd won six medals previously [junior, U19 and U23 level] but I'd never won one. I'd been second on numerous occasions but I'd never won one before. I'd been on the podium for a silver or bronze, standing there on the podium and they bring out the rainbow jersey and they put it on the world champion … I'd stood next to them and there's a bit of that, you know, you've come close but not quite there. You've ridden well of course but you haven't won. It's a disappointing experience to have the rainbow jersey come up to the guy next to you on the podium and it was something I'd seen on more than a few occasions.

It was very quiet and subdued afterwards. We had dinner at the restaurant and I went home. We had to drive past my house to get to the team hotel so I went home that night and slept in my own bed. I woke up the next day and the TV people were knocking on my front door in the morning, ringing the bell and so on.

I found that a little disappointing because I was still the same person. When I woke up on the Sunday morning before the race and then when woke up on Monday afterwards, I was still the same person. I rode for the same team but everyone's perception of you changes so much. If I'd got second place no one's perception would've changed despite me still having a good race. But win and everyone perceives you so differently because you are the world champion … but as a human being, on a human level, well, actually, I'm still the same person.

Evans' win meant that he wore the rainbow jersey throughout 2010, a year during which he won La Flèche Wallonne and the points jersey at the Giro.

Absolutely it is a special year. I had a little bit of bad luck that year, I had an injury at the Tour and got sick during the Giro but at both of them I was there, racing for the win. I had the pink jersey at the Giro, but then when lying second I got a fever. At the Tour I crashed and broke my elbow, rode to the finish and took the yellow jersey but I'd broken my arm. I was in a position to really do something. I'd won La Flèche Wallonne and I was having a good year but I had a bit of bad luck at crucial moments.

Being the world champion, everyone watches the jersey. I think sometimes the curse of the rainbow jersey gets a little bit out of proportion because whatever you do as the world champion, if you stop for a pee or whatever, everybody knows what you're doing so if anything bad happens, if you crash out the race or something and you're the world champion, then people see it. I don't think it brings added pressure but you are certainly a lot more observed by your competitors and that makes it harder to win wearing the rainbow jersey. I think it is more difficult.

In 2010 the Worlds were held in Australia for the first time with Evans as defending champion. Evans finished seventeenth with Allan Davis the best of the home riders in third.

There was a little bit more focus on me and more team belief. The Worlds was held on a course that suited me really well and I was away with Philippe Gilbert so there was nothing wrong. I hadn't done the Vuelta that year but I was riding well. That Worlds was the first without team radios and the nature of the course made it just a little bit of an unpredictable race. You didn't know if the break was going to come back or if the group behind was going to come up. As it turned out they did come up and when they caught us we ended up with less condition to follow on and to contest the sprint. But I certainly rode well, maybe a little bit too aggressively in hindsight, but I was there in my home country as the defending world champion and I didn't want to leave anything … I wanted to give myself every opportunity to perform again.

The most elating and amazing experience of my career was the last kilometre or two of the world championships to the finish in Mendrisio. Alongside riding on the Champs-Élysées in yellow of course, emotionally, on the bike, it was one of the most amazing experiences that I ever had in my life.

26

RACING AGAINST THE CLOCK

On 25 August 1994, Great Britain's Chris Boardman rolled down the ramp at the start of a 42-kilometre time trial in Sicily. Nine days earlier, on the track at Palermo, Boardman had won his first individual pursuit world title. Now he has switched focus to the road, the last rider in a field of fifty-seven to start the newly introduced men's individual time trial at the world championships.

The Sicilian sun bore down and the temperature nudged 42 degrees as Boardman blitzed a tough and technical course that proved worthy of a world championship race, with numerous direction changes, climbs and sections of cobbles in the battle for the right to claim the right to be the first man to wear a rainbow jersey as the individual time trial world champion.

Slightly down at the first time check, by the time he reached the 19.2-kilometre mark the Briton was more than16 seconds ahead of second placed Andrea Chiurato of Italy. Boardman, riding the famously pioneering Lotus bike that would later lead to suggestions that protests might be made over his saddle position, had worn yellow at the Tour the previous month after winning the prologue in Lille. Now he was ripping up the race in search of another jersey. As he crossed the line outside Catania's city hall the clock stopped at 49 minutes, 34.5 seconds. His margin over Chiurato was 48 seconds. Germany's Jan Ullrich, an amateur who would go on to win the Tour three years later, took third, nearly two minutes back. Boardman had destroyed the field to claim his second rainbow jersey in nine days, entering the record books as the first man to become the individual time trial world champion. He would make the podium on a further three occasions but never again as champion.

In the inaugural women's race, thirty-two-year-old Karen Kurreck of the USA took the jersey. A former gymnast and triathlete, Kurreck had only focused on cycling three years previously and was still working for a software company in California at the time of her win. Second was Canada's Anne Samplonius, while in third was a certain Frenchwoman called Jeannie Longo.

***

While Boardman and Kurreck took those inaugural titles it had not been the first time that racing against the clock had featured in the road world championships. When the UCI introduced the road Worlds for amateurs in 1921 the first races initially took the form of an individual time trial, much to the despair of the Italians who had been among the nations lobbying the UCI for the introduction of the event but who wanted a massed-start road race rather than a ride against the clock. As a result Italy boycotted the event which was first held in Copenhagen and won by Sweden's Gunnar Sköld. At 190 kilometres it was not for the faint-hearted and Sköld took more than six and a quarter hours to complete the course. The format was repeated in 1922 when Britain's Dave Marsh posted the fastest time after a 160-kilometre time trial. After that the championships adopted massed-start road races, only reverting to the time trial format once, in 1931.

In 1962 the UCI added an amateur men's team time trial to the world championship itinerary for the first time. Ridden by national teams of four the inaugural race was won by Italy and it remained a sporadic part of the programme until 1994 when the final race was held, also won by Italy. Somewhat ironically given the nation's initial resistance to the time trial format, of the twenty-seven times the men's amateur team time trial race was held, Italy won seven, the most of any country. A women's team time trial was introduced in 1987, which also ran until 1994. The Soviet Union and then Russia ruled supreme at the event, claiming four titles including both the first and last races. No other nation secured more than one win.

With individual time trials introduced in 1994, team-based tests against the clock were dropped from the event's programme. They returned in 2012 when a team time trial for trade teams was introduced, bringing a new dimension to the Worlds.

***

Longo's third place behind Kurreck in 1994 was an appetiser of what was to come from the Frenchwoman. Echoing her domination in the road race during the mid- to late-1980s, from 1995 through to 1997, Longo won three time trial titles in a row and added a fourth in 2001. The first of her victories came in Colombia with a win of more than one minute ahead of Canada's Clara Hughes. Just three days later Longo won her fifth road-race jersey to become the first rider to secure both road world titles in the same year. Other women to claim both titles, but in different years, are the Netherlands' Leontien van Moorsel and Germany's Judith Arndt. Spain's Abraham Olano is the only man to claim both titles, adding the 1998 time trial crown to his 1995 road-race win.

The men's event has been dominated over the years by three men: Australia's Michael Rogers, Switzerland's Fabian Cancellara and Germany's Tony Martin. Cancellara, also a two-time junior champion in the discipline, and Martin share the record for most titles with four apiece, while Rogers was crowned champion three years in a row (2003–2005), although his first win was confirmed nearly twelve months after he crossed the line in Hamilton, Canada after the man who had beaten him into second, Britain's David Millar, was stripped of his title after confessing to doping. In his book

Racing Through the Dark, Millar recounts standing on the podium listening to the national anthem. 'I was world time trial champion,' he writes, 'yet I felt almost nothing. I should have been choked, moved, just as other athletes were at such a moment. Instead. I just thought: "Job done."'[263]

Millar's disqualification meant that until 2010 no Briton had managed to follow Boardman in winning the time trial jersey. Then Emma Pooley won the women's title in Australia with a 15-second win over Arndt, crowning a terrific year in which she had also won the Tour de l'Aude and La Flèche Wallonne. Pooley was followed by Bradley Wiggins in 2014 who claimed a 26-second win ahead of Martin. Wiggins' win was his first road world title and the final major road win in a glittering career that had already included a yellow jersey at the Tour, multiple world and Olympic titles on the track and the Olympic time trial gold in London. 'To add the world title to the British title and the Olympic title means I've got the set,' Wiggins reflected afterwards. 'Along with the pursuit world titles, it's fantastic.'[264]

27

MARIANNE VOS
(2006, 2012, 2013)

Born in s-Hertogenbosch, the Netherlands, in 1987, Marianne Vos is perhaps the most complete rider in history, with multiple world titles across road, cyclo-cross and track cycling and Olympic gold on road and track. Vos is a five-times winner of the season-long World Cup (now the World Tour), has claimed the Giro d'Italia three times and holds the record for most wins at La Flèche Wallonne with five victories. She has stood on the podium of the elite road world championships eight times, equalling the record of Yvonne Reynders and Keetie van Oosten-Hage. On three of those occasions, Vos was on the top step.

In 2004 Vos rode her first world championships, riding in the junior road race in Verona. Vos was active right from the start and eventually escaped to win her first rainbow jersey at the first attempt. We start by talking about that first race.

***

Marianne Vos:

At seventeen I got into the Dutch road junior squad. We didn't have many international races so we didn't have a clue how we would perform internationally, but our national coach, Egon van Kessel, picked the best riders from our generation and we had our training camps for two or three days at the weekend – of course we still went to school then. He always said if we trained really hard then we'd be the best in the world championships. He had great faith and trust in our performance in Verona. We did some racing as well at the elite level and by the time we went to Italy for the Worlds we were pretty sure we were good because he had that much trust in us and, of course, we had put a lot of effort into our training. So we were pretty sure we would be able to go for the title.

We stayed in the same hotel as the elite riders in Bardolino, where the time trial was held. As a young rider it was very special to be there with the elite riders and all the big names from Dutch cycling. I stayed there the whole week because Roxane Knetemann and I rode the time trial as well. It was a really special experience. To have the combined championships was of huge value to me … it was big, all the big names were there, the tension was great.

I sort of sprinted from the gun, so I had a gap straightaway, but then I decided to save my energy until the final lap. I knew there was a chance because the climb, the Torricelle, in Verona, is pretty hard. I knew that if I waited for the right moment I could make a good move and then I would be able to keep it to the finish. Our national coach didn't want to give us roles, he wanted to keep the opportunities open for all the riders, of course he said give your best and don't bring each other back, but just try to go for the title. So we were there as a team but also trying to get the best result for ourselves. That was a bit of a weird situation looking back now as an elite rider, but as a junior it was like that every week, so it was normal.

I really wanted to become world champion and I remember crossing the line not really believing it had just happened. I was happy but the strange thing was that normally when I won races all the people around me would be just like, 'OK, that's nice', but all the Dutch team and everyone went through the roof, they were out of their minds. It was a weird experience actually. Then to have the national anthem played for you, and of course with another famous Dutch rider, Ellen Van Dijk, next to me on the podium … yeah, I remember all that.

I had to go to the podium through the mixed zone and then to the car park, it was about a kilometre. Every single Italian that I passed in that kilometre wanted to touch me or give me their hands or a kiss or whatever. It took for ever for me to get from the mixed zone to the car park. As a junior I'd never had that attention before but wearing the rainbow stripes, even as a Dutch junior girl, I realised the importance of the rainbow jersey and what it meant.

After turning professional in 2006, Vos enjoyed a terrific debut season, winning her first cyclo-cross world title before claiming a number of road races, including the under-23 European title and the Dutch national championships. In Salzburg for her first elite road Worlds, Vos twice joined the moves of Nicole Cooke and Nicole Brändli before winning in a sprint when those moves failed.

Early in the season I won a stage in the Gracia Tour and I won stages in Emakumeen Bira and a couple of classics in Holland, but I was mostly focused on the Dutch championships in Maastricht and the under-23 European championships. I wasn't really thinking about the Worlds; with the early wins in the season I knew maybe I would be selected … but the focus was on the nationals. Surprisingly I won that and then at the Europeans I was one of the favourites and won. Then I was sure about the selection for the Worlds.

Going into those world championships I was totally without pressure. I was an outsider, a first-year elite with nothing to prove. I just had to try my best. I knew I had a chance, I had already won against all the girls that were in the Worlds and it was a course that sort of suited me. I thought, 'OK, I might not be the biggest favourite but let's see. I might have a chance for a good result.'

Chantal Beltman was the most experienced rider on the team, she was with me with the national team at the Tour of Tuscany before the Worlds. That was good because then you get to know each other better. We knew each other but not as teammates so it was good to be together and have that experience in the build-up. I was pretty happy to have her at my side in Salzburg when we ended up in the break of seventeen. I remember Chantal saying to me, 'You're the best sprinter here, so be sure that you are ready and you can win.' She was the one who really pointed it out. From that moment we discussed things. Chantal wanted to try to escape to go solo and I said, 'OK, that's good because then we'll have a hard final and the others will have to bring you back. That will help me for the sprint if you are then brought back.' So we were trying to play our cards, to make the most of the possibilities and it worked out really well. I am very thankful to Chantal for getting me into that position.

It has always been one of my specialities to know the capacity of a rider and what they are capable of, but of course you aren't always able to get it right. Being in that front group I knew Nicole Brändli was the best climber and that Nicole Cooke was the most experienced, maybe the favourite to win the race because she had a good sprint but was also a very good classics rider – she had pressure on her. When they went on the attack I knew I had to go with them. Twice it was exactly the same three-rider break but it didn't really work, mostly because Nicole [Brändli] wasn't a sprinter and didn't want to go to the finish line along with two sprinters, which of course was totally right. Behind there was a chase – Svetlana Bubnenkova was there. She always wanted to ride.

In the final moments you have to rely on your team – I had to rely on Chantal, rely on myself. Also you have to decide where to go and when to move or not to move. I knew Nicole Cooke and Trixi Worrack were the riders to watch in that group for the sprint – and looking at the results I was right [Worrack finished second, Cooke third]. In that sprint I knew the last corner was slightly to the left and that if you were on the right-hand side you had to go around further, so I selected the left side. I didn't really think that they could maybe close the gap to the barriers and leave me no room. But if you feel good you make the right decision and I just felt that was the right side. I felt good that I was there and quite easy in the wheel of Trixie. I felt that I would just go when we passed the 200 metres sign.

Vos came off Worrack's wheel to win the sprint with some ease, winning her first elite road title.

It was an incredible sprint, especially if you look at the footage from above. It was pretty weird. Of course, I was one of the sprinters in a non-sprinter race. We had some fast girls in the group but not the real sprinters because they were dropped on the climb, that's where I got a little lucky. I didn't win any real bunch-sprint finishes that year, my first sprint win only came the season after. In a bunch sprint I wouldn't be too comfortable but from that group I knew I had a good chance.

I never thought about what would happen after the finish. I just thought I'll finish and I'll go where I have to go and if I win then they will take me. For me it always happens in a blur. Most of the time you go to the mixed zone or the podium ceremony, then to the anti-dope control, which is actually the first moment that you get some rest because you have to wait anyway. There you can let it sink in a bit but you still have a lot of people around and so it's not really the time for celebrations. It all takes a while. We drove back to the hotel and I remember getting back to my room with my jersey and medal and heading for a shower. Then you finally get some time to yourself and you can think about what has just happened. That was a really special moment for me.

We all went out as a team to celebrate. I was a nineteen-year-old in a group of somewhat older girls who were already prepared and with all their clothes to go out and party – totally ready. I was like, 'OK, let's see if I have some jeans – something to wear.' Then they forgot me! They were already on their way until at some point Chantal realised, 'Hey, where's Marianne?' So they came back to pick me up! I've never really been a girl that goes dancing or to clubs or whatever but of course it was fun to celebrate with the whole team, to have a drink and to have a party. But for me that moment, having that celebration … I found it a bit difficult because I'm not an outgoing person, I'm a bit shy, especially as a young girl in that group. I had some difficulties to find my place, but of course I didn't care because I was world champion and everything was cool.

Vos was only nineteen and with a single professional season behind her. Already she had the rainbow jersey on her back.

What I hadn't thought about was all the attention that would come. I just wanted to ride my bike, I wasn't thinking about getting famous or people wanting to know everything about me. That wasn't part of my goal, not at all. I just wanted to be the best and win races. So when I got more attention I really had to ask myself the question if I wanted this because it wasn't what I had been going for. I didn't want to be in the spotlight, I didn't want to be a famous Dutch person and I didn't want to have everyone having opinions about me. But I realised that if I wanted to continue racing, and if I wanted to have a career as a pro rider, then that would be part of it. So I tried to embrace it and make the best of it and to just be authentic and tell my story how I wanted to. It was pretty difficult, as an introvert you don't really like to share your story or your emotions, so it definitely took some time, but from that moment it was, 'OK, this is what I want and I'll try to deal with it in the best possible way.'

The attention comes because it's about winning races. If you lose it can be interesting but second place doesn't count. The next day, after you become world champion, you are in your hotel having breakfast with maybe a couple of people around, but really it is just a normal breakfast.

Then you go home that night and the next day nothing has changed really. And that is a good thing because really why should your world change if you've become world champion? But it is weird because you have a goal and you work really hard and long for it, and then once you have reached that goal, or not, but in this case reached it, then that's it. It's a weird feeling because now your goal is gone. So what do you do now on Monday morning after you've had breakfast?

At the beginning of my career I asked myself if I would be able to keep resetting my goals, because you have to suffer and you have to go through a lot of pain. I questioned myself on whether it was something I could do for long. I had no idea. But the competition gives me such a rush, maybe it is even a sort of addiction – if you win you know how it feels and you want that feeling again. For me that is the best explanation. It's not sort of, 'OK, now I've done that, I've been there, done it, never again.' It's more like, 'This is a great feeling and I want to have it again next year.'

Vos's 2006 win was the start of a remarkable run at the Worlds. Between 2007 and 2011 she claimed five silver medals in a row.

Those years at the world championships were pretty tough. Of course you know you can't be the world champion for ever and you can't win them every year. My first second place was when Marta Bastianelli won, when there was very strong competition from Italy. That race was really hard and I was really, really disappointed. Losing the jersey was tough but I'd had to deal with another country that was stronger at that moment and I didn't have the power to make the difference on my own. I had to deal with that, but one second place was okay. Then year after year I got second.

Getting silver never felt like winning a medal, instead it felt like, 'Hmm, lost again.' My fifth second place in Copenhagen was devastating because all the team worked for me and the Dutch team was very strong at that time, I even had Kirsten Wild as one of my lead-out girls and she was also one of the best sprinters in the world. I was very, very angry at myself not finishing off all the work that they had done. I was done with getting second. At Copenhagen I was so angry, I knew that OK, next year, at Valkenburg, whatever … I win.

In 2012 the Worlds were held in the Netherlands, returning to Valkenburg and the famous Cauberg climb. Vos entered the race as the winner of the season-long World Cup and as the Olympic champion after beating Lizzie Armitstead in the Olympic road race on the Mall in London.

The Olympic Games were my main goal that year and actually took the pressure off for the world championships in my home country. I wasn't nervous at all because I had reached my goal that year already. I remember in the build-up to the Olympic Games some of the Dutch media were asking my teammates, 'Aren't you afraid she will get second again?' At the time I found that a strange question but then if you looked back, OK … perhaps it wasn't that weird because if I'd come second in the past maybe I wasn't capable of winning at that high level, that very highest level of podium. But I trusted myself. I knew that I was in good shape and that I can win races all year, in every circumstance, on every course, it doesn't matter … so I thought I can win these Olympics too.

Those Olympics were something spectacular. Since Beijing I had wanted to win gold on the road and so the pressure was off. I wanted to use the shape I had at the end of July and make the best of it, to take it to the Worlds in Valkenburg.

There was some pressure, but it is how you take it. At that moment I felt really good. I remember a week before I'd felt bad and skipped the time trial because I needed the extra rest. It had been too much with the pressure for the Olympic Games and then afterwards meeting the Queen, having a dinner here and a celebration there. I was totally exhausted so I said to my coach that while I wanted to ride the time trial I didn't think it was smart to do so. As the road race got closer I started feeling better and better. We did the team time trial and I felt good in that and so from that moment I thought, 'OK, I'm ready to race here.'

Vos made her first move on the Cauberg, bridging across to her teammate Anna van der Breggen who had gone with an earlier break.

Our tactics were to send people up the road and then keep the front group at about 30 seconds so I could jump to the front and then be in the lead group. That worked really well with Anna van der Breggen who had a fantastic race. She was in that break, kept herself quiet and then the rest of the team set me up for the Cauberg. I know the Cauberg really well. It's a nasty climb if you're not in top shape but it's a really nice climb if you know you can attack it and then keep it going to the top. That day it felt like the latter. I just had to jump those 25 or 30 seconds and then, when I got to the front, Anna did a fantastic job.

It's quite honest on the Cauberg, you know that if you have good legs there aren't many girls who can follow. It was quite early it's true but I felt good and there was a perfect set-up. Also, it's a hard lap and so it gets in the legs of everybody, it's not like it is easy to follow in the group, so you know that if you dare and people do come across later then they have still done an effort as well, so we were quite keen on that early break.

Vos attacked on the final ride up the Cauberg and soloed to a famous win. She crossed the line holding aloft a Dutch flag she had grabbed from a fan.

It was a special moment. After finishing in London with that sprint against Lizzie and the emotion of that single moment crossing the line, here I had more time to celebrate, and in my home country. Obviously I was in a lot of pain because of the lactic acid that came from the Cauberg effort so the last 2 kilometres really hurt. But when I looked back I only saw one rider behind me, so OK, it was basically a time trial, one by one, and I had a good lead. It hurts but it's a nice feeling because you know that on the line it will all be done and this exhaustion will turn into a rainbow jersey. I was on the left side of the road and I saw a guy with a flag on the right side.

I didn't know him and he wasn't there ready for me or anything. I didn't really think about grabbing something but when I saw him I thought, 'This is going to be my moment, I want to take this flag because winning a world title on home soil is not something you do very often.' After five times getting silver I had got so disappointed in myself, even more so because the team was working so hard, that while I wanted it for myself in 2012 I also wanted it for the team. Of course the team knows you do your best and try your hardest, and even during those five years you still have a silver medal which shouldn't be a bad thing, but I felt I had to give something back. I really enjoyed that day. I was cool and calm, why? Probably because I really felt it was going to end well – I felt good.

The following year Vos travelled to Florence, again as the World Cup winner, and successfully defended her Worlds title. Her win crowned an incredible eight-year world championship run during which she never finished worse than second and claimed three rainbow jerseys.

In Florence I wanted to win but I didn't feel too good. I knew I had a chance and I thought maybe I could win, but I was less sure. I had a small injury in the build-up and had back problems. I was a lot more nervous. I remember crossing the line, knowing I'd won again, totally exhausted but maybe even happier because of the struggle and the effort that it took. The year before I was in pain but I had felt good and so it is much easier when everything comes together.

During the race I doubted whether I could win. Anna again did a great job setting me up for the perfect attack, but at one moment she nearly dropped me just by keeping a high pace. You don't feel very sure about yourself when your teammate is going better than you. We talked about it and agreed she would try to attack on the longer climb and I'd then try on the steeper part. Going to that steep climb, I knew I had to take the moment and go until the finish. I had Emma Johansson and Rossella Ratto behind me and of course they are good riders so I had to keep some pace. I was really exhausted when I crossed the finish. I remember coming off my bike and sitting against the barriers to catch my breath and get some air again. In Valkenburg it was pure joy but in Florence it was perhaps relief that, 'Yes, it is still possible.'

I definitely want to go for another title but I don't think about four or five or whatever. I'm not racing for the history books. I'm not racing for records. I'm racing for the moment.

RESULTS AND STATISTICS

Men's Elite (Professional) Road Race Podiums

Year	Host	First	Second	Third	Km	Starters	Finishers
1927	Nürburgring, Germany	Alfredo Binda (ITA) 6hr 37min 29sec	Costante Girardengo (ITA) @ 7min 16sec	Domenico Piemontesi (ITA) @ 10min 51sec	182.5	55	15
1928	Budapest, Hungary	Georges Ronsse (BEL) 6hr 20min 10sec	Herbert Nebe (GER) @ 19min 43sec	Bruno Wolke (GER) @ s.t.	191.7	16	8
1929	Zurich, Switzerland	Georges Ronsse (BEL) 6hr 48min 5sec	Nicolas Frantz (LUX) @ s.t.	Alfredo Binda (ITA) @ s.t.	200	16	16
1930	Liège, Belgium	Alfredo Binda (ITA) 7hr 30min 45sec	Learco Guerra (ITA) @ s.t.	Georges Ronsse (BEL) @ s.t.	210.6	23	17
1931	Copenhagen, Denmark	Learco Guerra (ITA) 4hr 53min 43sec	Ferdinand Le Drogo (FRA) @ 5min 17sec	Albert Buchi (SWI) @ 4min 48sec	172	17	13
1932	Rome, Italy	Alfredo Binda (ITA) 7hr 1min 28sec	Remo Bertoni (ITA) @ 15sec	Nicolas Frantz (LUX) @4 min 52 sec	206.1	21	17
1933	Monthléry, France	Georges Speicher (FRA) 7hr 8min 58sec	Antonin Magne (FRA) @ 5min 3sec	Marinus Valentijn (NED) @ 5min 4sec	250	28	13
1934	Leipzig, Germany	Karel Kaers (BEL) 5hr 56min 15.8sec	Learco Guerra (ITA) @ s.t.	Gustave Danneels (BEL) @ s.t.	225.6	26	15
1935	Floreffe, Belgium	Jean Aerts (BEL) 6hr 5min 19sec	Luciano Montero (ESP) @ 2min 57sec	Gustave Danneels (BEL) @ 5min 4sec	216	29	13
1936	Bern, Switzerland	Antonin Magne (FRA) 5hr 53min 32sec	Aldo Bini (ITA) @ 9min 27sec	Theo Middelkamp (NED) @ 9min 8sec	218.4	39	10
1937	Copenhagen, Denmark	Eloi Meulenberg (BEL) 7hr 59min 48sec	Emil Kijewski (GER) @ s.t.	Paul Egli (SWI) @ s.t.	297.5	34	9
1938	Valkenburg, Netherlands	Marcel Kint (BEL) 7hr 53min 25sec	Paul Egli (SWI) @ s.t.	Leo Amberg (SWI) @ s.t.	273	36	8
1946	Zurich, Switzerland	Hans Knecht (SWI) 7hr 24min 28sec	Marcel Kint (BEL) @ 10sec	Rik Van Steenbergen (BEL) @ 59sec	270	32	17

Year	Location	Winner	Second	Third	Distance	Starters	Finishers
1947	Reims, France	Theo Middelkamp (NED) 7hr 28min 17sec	Albert Sercu (BEL) @ 10sec	Jefke Janssen (NED) @ s.t.	273.9	31	7
1948	Valkenburg, Netherlands	Alberic Schotte (BEL) 7hr 30min 42sec	Jean-Apotre Lazarides (FRA) @ 1sec	Lucien Teisseire (FRA) @ 3min 41sec	266.8	37	10
1949	Copenhagen, Denmark	Rik Van Steenbergen (BEL) 7hr 33min 44sec	Ferdi Kübler (SWI) @ s.t.	Fausto Coppi (ITA) @ s.t.	290	35	22
1950	Moorslede, Belgium	Alberic Schotte (BEL) 7hr 49min 54sec	Theo Middelkamp (NED) @ 1min 1sec	Ferdi Kübler (SWI) @ 1min 48sec	284	40	12
1951	Varese, Italy	Ferdi Kübler (SWI) 8hr 28min 28sec	Fiorenzo Magni (ITA) @ s.t.	Antonio Bevilacqua (ITA) @ s.t.	295.2	45	24
1952	Luxembourg	Heinz Müller (GER) 7hr 5min 51.4sec	Gottfried Weilenmann (SWI) @ s.t.	Ludwig Hormann (GER) @ s.t.	280	48	38
1953	Lugano, Switzerland	Fausto Coppi (ITA) 7hr 30min 59sec	Germain Derycke (BEL) @ 6min 22sec	Stan Ockers (BEL) @ 7min 33sec	270	70	27
1954	Solingen-Klingenring, Germany	Louison Bobet (FRA) 7hr 24min 36sec	Fritz Schär (SWI) @ 12sec	Charly Gaul (LUX) @ 2min 12sec	240	71	22
1955	Frascati, Italy	Stan Ockers (BEL) 8hr 43min 29sec	Jean-Pierre Schmitz (LUX) @ 1min 3sec	Germain Derycke (BEL) @ 1min 15sec	293.1	65	21
1956	Copenhagen, Denmark	Rik Van Steenbergen (BEL) 7hr 26min 15sec	Rik Van Looy (BEL) @ s.t.	Gerrit Schulte (NED) @ s.t.	285.1	71	27
1957	Waregem, Belgium	Rik Van Steenbergen (BEL) 7hr 43min 10sec	Louison Bobet (FRA) @ s.t.	André Darrigade (FRA) @ s.t.	290.2	70	41
1958	Reims, France	Ercole Baldini (ITA) 7hr 29min 32sec	Louison Bobet (FRA) @ 2min 9sec	André Darrigade (FRA) @ 3min 47sec	276.8	67	26
1959	Zandvoort, Netherlands	André Darrigade (FRA) 7hr 30min 43sec	Michele Gismondi (ITA) @ s.t.	Nöel Foré (BEL) @ s.t.	292	69	44
1960	Hohenstein-Sachsenring, East Germany (DDR)	Rik Van Looy (BEL) 7hr 47min 27sec	André Darrigade (FRA) @ s.t.	Pino Cerami (BEL) @ s.t.	279.4	67	32

Year	Location	1st	2nd	3rd	Distance		
1961	Bern, Switzerland	Rik Van Looy (BEL) 7hr 46min 35sec	Nino Defilippis (ITA) @ s.t.	Raymond Poulidor (FRA) @ s.t.	285.3	71	32
1962	Salo, Italy	Jean Stablinski (FRA) 7hr 34min 11sec	Seamus Elliott (IRL) @ 1min 22sec	Jos Hoevenaars (BEL) @ 1min 44sec	296.2	69	36
1963	Renaix / Ronse, Belgium	Benoni Beheyt (BEL) 7hr 25min 26sec	Rik Van Looy (BEL) @ s.t.	Jo De Haan (NED) @ s.t.	278.8	70	36
1964	Sallanches, France	Jan Janssen (NED) 7hr 35min 52sec	Vittorio Adorni (ITA) @ s.t.	Raymond Poulidor (FRA) @ s.t.	290	62	40
1965	Lasarte (San Sebastián), Spain	Tom Simpson (GBr) 6hr 38min 19sec	Rudi Altig (GER) @ s.t.	Roger Swerts (BEL) @ 3min 40sec	267.4	74	56
1966	Nürburgring, Germany	Rudi Altig (GER) 7hr 21min 10sec	Jacques Anquetil (FRA) @ s.t.	Raymond Poulidor (FRA) @ s.t.	273.7	74	22
1967	Heerlen, Netherlands	Eddy Merckx (BEL) 6hr 44min 42sec	Jan Janssen (NED) @ s.t.	Ramon Saez (ESP) @ s.t.	265.2	70	44
1968	Imola, Italy	Vittorio Adorni (ITA) 7hr 27min 39sec	Herman Van Springel (BEL) @ 9min 50sec	Michele Dancelli (ITA) @ 10min 18sec	277.3	84	19
1969	Zolder, Belgium	Harm Ottenbros (NED) 6hr 23min 44sec	Julien Stevens (BEL) @ s.t.	Michele Dancelli (ITA) @ 2min 18sec	262.8	93	62
1970	Leicester, Great Britain	Jean-Pierre Monsere (BEL) 6hr 33min 58sec	Leif Mortensen (DEN) @ 2sec	Felice Gimondi (ITA) @ s.t.	271.9	95	69
1971	Mendrisio, Switzerland	Eddy Merckx (BEL) 6hr 39min 6sec	Felice Gimondi (ITA) @ s.t.	Cyrille Guimard (FRA) @ 1min 13sec	268.8	93	57
1972	Gap, France	Marino Basso (ITA) 7hr 5min 59sec	Franco Bitossi (ITA) @ s.t.	Cyrille Guimard (FRA) @ s.t.	272.5	89	42
1973	Barcelona, Spain	Felice Gimondi (ITA) 6hr 31min 26sec	Freddy Maertens (BEL) @ s.t.	Luis Ocaña Pernía (ESP) @ s.t.	248.6	88	39
1974	Montreal, Canada	Eddy Merckx (BEL) 6hr 52min 22sec	Raymond Poulidor (FRA) @ 2sec	Mariano Martinez (FRA) @ 37sec	262.5	70	18

Year	Location	Winner	Second	Third	Dist	Start	Fin
1975	Yvoir, Belgium	Hennie Kuiper (NED) 6hr 39min 19sec	Roger De Vlaeminck (BEL) @17sec	Jean-Pierre Danguillaume (FRA) @s.t.	266	79	28
1976	Ostuni, Italy	Freddy Maertens (BEL) 7hr 6min 10sec	Francesco Moser (ITA) @s.t.	Constantino Conti (ITA) @11sec	288	85	53
1977	San Cristóbal, Venezuela	Francesco Moser (ITA) 6hr 36min 24sec	Dietrich Thurau (GER) @s.t.	Franco Bitossi (ITA) @1min 19sec	255	89	33
1978	Nürburgring, Germany	Gerrie Knetemann (NED) 7hr 32min 4sec	Francesco Moser (ITA) @s.t.	Jørgen Marcussen (DEN) @20sec	273.7	111	31
1979	Valkenburg, Netherlands	Jan Raas (NED) 7hr 3min 9sec	Dietrich Thurau (GER) @s.t.	Jean-Rene Bernaudeau (FRA) @s.t.	274.8	114	44
1980	Sallanches, France	Bernard Hinault (FRA) 7hr 32min 16sec	Gianbattista Baronchelli (ITA) @1min 1sec	Juan Fernandez (ESP) @4min 25sec	268	107	15
1981	Prague, Czechoslovakia	Freddy Maertens (BEL) 7hr 21min 59sec	Giuseppe Saronni (ITA) @s.t.	Bernard Hinault (FRA) @s.t.	281.4	112	69
1982	Goodwood, Great Britain	Giuseppe Saronni (ITA) 6hr 42min 22sec	Greg LeMond (USA) @5sec	Sean Kelly (IRL) @10sec	275.1	136	55
1983	Altenrhein, Switzerland	Greg LeMond (USA) 7hr 1min 21sec	Adri van der Poel (NED) @1min 11sec	Stephen Roche (IRL) @s.t.	269.9	117	46
1984	Barcelona, Spain	Claude Criquielion (BEL) 6hr 46min 46sec	Claudio Corti (ITA) @14sec	Steve Bauer (CAN) @1min 1sec	255.5	119	31
1985	Giavera del Montello, Italy	Joop Zoetemelk (NED) 6hr 26min 38sec	Greg LeMond (USA) @3sec	Moreno Argentin (ITA) @s.t.	265.5	149	66
1986	Colorado Springs, USA	Moreno Argentin (ITA) 6hr 32min 38sec	Charles Mottet (FRA) @1sec	Giuseppe Saronni (ITA) @9sec	261.8	141	87
1987	Villach, Austria	Stephen Roche (IRL) 6hr 50min 2sec	Moreno Argentin (ITA) @1sec	Juan Fernandez (ESP) @s.t.	276	168	71
1988	Renaix / Ronse, Belgium	Maurizio Fondriest (ITA) 7hr 2min 11sec	Martial Gayant (FRA) @27sec	Juan Fernandez (ESP) @41sec	271.4	178	79

Year	Location	Winner	Second	Third	Distance (km)		
1989	Chambéry, France	Greg LeMond (USA) 6hr 45min 59sec	Dimitri Konyshev (RUS) @ s.t.	Sean Kelly (IRL) @ s.t.	259.3	190	42
1990	Utsunomiya, Japan	Rudy Dhaenens (BEL) 6hr 51min 59sec	Dirk De Wolf (BEL) @ s.t.	Gianni Bugno (ITA) @ 8sec	261	145	57
1991	Stuttgart, Germany	Gianni Bugno (ITA) 6hr 20min 23sec	Steven Rooks (NED) @ s.t.	Miguel Indurain (ESP) @ s.t.	252.8	191	96
1992	Benidorm, Spain	Gianni Bugno (ITA) 6hr 34min 28sec	Laurent Jalabert (FRA) @ s.t.	Dimitri Konyshev (RUS) @ s.t.	261.6	193	90
1993	Oslo, Norway	Lance Armstrong (USA) 6hr 17min 10sec	Miguel Indurain (ESP) @ 19sec	Olaf Ludwig (GER) @ s.t.	257.6	171	66
1994	Agrigento, Italy	Luc Leblanc (FRA) 6hr 33min 54sec	Claudio Chiappucci (ITA) @ 9sec	Richard Virenque (FRA) @ s.t.	251.7	170	57
1995	Duitama, Colombia	Abraham Olano (ESP) 7hr 9min 55sec	Miguel Indurain (ESP) @ 35sec	Marco Pantani (ITA) @ s.t.	265.5	98	20
1996	Lugano, Switzerland	Johan Museeuw (BEL) 6hr 23min 50sec	Mauro Gianetti (SWI) @ 1sec	Michele Bartoli (ITA) @ 29sec	252	151	49
1997	San Sebastián, Spain	Laurent Brochard (FRA) 6hr 16min 48sec	Bo Hamburger (DEN) @ 9sec	Leon Van Bon (NED) @ s.t.	256.5	161	87
1998	Valkenburg, Netherlands	Oskar Camenzind (SWI) 6hr 1min 30sec	Peter Van Petegem (BEL) @ 23sec	Michele Bartoli (ITA) @ 24sec	258	152	66
1999	Verona, Italy	Oscar Freire (ESP) 6hr 19min 29sec	Markus Zberg (SWI) @ 4sec	Jean-Cyril Robin (FRA) @ s.t.	260	173	49
2000	Plouay, France	Romans Vainsteins (LAT) 6hr 15min 28sec	Zbigniew Spruch (POL) @ s.t.	Oscar Freire (ESP) @ s.t.	268.9	168	109
2001	Lisbon, Portugal	Oscar Freire (ESP) 6hr 7min 21sec	Paolo Bettini (ITA) @ s.t.	Andrej Hauptman (SLO) @ s.t.	254.1	171	94
2002	Zolder, Belgium	Mario Cipollini (ITA) 5hr 30min 3sec	Robbie McEwen (AUS) @ s.t.	Erik Zabel (GER) @ s.t.	256	201	168

Year	Location	Winner	Second	Third	Distance (km)		
2003	Hamilton, Canada	Igor Astarloa (ESP) 6hr 30min 19sec	Alejandro Valverde (ESP) @ 5sec	Peter Van Petegem (BEL) @ s.t.	260.4	180	112
2004	Verona, Italy	Oscar Freire (ESP) 6hr 57min 15sec	Erik Zabel (GER) @ s.t.	Luca Paolini (ITA) @ s.t.	265.5	200	88
2005	Madrid, Spain	Tom Boonen (BEL) 6hr 26min 10sec	Alejandro Valverde (ESP) @ s.t.	Anthony Geslin (FRA) @ s.t.	273	193	188
2006	Salzburg, Austria	Paolo Bettini (ITA) 6hr 15min 36sec	Erik Zabel (GER) @ s.t.	Alejandro Valverde (ESP) @ s.t.	265.9	198	126
2007	Stuttgart, Germany	Paolo Bettini (ITA) 6hr 44min 43sec	Alexandr Kolobnev (RUS) @ s.t.	Stefan Schumacher (GER) @ s.t.	267.4	197	72
2008	Varese, Italy	Alessandro Ballan (ITA) 6hr 37min 30sec	Damiano Cunego (ITA) @ 3sec	Matti Breschel (DEN) @ s.t.	260.2	205	77
2009	Mendrisio, Switzerland	Cadel Evans (AUS) 6hr 56min 26sec	Alexandr Kolobnev (RUS) @ 27sec	Joaquim Rodriguez (ESP) @ s.t.	262.2	202	108
2010	Melbourne, Australia	Thor Hushovd (NOR) 6hr 21min 49sec	Matti Breschel (DEN) @ s.t.	Allan Davis (AUS) @ s.t.	257.2	178	99
2011	Copenhagen, Denmark	Mark Cavendish (GBr) 5hr 40min 27sec	Matthew Goss (AUS) @ s.t.	André Greipel (GER) @ s.t.	266	209	177
2012	Valkenburg, Netherlands	Philippe Gilbert (BEL) 6hr 10min 41sec	Edvald Boasson Hagen (NOR) @ 4sec	Alejandro Valverde (ESP) @ 5sec	261	207	122
2013	Tuscany, Italy	Rui Costa (POR) 7hr 35min 44sec	Joaquim Rodriguez (ESP) @ s.t.	Alejandro Valverde (ESP) @ 15sec	272.3	208	61
2014	Ponferrada, Spain	Michal Kwiatkowski (POL) 6hr 29min 7sec	Simon Gerrans (AUS) @ 1sec	Alejandro Valverde (ESP) @ s.t.	254.8	204	95
2015	Richmond, VA, USA	Peter Sagan (SVK) 6hr 14min 37sec	Michael Matthews (AUS) @ 3sec	Ramunas Navardauskas (LTU) @ s.t.	261.4	191	110
2016	Doha, Qatar	Peter Sagan (SVK) 5hr 40min 43sec	Mark Cavendish (GBr) @ s.t.	Tom Boonen (BEL) @ s.t.	257.3	197	53

Men's Elite Individual Time Trial Podiums

Year	Host	First	Second	Third	Km
1994	Catania, Italy	Chris Boardman (GBr) 49min 34sec	Andrea Chiurato (ITA) @ 48sec	Jan Ullrich (GER) @ 1min 51 sec	42
1995	Tunja, Colombia	Miguel Indurain (ESP) 55 min 30sec	Abraham Olano (ESP) @ 49sec	Uwe Peschel (GER) @ 2min 3sec	43
1996	Lugano, Switzerland	Alex Zülle (SWI) 48min 13sec	Chris Boardman (GBr) @ 40sec	Tony Rominger (SWI) @ 42sec	40.4
1997	San Sebastián, Spain	Laurent Jalabert (FRA) 52min 1sec	Sergei Gonchar (UKR) @ 3sec	Chris Boardman (GBr) @ 20sec	42.6
1998	Valkenburg, Netherlands	Abraham Olano (ESP) 54min 32sec	Melchor Mauri (ESP) @ 37sec	Sergei Gonchar (UKR) @ 47sec	43.5
1999	Treviso, Italy	Jan Ullrich (GER) 1hr 28sec	Michael Andersson (SWE) @14sec	Chris Boardman (GBr) @ 58sec	50.6
2000	Plouay, France	Sergei Gonchar (UKR) 56min 21sec	Michael Rich (GER) @10sec	Laszlo Bodrogi (HUN) @24sec	47.6
2001	Lisbon, Portugal	Jan Ullrich (GER) 51 min 49sec	David Millar (GBr) @ 7sec	Santiago Botero (COL) @ 12sec	38.7
2002	Zolder, Belgium	Santiago Botero (COL) 48min 4sec	Michael Rich (GER) @ 8sec	Igor Gonzalez De Galdeano (ESP) @ 17sec	40.4
2003	Hamilton, Canada	Michael Rogers (AUS) 52min 42sec	Uwe Peschel (GER) @ 0.5sec	Michael Rich (GER) @ 10sec	41.6
2004	Verona, Italy	Michael Rogers (AUS) 57min 30sec	Michael Rich (GER) @ 1min 12sec	Alexandre Vinokourov (KAZ) @ 1min 25sec	46.7

Year	Location				
2005	Madrid, Spain	Michael Rogers (AUS) 53min 34sec	José Iván Gutiérrez (ESP) @ 24sec	Fabian Cancellara (SWI) @ 24sec	44
2006	Salzburg, Austria	Fabian Cancellara (SWI) 1hr 11sec	David Zabriskie (USA) @ 1min 30sec	Alexandre Vinokourov (KAZ) @ 1min 50sec	50.8
2007	Stuttgart, Germany	Fabian Cancellara (SWI) 55min 41sec	Laszlo Bodrogi (HUN) @ 52sec	Stef Clement (NED) @ 58sec	44.9
2008	Varese, Italy	Bert Grabsch (GER) 52min 1sec	Svein Tuft (CAN) @ 43sec	David Zabriskie (USA) @ 52sec	43.7
2009	Mendrisio, Switzerland	Fabian Cancellara (SWI) 57min 55sec	Gustav Erik Larsson (SWE) @ 1min 27sec	Tony Martin (GER) @ 2min 30sec	49.8
2010	Melbourne, Australia	Fabian Cancellara (SWI) 8min 9sec	David Millar (GBr) @ 1min 2sec	Tony Martin (GER) @ 1min 12sec	45.6
2011	Copenhagen, Denmark	Tony Martin (GER) 53min 53sec	Bradley Wiggins (GBr) @ 1min 15sec	Fabian Cancellara (SWI) @ 1min 20sec	46.4
2012	Valkenburg, Netherlands	Tony Martin (GER) 58min 38sec	Taylor Phinney (USA) @ 5sec	Vasil Kiryienka (BLR) @ 1min 44sec	45.7
2013	Tuscany, Italy	Tony Martin (GER) 1hr 5min 36sec	Bradley Wiggins (GBr) @ 46sec	Fabian Cancellara (SWI) @ 48sec	57.9
2014	Ponferrada, Spain	Bradley Wiggins (GBr) 56min 25sec	Tony Martin (GER) @ 26sec	Tom Dumoulin (NED) @ 40sec	47.1
2015	Richmond, VA, USA	Vasil Kiryienka (BLR) 1hr 2min 29sec	Adriano Malori (ITA) @ 9sec	Jerome Coppel (FRA) @ 27sec	53.5
2016	Doha, Qatar	Tony Martin (GER) 44min 42sec	Vasil Kiryienka (BLR) @ 45sec	Jonathan Castroviejo (ESP) @ 1min 10sec	40

Women's Elite Road Race Podiums

Year	Host	First	Second	Third	Km	Starters	Finishers
1958	Reims, France	Elsy Jacobs (LUX) 1hr 50min 5sec	Tamara Novikova (URS) @ 2min 51sec	Maria Lukchina (URS) @ s.t.	59.3	29	26
1959	Rotheux, Belgium	Yvonne Reynders (BEL) 1hr 53min 32sec	Aina Puronen (URS) @ s.t.	Vera Gorbatcheva (URS) @ s.t.	72	34	29
1960	Hohenstein-Sachsenring, East Germany (DDR)	Beryl Burton (GBr) 1hr 54min 39sec	Rosa Sels (BEL) @ 3min 57sec	Elisabeth Kleinhans-Eicholz (GER) @ s.t.	61.1	30	30
1961	Douglas, Isle of Man, Great Britain	Yvonne Reynders (BEL) 1hr 58min 6sec	Beryl Burton (GBr) @ 2sec	Elsy Jacobs (LUX) @ 5sec	62.4	33	26
1962	Salo, Italy	Marie-Rose Gaillard (BEL) 1hr 53min 56sec	Yvonne Reynders (BEL) @ 2min 31sec	Marie-Therese Naessens (BEL) @ s.t.	64.4	31	29
1963	Renaix / Ronse, Belgium	Yvonne Reynders (BEL) 2hr 3min 18sec	Rosa Sels (BEL) @ s.t.	Aina Puronen (URS) @ s.t.	65.6	27	25
1964	Sallanches, France	Emilia Sonka (URS) 1hr 44min 37sec	Galina Yudina (URS) @ s.t.	Rosa Sels (BEL) @ s.t.	58	25	25
1965	Lasarte (San Sebastián), Spain	Elisabeth Kleinhans-Eicholz (GER) 1hr 31min 4sec	Yvonne Reynders (BEL) @ s.t.	Aina Puronen (URS) @ s.t.	51.9	34	32
1966	Nürburgring, Germany	Yvonne Reynders (BEL) 1hr 27min 21sec	Keetie Hage (NED) @ s.t.	Aina Puronen (URS) @ s.t.	46.5	40	36
1967	Heerlen, Netherlands	Beryl Burton (GBr) 1hr 26min 30sec	Lyubov Zadorozhnaya (URS) @ 1min 47sec	Anna Konkina (URS) @ 5min 47sec	53	41	38
1968	Imola, Italy	Keetie Hage (NED) 1hr 29min 6sec	Bajba Tsaune (URS) @ s.t.	Morena Tartagni (ITA) @ s.t.	55.2	44	28
1969	Brno, Czechslovakia	Audrey McElmury (USA) 2hr 4min 2sec	Bernadette Swinnerton (GBr) @ 1min 10sec	Nina Trofimova (URS) @ s.t.	69.7	43	33
1970	Leicester, Great Britain	Anna Konkina (URS) 1hr 39min 54sec	Morena Tartagni (ITA) @ s.t.	Raisa Obodovskaja (URS) @ s.t.	61.5	41	35
1971	Mendrisio, Switzerland	Anna Konkina (URS) 1hr 24min 2sec	Morena Tartagni (ITA) @ s.t.	Keetie Hage (NED) @ s.t.	50.4	42	39

Year	Location	Winner	Second	Third			
1972	Gap, France	Geneviéve Gambillon (FRA) 1hr 38min 41sec	Lyubov Zadorozhnaya (URS) @1sec	Anna Konkina (URS) @s.t.	60.6	45	38
1973	Barcelona, Spain	Nicole Van den Broeck (BEL) 1hr 31min 8sec	Keetie Van Oosten-Hage (NED) @s.t.	Valentina Rebrovskaja (URS) @s.t.	55	43	34
1974	Montreal, Canada	Geneviéve Gambillon (FRA) 1hr 47min 36sec	Bajba Tsaune (URS) @s.t.	Keetie Van Oosten-Hage (NED) @s.t.	60	38	30
1975	Mettet, Belgium	Tineke Kole-Fopma (NED) 1hr 32min 36sec	Geneviéve Gambillon (FRA) @1sec	Keetie Van Oosten-Hage (NED) @s.t.	54.1	44	42
1976	Ostuni, Italy	Keetie Van Oosten-Hage (NED) 1hr 39min 14sec	Luigina Bissoli (ITA) @s.t.	Yvonne Reynders (BEL) @s.t.	62	46	40
1977	San Cristóbal, Venezuela	Josiane Bost (FRA) 1hr 22min 41sec	Connie Carpenter (USA) @1min 48sec	Minnie Brinkhof-Nieuwenhuis (NED) @s.t.	49.7	32	29
1978	Brauweiler, Germany	Beate Habetz (GER) 1hr 45min 2sec	Keetie Van Oosten-Hage (NED) @s.t.	Emanuelle Lorenzon (ITA) @s.t.	70.5	59	55
1979	Valkenburg, Netherlands	Petra De Bruin (NED) 1hr 43min 57sec	Jenny De Smet (BEL) @s.t.	Beate Habetz (GER) @26sec	64	61	57
1980	Sallanches, France	Beth Heiden (USA) 1hr 45min 15sec	Tuulikki Jahre (SWE) @s.t.	Mandy Jones (GBr) @s.t.	53.6	72	61
1981	Prague, Czechoslovakia	Ute Enzenauer (GER) 1hr 30min 2sec	Jeannie Longo (FRA) @s.t.	Connie Carpenter (USA) @s.t.	53.6	75	73
1982	Goodwood, Great Britain	Mandy Jones (GBr) 1hr 31min	Maria Canins (ITA) @s.t.	Gerda Sierens (BEL) @s.t.	61.1	81	69
1983	Altenrhein, Switzerland	Marianne Berglund (SWE) 1hr 38min 17sec	Rebecca Twigg (USA) @s.t.	Maria Canins (ITA) @s.t.	60	75	69
1984	No race						
1985	Giavera del Montello, Italy	Jeannie Longo (FRA) 1hr 53min 10sec	Maria Canins (ITA) @s.t.	Sandra Schumacher (GER) @47sec	73.7	91	82
1986	Colorado Springs, USA	Jeannie Longo (FRA) 1hr 38min 56sec	Janelle Parks (USA) @10sec	Alla Iakovleva (URS) @s.t.	61.6	82	77

Year	Location						
1987	Villach, Austria	Jeannie Longo (FRA) 1hr 46min 40sec	Heleen Hage (NED) @ 21sec	Connie Meijer (NED) @ s.t.	72	111	87
1988	No race						
1989	Chambéry, France	Jeannie Longo (FRA) 1hr 56min 41sec	Catherine Marsal (FRA) @ 4min 5sec	Maria Canins (ITA) @ s.t.	74.1	106	89
1990	Utsunomiya, Japan	Catherine Marsal (FRA) 2hr 7sec	Ruthie Matthes (USA) @ 3min 24sec	Luisa Seghezzi (ITA) @ s.t.	72.5	75	65
1991	Stuttgart, Germany	Leontien Van Moorsel (NED) 2hr 9min 47sec	Inga Thompson (USA) @ 1min 54sec	Alison Sydor (CAN) @ 2min 46sec	79	113	103
1992	No race						
1993	Oslo, Norway	Leontien Van Moorsel (NED) 2hr 21min 20sec	Jeannie Longo (FRA) @ s.t.	Laura Charameda (USA) @ 4sec	92	118	113
1994	Capo d'Orlando, Italy	Monica Valen (NOR) 2hr 8min 3sec	Patsy Maegerman (BEL) @ s.t.	Jeanne Golay (USA) @ s.t.	86.4	91	73
1995	Duitama, Colombia	Jeannie Longo (FRA) 2hr 37min 45sec	Catherine Marsal (FRA) @ 38sec	Edita Pucinskaite (LTU) @ 1min 56sec	88.5	99	88
1996	Lugano, Switzerland	Barbara Heeb (SWI) 2hr 53min 5sec	Rasa Polikeviciute (LTU) @ 17sec	Linda Jackson (CAN) @ 37sec	100.8	93	73
1997	San Sebastián, Spain	Alessandra Cappellotto (ITA) 2hr 44min 37sec	Elizabeth Tadich (AUS) @ s.t.	Catherine Marsal (FRA) @ s.t.	108	108	85
1998	Valkenburg, Netherlands	Diana Ziliute (LTU) 2hr 35min 35sec	Leontien Van Moorsel (NED) @ s.t.	Hanka Kupfernagel (GER) @ s.t.	103.2	120	95
1999	Verona, Italy	Edita Pucinskaite (LTU) 2hr 59min 49sec	Anna Millward-Wilson (AUS) @ 18sec	Diana Ziliute (LTU) @ s.t.	113.7	120	93
2000	Plouay, France	Zinaida Stahurskaya (BLR) 3hr 17min 39sec	Chantal Beltman (NED) @ 1min 27sec	Madeleine Lindberg (SWE) @ 1min 50sec	127.4	110	60
2001	Lisbon, Portugal	Rasa Polikeviciute (LTU) 3hr 12min 5sec	Edita Pucinskaite (LTU) @ s.t.	Jeannie Longo (FRA) @ s.t.	121	106	63
2002	Zolder, Belgium	Susanne Ljungskog (SWE) 2hr 59min 15sec	Nicole Brändli (SWI) @ s.t	Joane Somarriba Arrola (ESP) @ s.t.	128	114	90

Year	Location	1st	2nd	3rd			
2003	Hamilton, Canada	Susanne Ljungskog (SWE) 3hr 16min 6sec	Mirjam Melchers-Van Poppel (NED) @ s.t.	Nicole Cooke (GBr) @ s.t.	124	90	67
2004	Verona, Italy	Judith Arndt (GER) 3hr 44min 38sec	Tatiana Guderzo (ITA) @ 10sec	Anita Valen-De Vries (NOR) @ 12sec	132.7	118	74
2005	Madrid, Spain	Regina Schleicher (GER) 3hr 8min 52sec	Nicole Cooke (GBr) @ s.t.	Oenone Wood (AUS) @ s.t.	126	131	107
2006	Salzburg, Austria	Marianne Vos (NED) 3hr 20min 26sec	Trixi Worrack (GER) @ s.t.	Nicole Cooke (GBr) @ s.t.	132.9	136	94
2007	Stuttgart, Germany	Marta Bastianelli (ITA) 3hr 46min 34sec	Marianne Vos (NED) @ 6sec	Giorgia Bronzini (ITA) @ s.t.	133.7	142	81
2008	Varese, Italy	Nicole Cooke (GBr) 3hr 42min 11sec	Marianne Vos (NED) @ s.t.	Judith Arndt (GER) @ s.t.	138.8	137	91
2009	Mendrisio, Switzerland	Tatiana Guderzo (ITA) 3hr 33min 25sec	Marianne Vos (NED) @ 19sec	Noemi Cantele (ITA) @ s.t.	124.2	127	56
2010	Melbourne, Australia	Giorgia Bronzini (ITA) 3hr 32min 1sec	Marianne Vos (NED) @ s.t.	Emma Johansson (SWE) @ s.t.	127.2	123	76
2011	Copenhagen, Denmark	Giorgia Bronzini (ITA) 3hr 21min 28sec	Marianne Vos (NED) @ s.t.	Ina-Yoko Teutenberg (GER) @ s.t.	140	146	120
2012	Valkenburg, Netherlands	Marianne Vos (NED) 3hr 14min 29sec	Rachel Neylan (AUS) @ 10sec	Elisa Longo Borghini (ITA) @ 18sec	128.8	132	80
2013	Tuscany, Italy	Marianne Vos (NED) 3hr 44min	Emma Johansson (SWE) @ 15sec	Rossella Ratto (ITA) @ s.t.	140	141	46
2014	Ponferrada, Spain	Pauline Ferrand-Prevot (FRA) 3hr 29min 21sec	Lisa Brennauer (GER) @ s.t.	Emma Johansson (SWE) @ s.t.	127.4	134	59
2015	Richmond, VA, USA	Elizabeth Armitstead (GBr) 3hr 23min 26sec	Anna Van Der Breggen (NED) @ s.t.	Megan Guarnier (USA) @ s.t.	129.6	135	88
2016	Doha, Qatar	Amalie Dideriksen (DEN) 3hr 10min 27sec	Kirsten Wild (NED) @ s.t.	Lotta Lepistö (FIN) @ s.t	134.1	142	103

Women's Elite Individual Time Trial Podiums

Year	Host	First	Second	Third	Km
1994	Catania, Italy	Karen Kurreck (USA) 38min 22sec	Anne Samplonius (CAN) @ 45sec	Jeannie Longo (FRA) @ 1min 22sec	30
1995	Tunja, Colombia	Jeannie Longo (FRA) 44min 27sec	Clara Hughes (CAN) @ 1min 11sec	Kathryn Watt (AUS) @ 1min 25sec	26
1996	Lugano, Switzerland	Jeannie Longo (FRA) 35min 16sec	Catherine Marsal (FRA) @ 48sec	Alessandra Cappellotto (ITA) @ 54sec	26.4
1997	San Sebastián, Spain	Jeannie Longo (FRA) 39min 15sec	Zulfiya Zabirova (KAZ) @ 0.85sec	Judith Arndt (GER) @ 29sec	28
1998	Valkenburg, Netherlands	Leontien Van Moorsel (NED) 31min 51sec	Zulfiya Zabirova (KAZ) @ 0.38sec	Hanka Kupfernagel (GER) @ 2sec	23
1999	Treviso, Italy	Leontien Van Moorsel (NED) 32min 31sec	Anna Wilson (AUS) @ 4sec	Edita Pucinskaite (LTU) @ 31sec	25.8
2000	Plouay, France	Mari Holden (USA) 33min 14sec	Jeannie Longo (FRA) @ 4sec	Rasa Polikeviciute (LTU) @ 47sec	25
2001	Lisbon, Portugal	Jeannie Longo (FRA) 29min 8sec	Nicole Brändli (SWI) @ 40sec	Teodora Ruano Sanchon (ESP) @ 44sec	19.2
2002	Zolder, Belgium	Zulfiya Zabirova (KAZ) 30min 2sec	Nicole Brändli (SWI) @ 14.7sec	Karin Thürig (SWI) @ 15.6sec	23.2
2003	Hamilton, Canada	Joane Somarriba (ESP) 28min 23sec	Judith Arndt (GER) @ 11sec	Zulfiya Zabirova (KAZ) @ 26sec	20.8
2004	Verona, Italy	Karin Thürig (SWI) 30min 53sec	Judith Arndt (GER) @ 52sec	Zulfiya Zabirova (KAZ) @ 57sec	24

Year	Location	Winner	Second	Third	
2005	Madrid, Spain	Karin Thürig (SWI) 28min 51sec	Joana Somarriba (ESP) @ 5sec	Kristin Armstrong (USA) @ 39sec	22
2006	Salzburg, Austria	Kristin Armstrong (USA) 35min 5sec	Karin Thürig (SWI) @ 26sec	Christine Thorburn (USA) @ 29sec	26.1
2007	Stuttgart, Germany	Hanka Kupfernagel (GER) 34min 44sec	Kristin Armstrong (USA) @ 23sec	Christiane Söder (AUT) @ 41sec	25.1
2008	Varese, Italy	Amber Neben (USA) 33min 51sec	Christiane Söder (AUT) @ 7sec	Judith Arndt (GER) @ 22sec	25.1
2009	Mendrisio, Switzerland	Kristin Armstrong (USA) 35min 26sec	Noemi Cantele (ITA) @ 55sec	Linda Melanie Villumsen (NZL) @ 58sec	26.8
2010	Melbourne, Australia	Emma Pooley (GBr) 32min 48sec	Judith Arndt (GER) @ 15sec	Linda Melanie Villumsen (NZL) @ 16sec	22.9
2011	Copenhagen, Denmark	Judith Arndt (GER) 37min 7sec	Linda Melanie Villumsen (NZL) @ 22sec	Emma Pooley (GBr) @ 24sec	27.8
2012	Valkenburg, Netherlands	Judith Arndt (GER) 32min 26sec	Evelyn Stevens (USA) @ 34sec	Linda Melanie Villumsen (NZL) @ 41sec	24.1
2013	Tuscany, Italy	Ellen Van Dijk (NED) 27min 48sec	Linda Melanie Villumsen (NZL) @ 24sec	Carmen Small (USA) @ 28sec	25.3
2014	Ponferrada, Spain	Lisa Brennauer (GER) 38min 48sec	Hanna Solovey (UKR) @ 18sec	Evelyn Stevens (USA) @ 21sec	29.5
2015	Richmond, VA, USA	Linda Melanie Villumsen Serup (NZL) 40min 30sec	Anna Van Der Breggen (NED) @ 3sec	Lisa Brennauer (GER) @ 6sec	30
2016	Doha, Qatar	Amber Neben (USA) 36min 37sec	Ellen Van Dijk (NED) @ 6sec	Katrin Garfoot (AUS) @ 8sec	28.9

AUTHOR ACKNOWLEDGEMENTS

A huge thanks to all of the following who helped with arranging or supported interviews and, of course, the riders who gave up their time to share their stories with me: Leo Aquina, Robert Arnold, Simon Barnes, Mandy Bishop, Nicole Cooke, Troy De Haas, Maurizio Evangelista, Cadel Evans, Antonio Freire, Oscar Freire, Felice Gimondi, José Manuel Gonzáles, Barry Hoban, Andy Hood, Marniek Kint, Christoffer Lehmann, Georges Luechinger, Catherine Marsal, Eric Peeters, Yvonne Reynders, Christel Roche, Stephen Roche, Lee Rodgers, Chris Sidwells, Paul Van Bommel, Keetie Van Oosten-Hage and Marianne Vos.

Thanks to all at Aurum Press, specifically Lucy Warburton for believing in the project and guiding me through the entire process and to Ru Merritt for unearthing the images that grace the book. Thanks to Richard Whitehead for shaping the final text and to the staff at the British Library for their advice and assistance and willingness to go and find yet another trolley-full of periodicals.

Finally, but most importantly, I owe a huge debt of gratitude to my wonderful partner Karen. Without her continued enthusiasm and unwavering support this book simply would not have been possible. Karen, as ever, thank you.

BIBLIOGRAPHY

This book draws on a wide range of sources. The following are worthy of special mention:

Armstrong, Lance: *It's Not About the Bike,* Yellow Jersey Press, 2001.

Cavendish, Mark: *At Speed,* Ebury Press, 2013.

Chany, Pierre: *La Fabuleuse Histoire des Classiques et des Championnats du Monde,* Editions ODIL, 1979.

Cooke, Nicole: *The Breakaway,* Simon & Schuster, 2014.

Cossins, Peter: *The Monuments: The Grit and the Glory of Cycling's Greatest One-Day Races,* Bloomsbury Publishing, 2014.

Fotheringham, William: *Fallen Angel: The Passion of Fausto Coppi,* Yellow Jersey Press, 2009.

Friebe, Daniel: *Eddy Merckx, The Cannibal,* Ebury Press, 2012.

Howard, Paul: *Sex, Lies and Handlebar Tape: The remarkable life of Jacques Anquetil,* Mainstream Publishing, 2011.

Jacobs, Rene and Mahau, Hector: *Van de Nurburgring tot Zolder,* de Eecloonaar, 2002.

Roche, Stephen: *Born to Ride, The Autobiograpy of Stephen Roche,* Yellow Jersey Press, 2012.

Sykes, Herbie: *Maglia Rosa,* Rouleur Books, Bloomsbury Publishing, 2013.

Van Landeghem, Jos: *Onsterfelijke Wereldkampioenen Wielrennen,* de Eecloonaar, 2001.

Weidenfield and Nicolson: *The Official Tour de France Centenniel,* Orion Publishing Group, 2003.

The archives of: Cycling, Cycling and Mopeds, Cycling Weekly, Ride Cycling Review, Miroir des Sports, the Guardian, the Telegraph, the Independent, La Stampa, Le Petit journal, Paris-Soir, Gazette de Lausanne, Journal de Genève, Le Monde, Leidsch Dagblad, ABC, Corriere della Sera, l'Equipe, La Gazzetta dello Sport, New York Times.

The following websites: cyclebase.nl, cq.com, cyclingnews.com, velonews.com.

ENDNOTES

Chapter One
1 Financial Times; 3 April 2015
2 Jackson: Sacred Hoops (Hyperion) 1995, p24
3 Chany: La Fabuleuse Histoire des Classiques et des Championnats du Monde (Editions Odil) 1979, p703
4 http://oldsite.uci.ch/imgarchive/AboutUCI/Mission/Reglesgouvernanceenglishversion.pdf
5 http://www.ridemedia.com.au/features/despatch-from-doha-an-overview-of-the-championships/

Chapter Two
6 http://www.nuerburgring.de/en/fans-info/history/the-legend-nuerburgring.html
7 Jacobs and Mahau: Van de Nurburgring tot Zolder (2002), p19
8 La Stampa; 20 July 1927
9 Paris Soir; 16 July 1927
10 Chany: La Fabuleuse Histoire des Classiques et des Championnats du Monde (Editions Odil) 1979
11 Paris Soir; 23 July 1927
12 Cycling; 27 July 1927
13 La Stampa; 22 July 1927

Chapter Three
14 Corriere della Sera; 22 August 1928
15 La Stampa; 22 August 1928
16 Cycling; 31 August 1928
17 La Stampa; 22 August 1928
18 La Stampa; 22 August 1928
19 Corriere Della Sera; 23 August 1928
20 Corriere Della Sera; 27 October 1928
21 La Stampa; 18 August 1929
22 Cycling; 23 August 1929
23 Jacobs and Mahau: Van de Nurburgring tot Zolder (The Eeclonaar) 2002
24 Sykes: Maglia Rosa (Bloomsbury) 2013, p51
25 Chany: La Fabuleuse Histoire du Tour de France (Minerva) 2003, p240
26 Chany: La Fabuleuse Histoire du Tour de France (Minerva) 2003, p240
27 La Stampa; 28 July 1930
28 La Stampa; 31 August 1930
29 Cycling; 4 September 1931
30 Chany: La Fabuleuse Histoire des Classiques et des Championnats du Monde (Editions Odil) 1979, p718
31 Corriere della Sera; 27 August 1931
32 Foot: Pedalare! Pedalare! (Bloomsbury) 2011
33 Chany: La Fabuleuse Histoire des Classiques et des Championnats du Monde (Editions Odil) 1979, p718
34 Chany: La Fabuleuse Histoire des Classiques et des Championnats du Monde (Editions Odil) 1979, p481
35 La Stampa; 1 September 1932
36 Cycling; 9 September 1932
37 Chany: La Fabuleuse Histoire des Classiques et des Championnats du Monde (Editions Odil) 1979, p722
38 Paris Soir; 16 August 1933
39 Chany: La Fabuleuse Histoire des Classiques et des Championnats du Monde (Editions Odil) 1979, p724
40 Cycling; 24 August 1934
41 Cycling; 21 August 1935

42 Paris-Soir; 8 September 1936
43 Paris-Soir; 8 September 1936
44 Paris-Soir; 8 September 1936
45 Chany: La Fabuleuse Histoire des Classiques et des Championnats du Monde (Editions Odil) 1979, p729
46 Chany: La Fabuleuse Histoire des Classiques et des Championnats du Monde (Editions Odil) 1979, p732
47 La Stampa; 5 September 1938
48 Jacobs and Mahau: Van de Nurburgring tot Zolder (The Eeclonaar) 2002
49 Jacobs and Mahau: Van de Nurburgring tot Zolder (The Eeclonaar) 2002

Chapter Four
50 Cossins: The Monuments (Bloomsbury) 2014

Chapter Five
51 Gazette de Lausanne; 11 February 1946
52 Gazette de Lausanne; 11 February 1946
53 Thonon: Campionissimes (Editions Arts & Voyages) 1974, p50
54 Le Monde; 5 August 1947
55 Leidsch Dagblad; 23 August 1948
56 Cycling; 25 August 1948
57 Cycling; 25 August 1948
58 Fotheringham: Fallen Angel: the Passion of Fausto Coppi (Yellow Jersey Press) 2009, p107
59 Le Monde; 24 August 1948
60 La Stampa; 23 August 1948
61 Chany: La Fabuleuse Histoire des Classiques et des Championnats du Monde (Editions Odil) 1979, p738
62 Cycling; 25 August 1949
63 Cycling; 25 August 1949

Chapter Six
64 Cycling; 26 August 1954
65 Le Miroir des Sports; 23 August 1954
66 Le Miroir des Sports; 23 August 1954
67 Chany: La Fabuleuse Histoire des Classiques et des Championnats du Monde (Editions Odil) 1979, p750
68 Chany: La Fabuleuse Histoire des Classiques et des Championnats du Monde (Editions Odil) 1979, p740
69 Fotheringham: Fallen Angel: the Passion of Fausto Coppi (Yellow Jersey Press) 2009, p157
70 Journal de Genève; 3 September 1951
71 Cycling; 28 August 1952
72 La Stampa; 31 August 1953
73 La Corriere della Sera Stampa; 31 August 1953
74 Cycling; 3 September 1953
75 Chany: La Fabuleuse Histoire des Classiques et des Championnats du Monde (Editions Odil) 1979, p743
76 Cycling; 3 September 1953
77 La Stampa; 31 August 1953
78 Fotheringham: Fallen Angel: the Passion of Fausto Coppi (Yellow Jersey Press) 2009, p183
79 Cycling; 31 August 1955
80 La Stampa; 30 August 1958
81 La Stampa; 30 August 1958
82 La Stampa; 1 September 1958
83 La Stampa; 1 September 1958
84 Cycling and Mopeds; 19 August 1959

Chapter Seven

85   La Stampa; 29 November 1957
86   La Stampa; 2 March 1958
87   Hermans: Yvonne Reynders, zeven maal in de zevende hemel (Boek & media publishing) 2002

Chapter Nine

88   Cycling and Mopeds; 6 September 1961
89   La Stampa; 16 May 1962
90   Cycling and Mopeds; 14 August 1963
91   Chany: La Fabuleuse Histoire des Classiques et des Championnats du Monde (Editions Odil) 1979, p769
92   https://www.flickr.com/photos/67394469@N06/20958468875/
93   Howard: Sex Lies and Handlebar Tape (Mainstream Publishing) 2008
94   Cycling and Mopeds; 5 September 1962
95   Le Monde; 4 September 1962
96   Procycling; October 2014
97   Procycling; October 2014
98   Cycling; 5 September 1964
99   Chany: La Fabuleuse Histoire des Classiques et des Championnats du Monde (Editions Odil) 1979, p770
100 Cycling; 12 September 1964

Chapter Ten

101 Cycling and Mopeds; 17 August 1960
102 The Daily Express; 15 August 1960
103 http://www.cyclingweekly.co.uk/news/latest-news/beryl-burton-british-legend-62824
104 Cycling; 9 September 1967
105 Cycling; 9 September 1967
106 Clemitson: Ride the Revolution (Bloomsbury) 2015, p11
107 Hermans: Yvonne Reynders, zeven maal in de zevende hemel (Boek & media publishing) 2002
108 Cycling; 3 September 1966
109 Leidsch Dagblad; 28 August 1967
110 Cycling; 9 September 1967
111 Cycling; 11 September 1965
112 Fotheringham: Put Me Back on my Bike, In Search of Tom Simpson (Yellow Jersey Press) 2002
113 Cycling; 11 September 1965
114 Le Monde; 7 September 1965
115 Cycling; 11 September 1965
116 The Daily Express; 6 September 1965
117 Cycling; 11 September 1965
118 Cycling; 11 September 1965
119 La Stampa; 17 October 1965
120 Howard: Sex Lies and Handlebar tape (Mainstream Publishing) 2008
121 Howard: Sex Lies and Handlebar tape (Mainstream Publishing) 2008

Chapter Twelve

122 Perneger; BMJ 2015;351:h6304 14 December 2015 http://www.bmj.com/content/351/bmj.h6304
123 Perneger; BMJ 2015;351:h6304 14 December 2015 http://www.bmj.com/content/351/bmj.h6304
124 La Stampa; 19 August 1970
125 Cycling; 22 August 1970
126 La Stampa; 17 August 1970
127 De Volkskant; 20 July 1995
128 La Stampa; 18 August 1970
129 The Official Tour de France Centenniel (Weidenfeld and Nicolson) 2003

130 Cycling; 11 September 1971
131 Chany: La Fabuleuse Histoire des Classiques et des Championnats du Monde (Editions Odil) 1979, p784
132 Cycling; 11 September 1971
133 Cycling; 12 August 1972
134 Cycling; 12 August 1972
135 Cycling; 8 September 1973
136 Corriere dell Sera; 3 September 1973
137 Chany: La Fabuleuse Histoire des Classiques et des Championnats du Monde (Editions Odil) 1979, p789

Chapter Fifteen
138 New York Times; 19 January 1974
139 The Montreal Gazette; 26 August 1974
140 Cycling; 31 August 1974
141 Cycling; 31 August 1974
142 Cycling; 31 August 1974
143 Le Monde; 27 August 1974
144 Cycling; 31 August 1974
145 Chany: La Fabuleuse Histoire des Classiques et des Championnats du Monde (Editions Odil) 1979, p791
146 Cycling; 13 September 1975
147 Cycling; 13 September 1975
148 Chany: La Fabuleuse Histoire des Classiques et des Championnats du Monde (Editions Odil) 1979, p793
149 Leidsch Dagblad; 28 August 1975
150 Chany: La Fabuleuse Histoire des Classiques et des Championnats du Monde (Editions Odil) 1979, p794
151 Chany: La Fabuleuse Histoire des Classiques et des Championnats du Monde (Editions Odil) 1979, p794
152 Cycling; 11 September 1976
153 Cycling; 11 September 1976
154 La Stampa; 6 September 1976
155 http://bikeraceinfo.com/oralhistory/freddy-maertens.html
156 Chany: La Fabuleuse Histoire des Classiques et des Championnats du Monde (Editions Odil) 1979, p799
157 Chany: La Fabuleuse Histoire des Classiques et des Championnats du Monde (Editions Odil) 1979, p801
158 Leidsch Dagblad; 5 September 1977

Chapter Sixteen
159 Le Monde; 2 September 1980
160 La Stampa; 1 September 1980
161 La Stampa; 4 September 1980
162 Cycling; 6 September 1980
163 Jacobs and Mahau: Van de Nurburgring tot Zolder (The Eeclonaar) 2002, p335
164 Cycling; 6 September 1980
165 La Stampa; 1 September 1981
166 La Stampa; 1 September 1981
167 La Stampa; 1 September 1981
168 Cycling; 11 September 1982
169 Cycling; 11 September 1982
170 Cycling; 10 September 1983
171 New York Times; 30 October 1983
172 Cycling Weekly; 11 September 1986
173 Cycling Weekly; 31 August 1989

174 Cycling Weekly; 10 September 1987
175 Cycling Weekly; 10 September 1987
176 La Stampa; 7 September 1987
177 Leidsch Dagblad; 29 August 1988
178 Leidsch Dagblad; 29 August 1988
179 Los Angeles Times; 21 April 1987
180 Cycling Weekly; 21 August 1989

Chapter Nineteen
181 Cycling Weekly; 14 October 1995
182 Le Monde; 10 October 1995
183 ABC; 9 October 1995
184 Cycling Weekly; 13 September 1990
185 Cycling; 13 September 1990
186 Le Monde; 2 September 1990
187 Cycling; 13 September 1990
188 Cycling; 13 September 1990
189 La Stampa; 24 August 1991
190 Cycling Weekly; 31 August 1991
191 La Stampa; 26 August 1991
192 La Stampa; 26 August 1991
193 ABC; 6 September 1992
194 De Telegraaf; 26 Aug 1991
195 Armstrong: It's Not About the Bike (Yellow Jersey Press) 2000, p61
196 Cycling Weekly; 4 September 1993
197 Cycling Weekly; 3 September 1994
198 Le Monde; 25 August 1994
199 Cycling Weekly; 14 October 1995
200 www.nrc.nl/nieuws/1996/10/07/johan-museeuw-verliest-goesting-in-de-wielersport-7326998-a1023190
201 www.nrc.nl/nieuws/1996/10/07/johan-museeuw-verliest-goesting-in-de-wielersport-7326998-a1023190
202 http://autobus.cyclingnews.com/results/archives/oct96/mrr.html
203 www.dezondag.be/johan-museeuw-zwijgt-niet-meer-wilfried-peeters-wist-alles/
204 Cycling Weekly; 16 October 1999
205 Cycling Weekly; 16 October 1999

Chapter Twenty-One
206 http://autobus.cyclingnews.com/results/2001/oct01/oct14news.php
207 http://autobus.cyclingnews.com/results/2001/oct01/oct15news.php
208 La Stampa; 15 October 2001
209 Cycling Weekly; 20 October 2001
210 La Stampa; 12 October 2002
211 http://autobus.cyclingnews.com/news/?id=2002/jul02/jul10news
212 http://autobus.cyclingnews.com/news/?id=2002/jul02/jul16news
213 Cycling Weekly; 19 October 2002
214 http://www.cyclingnews.com/news/cipollini-celebrates-his-2002-zolder-world-title/
215 http://www.velonation.com/Photos/Photo-Album/mmid/614/mediaid/1788.aspx.
216 http://www.cyclingnews.com/features/mario-cipollini-the-wounded-lion-king/
217 Cycling Weekly; 16 October 1999
218 La Stampa; 1 October 2004
219 ABC; 4 October 2004
220 http://autobus.cyclingnews.com/road/2004/worlds04/?id=results/worlds049
221 http://www.cyclingnews.com/news/belgian-worlds-selection-some-opinions/
222 La Stampa; 25 September 2005
223 http://www.cyclingnews.com/news/hammond-cramps-questions-teams-tactics/

224 La Stampa; 26 September 2005
225 Cycling Weekly; 27 December 2011
226 http://www.velonews.com/2005/09/news/road/germanys-schleicher-grabs-road-title_8956#g5GUzTsv4cyj6ZQo.99
227 Cooke: The Breakaway (Simon & Schuster) 2014
228 www.velonews.com/2006/09/news/road/vos-scores-womens-road-title_10924#LP2k63i74Ws8wStO.99
229 NRC.nl; 25 September 2006
230 http://www.velonews.com/2006/09/news/road/better-than-ever-a-conversation-with-paolo-bettini_10921#xHaKoV9JllG42Lpb.99
231 http://autobus.cyclingnews.com/road/2006/worlds06/index.php?id=/features/2006/italians_preworlds
232 La Stampa; 25 September 2006
233 La Stampa; 25 September 2006
234 The Daily Telegraph; 30 September 2007
235 La Stampa; 1 October 2007

Chapter Twenty-Three

236 La Gazzetta dello Sport; 27 September 2008
237 La Gazzetta dello Sport; 27 September 2008
238 http://www.eurosport.com/cycling/bettini-happy-to-help_sto1713685/story.shtml
239 http://www.eurosport.com/cycling/bettini-happy-to-help_sto1713685/story.shtml
240 Ride Cycling Review #46
241 Ride Cycling Review #46
242 Ride Cycling Review #46
243 Ride Cycling Review #46
244 The Sydney Morning Herald; 28 September 2009
245 Cycling Weekly; 15 December 2008
246 Cavendish: At Speed (Random House) 2013
247 Cavendish: At Speed (Random House) 2013
248 Cavendish: At Speed (Random House) 2013
249 http://www.cyclingnews.com/races/uci-road-world-championships-2011/elite-men-road-race/results/
250 http://www.cyclingnews.com/news/bettini-defends-italian-team-despite-poor-result-in-valkenburg/
251 www.velonews.com/2012/09/analysis/grande-gilbert-delivers-dream-ride_239805#i3J2OfLpTgiIdlau.99
252 http://www.lequipe.fr/Cyclisme-sur-route/Actualites/Gilbert-je-ne-comprenais-pas/402249
253 http://uk.reuters.com/article/uk-oly-cycl-wroad-day2-preview-idUKBRE86Q0WV20120727?feedType=RSS&feedName=sportsNews
254 http://pelotonmagazine.com/travel-culture/inside-peloton-cannibal/
255 The Guardian; 1 April 2017
256 http://www.dohacycling2016.com/dideriksen-spoils-dutch-birthday-party/
257 https://dennikn.sk/178348/jazdil-so-saganom-porazal-nas-aj-na-starom-bicykli-od-sestry/
258 Cyclist; 21 April 2015
259 http://www.cyclingnews.com/races/uci-road-world-championships-2015/elite-men-road-race/results/
260 Rouleur #66
261 Ride Cycling Review #74
262 http://www.ridemedia.com.au/features/despatch-from-doha-an-overview-of-the-championships/

Chapter Twenty-Six

263 Millar: Racing Through the Dark (Orion Books) 2011, p196
264 http://www.cyclingnews.com/races/uci-road-world-championships-2014/mens-elite-individual-time-trial/results/

INDEX